Jesus said to the people who believed in him, "You are truly my disciples if you remain faithful to my teachings. **32** And you will know the truth, and the truth will set you free."

John 8:31-32 (NLT)

Kylee,
So glad you are a disciple of Jesus, little sister!
Blessings!

DISCIPLE-*ing*

**Being a Disciple, Making Disciples,
and Living Out Our Purpose**

Steven R. Harbaugh

DISCIPLE-*ing* - Being a Disciple, Making Disciples, and Living Out Our Purpose

ISBN   978-1-7373078-0-8 Paperback
           978-1-7373078-1-5 Hardcover
           978-1-7373078-2-2 eBook

Dedication

This book was inspired by and is dedicated to Jesus Christ, the Lord God Almighty, God incarnate, the Image of the invisible God, *Yeshua Hamashiach*, Jesus Messiah, the Son of God, who came to save all who would trust in and follow Him as a disciple.

Jesus, this book is for your glory.

Acknowledgements

To the many friends and family that have supported this effort and the many hours of interviews, writing, talking about it, and all the edits - Thank you for your love and friendship.

To my wife, best friend, and biggest cheerleader, Tracey Harbaugh: thank you for tolerating the crazy hours of working through this material and for talking through ideas. I praise God for your help, love, and support during this project and in our lives together. I love you with every fiber in my being - you are truly a blessing from the Lord to me and so many.

To my Pastor, mentor, and friend, Woody Cumbie: thank you for being a bounce-board, encourager, and an example of what a disciple and disciple-maker looks like.

To my friend and spiritual mentor in the Lord, Dr. Marcus Warner: thank you for your friendship, insights, encouragement, and for helping me think through the process.

To Kari Ownbey: thank you for your diligent work at transcribing most of the interviews and proof-reading.

To Adam M., Andrew, Dr. Barb Haehner, David Harbaugh, Devon McDonald, Don and Karol, Jeff Carson, Jim Laidlaw, Jim and Anita VarnHagen, John Gidman, Kyle Condra, and Scott Beck: Thank you for your contributions to this effort through your interviews, your love of the Lord Jesus, and willingness to share your life and insights. You are a blessing to me, and to those who will read this book in the future. Praise the Lord for you. Thanks to my Mother, Diana Dicken, for proof reading, and to Mike Harbaugh and Derek Parker for the cover art!

To my mother, Diana Dicken, and my father, Dr. Glenn Harbaugh: thank you for instilling in me a love of reading, the joy of a good story, the arts, and teaching me to dream big.

Contents

Introduction: Why DISCIPLE-*ing*?

Jesus is Lord is the essential belief statement of Biblical Christianity – that JESUS IS LORD. That He is the Son of God, the Christ, the Jewish Messiah prophesied to come, the second part of the triunity of the Godhead - that Jesus is Deity in the flesh, *Emmanuel*, "God with us"- who came to save us from our sinful state and restore us to relational fellowship with the one true God. With that comes the understanding that Jesus is our Redeemer, our Savior - that Jesus is LORD. And, because of that belief, we choose to follow Him, his teachings, his words as preserved for us in the Word of God, the Holy Bible. Thus, we are following him as a *disciple*.

The Apostle John records an important statement of Jesus regarding being a disciple in John 8:31-32 (ESV):

'**So Jesus said to the Jews who had believed him,** *"If you abide in my word, you are truly my disciples, and you will know the truth, and the truth will set you free."*

A powerful statement, with several critical points to consider for any believer in Jesus Christ, or anyone seeking the truth that is in Christ:

1. First, he was speaking to Jewish believers, who were followers of Jesus – who had recognized Jesus as the Messiah – listening to and learning from Jesus.
2. Secondly, he used the conditional particle phrase of *"...If you abide in my word, you are truly my disciples...".* The conditional 'IF' is clearly present in the Greek text, "if you abide in my word",

explaining that we need to "abide" (to stay, continue, dwell, endure, stand) in His word, (the teachings of Christ, His words in Scripture).

3. Thirdly, that IF we abide/stay in His word we would truly be His disciples, and *"...you will know the truth, and the truth will set you free."* By staying in Jesus' teachings we would truly be a disciple, and **by that** we will know the truth. Anyone familiar with the Gospel of John would probably think of Jesus' statement in John 14:6 *"I am the way, and the truth, and the life. No one comes to the Father except through me."* Being a disciple by staying in Jesus' word will teach us the truth. As the rest of the New Testament teaches, we are set free from death, from the penalties of sin, from bondage to sin, and we are released to live a life in-Christ, and are given eternal life in the presence of God.

Thus, being a disciple is important – with eternal consequences! It is not just an academic pursuit, or a religious ritual, or the occasional attendance on a Saturday night or Sunday morning church service. Being a disciple of Jesus Christ is a vital calling. And it is not something we only *do* – it is who we *are*. Full time, 24/7, seven-days-a-week. It should become our identity ("I am a disciple of Jesus Christ", "I am a child of God", "I am a forgiven, saved, justified, sanctified, new-creation, follower of Jesus Christ").

But the questions are continually there:

"What IS a disciple?"

"What does it mean to be a disciple?"

"Why would I want to be a disciple?"

"How do I know if I'm disciple?"

"How can I help my family and friends to become disciples?"

"How do I live out my personal life as a disciple?"

"How do I live out my professional vocational life as a disciple?"

"How do I grow deeper in my personal relationship with Christ as a disciple?"

There are many people in this world that claim to be "of the Christian religion", yet who do not live out the characteristics or perceptions of being a disciple. It could be that they are *cultural Christians* (grew up in a Christian home, but who may not actually believe the Bible, or in Christ), or *social Christians* (identify as a Christian to fit into a societal norm or to make their spouses or friends feel better, but whom don't really believe), or they may be true believers in Jesus Christ, but their faith is superficial and lacking in depth of relationship with Christ. Whatever the case may be, something seems amiss.

The Purpose of This Book

The purpose of this book is to examine what it means to *BE a disciple* of Jesus Christ - and how we are instructed to *make disciples* as we travel in this life. What that looks like, feels like, and sounds like, and to understand our purpose and calling in being a disciple of Jesus Christ. And, not just in our personal lives, but also in our public and professional lives as well.

When I felt God's prompting to write this book, a clear image was burning in my mind. It is currently hanging on my wall, as a reminder of that vision and as a motivation to push through the hours and finish this book. That image was of a book cover that had people from all different walks of life and professions – police officers, firemen, nurses, teachers, business people, electricians, etc. What I would call *normal people* – yet *amazing people! Disciples.* Everyday people who are disciples of Jesus Christ, who share their stories, their insights, and how God has moved in their lives to both *Be Disciples*, and to *Make Disciples.*

The *Great Commission* in the Gospel of Matthew 28 was given to us by Jesus after his ministry, crucifixion, death, burial, and resurrection. Speaking to his disciples:

> **And Jesus came and said to them, "*All authority in heaven and on earth has been given to me. Go therefore and make disciples of all nations, baptizing them in the name of the Father and of the Son and of the Holy Spirit, teaching them to observe all that I have commanded you. And behold, I am with you always, to the end of the age.*"** *Matthew 28:18-20, ESV*

Not only are we called to BE disciples… we are commanded to "*make disciples of all nations, baptizing them in the name of the Father and of the Son and of the Holy Spirit, teaching them to observe all that I have commanded you…*".

Thus, the Purpose of this Book is to:

1. Help the reader understand the importance of being a disciple of Jesus Christ in both our personal lives and in our public/professional lives

2. Help the reader grow in a deeper personal relationship with Jesus Christ (whether a new believer or a life-long believer; we all can grow through continued focus, prayer, fellowship, and study, and through other's stories and examples).
3. Help the reader learn, through Scripture and the examples of other disciples, how to live out the life of Christ-centered discipleship – in both *being a disciple* and *making disciples.*

Twelve Stories

We will explore the lives of fourteen people who met with me, shared their story, and discussed how they follow God's leading in living out a life of being a disciple, and leading others to know Christ personally. This was done in twelve interviews which were recorded, and then carefully transcribed.

The dear people who you will read about come from different backgrounds, professions, and even from different countries. Older and younger, men and women, who love the Lord Jesus. Vocations include: police officer, fireman, former NFL player turned businessman, doctor, teachers, business owner, entrepreneurs, factory worker, software industry consultant, carpenter, electrician, engineer and mission leaders, government employee, and retired military.

Discussion & Application Questions

At the end of each chapter there is a series of *Discussion & Application Questions.* These are provided for personal study and reflection, small bible-study or life-group meetings - to help us to examine the story or the chapter and to identify:

- Key observations
- How God spoke to you through the chapter or story
- Application points that you want to make sure to remember and apply
- ACTION items to implement – (the professional coach in me can't help but to state that good ideas without a plan to take action are just wishes…. Taking action brings them to reality!)

Book Structure

The book is laid out in four sections on purpose, for **you**, the reader – whether for personal reading, life group discussion, other small group Bible study, book club, etc.:

1. *Section One*: The interview stories, with reflection questions at the end of each chapter to evaluate how it impacted you, what your key take-aways were, and to reflect on how God wants **you** to apply the principles in your life – personal or professional.
2. *Section Two*: Principles identified by the author
3. *Section Three*: Principles of discipleship categorized and systematized into what we are calling the *DISCIPLE-ing Matrix.* A model showing the interconnectedness of BE-ing a disciple and MAKE-ing disciples…as we are on the journey of life, work, family, socialization, etc.
4. *Section Four*: Final thoughts, conclusions, an ACTION plan for DISCIPLE-ing, and an examination of: *Spirit vs. Flesh – Choices & Consequences, and the Good News of Jesus Christ*

Section One:

Interviews

DISCIPLE-ing

Chapter 1

Adam M.
Police Lieutenant
Disciple of Jesus Christ

Adam is a warrior: a friendly, kind, helpful, compassionate, and gentle warrior. He is a family man, a husband, a
father, a brother, and a great friend. He loves to help
people, to serve his community, his church, and various
ministry organizations. He has a friendly smile and warm
eyes. He is also a protector – *a Sheepdog* – *"protecting the
sheep from the wolves"*. When the innocent are threatened,
Adam and his colleagues rush in to serve and protect the
public from those who would do them harm – even at the
risk of their own lives. As we read in John 15:13 *"Greater
love has one than this, that someone lay down his life for
his friends"* – and Adam has dedicated his life to protect
others. He is a leader, and commands a great deal of
respect from those who have been blessed to get to know
him. As his friend, I can also tell you that he has a great
sense of humor, loves to laugh, tell funny stories, and spend
time with those he cares about. And, most importantly,
Adam is a disciple of Jesus Christ. Adam was the first
person that the Lord led me to invite to interview in the
process of writing this book, and you will be greatly
blessed by this interview:

Interview with Adam - April 25th, 2019

Steve: In your personal life, how do you live out your faith? I know you're real active in your church and in your security team and Great Banquet, but tell me a little bit about how you live out your faith in your personal life?

Adam: I'm a very introverted person. In my life since accepting Christ, when I see a stranger, I try to smile and say "hi" to them. Little things like that is sharing the love of Christ with others. Just by engaging others with eye contact or smiles, trying to be more inviting. People were drawn to Jesus because He seemed to be easy to talk to or fun to be around. It didn't always have to be something he was saying, it was just His persona. So, I'm trying to embody that more. Before, I would be very closed off. I wouldn't make eye contact. I really didn't care if I interacted with people since I'm such an introvert. In the real world, once I know you I'm not, but really stepping out of my comfort zone and being drawn to share that love and engage, not by some big speech, but by being warm and loving...

Steve: and *real...*

Adam: Exactly, being *real.* It's amazing to see the surprise. Some people are very surprised to see it, even more so when I'm in uniform. On a day to day basis, dressed like a normal person, people aren't used to strangers being nice or just engaging. That's really pushed me to know more of what Christ was like.

Steve: That is amazing that you're *out-of-the-ordinary* if you're nice to people.

Adam: Yeah.

Steve: If you actually wave at people or make eye contact or speak to them in the store and are friendly...It sets you apart, especially with younger people. Wow, that's weird.

Adam: Yeah, unfortunately, today there is a lot less personal interaction than there used to be. Part of it is society, part of it is technology. We've gotten to be a culture of not engaging each other and that's sort of what I miss about...I wish I had grown up in the 40's or 50's because it seemed like people were more engaged with each other. We've lost that.

Steve: So, you're active in your church. Tell me about that; what do you do in your church life?

Adam: I used to operate the soundboard for the worship team. I love music, but I'm not up to their level of playing. My schedule prevents me from doing that now. The Sundays I'm off, I make it a priority to go to church. I don't like lying in bed and taking a day off. Sometimes my wife and kids will sometimes say "let's skip", but If I'm off, I feel I need to be there! Because the way my schedule is, I'm only off every other weekend as it is, so I just feel compelled to be there and to be a part of the Christian community. There are some days when I go alone. I'm really involved in the Bible Study Fellowship and a couple's small group through my church.

Steve: You've been doing that a long time, right?

Adam: Yeah, I've been doing BSF for about nine years or so.

Steve: Nine years. Wow.

Adam: Yeah. It's really a blessing... I love it because it makes me stay intentional. We get summers off, so it's like being in school. Over those 30 weeks, I'm accountable, not just to myself, but to all the men in the group because you have a small group, and if you don't do the lesson, it's pretty obvious. Because we start discussing stuff and if you're not talking and they call on you and you go, "uh, well, I didn't do my studies", so I...

Steve: be prepared...

Adam: I feel very compelled to really be in the Word, and that's something I need. I still feel really young in the discipleship walk, so I needed something...have something to keep me on task. Every morning, I start on the Bible-app. I pull up a different devotion. Either it's a week-long devotion. Sometimes I've done 30-day devotionals, but the first thing I do in the morning before I start hitting Facebook and all that kind of stuff when I get up, I open up the devotional. I spend a few minutes getting started with some prayer. I actually started that last year. I had a devotional with 365 devotions. Every day, even if I went on vacation, I took the devotion with me, and I try to get very intentional, and after that first year, I just kept with it.

Steve: It was routine.

Adam: I love how it starts my day that way. If I get out of sync, or for some reason, forget to do it, I notice it right away. My day's not right, so I have to stop, and since I always have my phone with me, I never have an excuse not to do it.

Steve: There you go! So, how does it translate from when you're with your family and church and personal life....to then putting on your uniform, and jumping in a police car and going out and serving the community in that capacity.

How does that translate? How do you live out your faith in your professional life?

Adam: Well, it's funny because now the way I look at it, there is no difference. When I put on that uniform, what I see is, a profound response from strangers. When they see a police officer walk into a store and I make eye contact with somebody and say, "hi, how are you doing?" they're shocked by a police officer being approachable because we're typically like robots.

Steve: Stoic.

Adam: Yeah, so before I really accepted Christ, there was no change at home. Maybe I was more, you know, impatient, more likely not to go to church, and same way at work. I was a little looser with the little things like taking some pens home, or grabbing batteries. It's Christmas time, we have batteries at work, so grab some batteries because your kids' toys are going to need batteries. Ethically, that's just not right. Before, I wouldn't have thought twice about it. I didn't, but after I made that conscious decision to start to be more Christ-like, at work, in little things like that, I know God is watching, so I feel like somebody's going to catch me. So, it doesn't matter if I'm at home or work, it's that same, I'm accountable to God, whether somebody's watching or not. That's the biggest thing now. I do the right thing, even when nobody's watching.

Steve: That's *character*, right?

Adam: Exactly. I try to impress that upon my kids and my *work kids*, the young officers that work for me, to always to be accountable even when nobody's watching. Do the right thing. You'll never go wrong that way. It keeps you on the right path. It's that faith and my desire to be a disciple. My prayer every day is to be a little more Christ-like. I have issues with my patience, self-control, my mouth; I can be pretty hurtful with my words really quick. Before I wouldn't think twice about it, now I feel guilty about it. I'll apologize. I'll ask for forgiveness if I've upset somebody. It goes the same way with work; I need to be more patient. I need to watch my words more carefully, because being a Lieutenant now, I've got a bunch of guys, I call them *kids* because I've started to figure out how they look at me; I'm on a pedestal to them.

Steve: Gray hair and everything. [laughs]

Adam: Yeah, So, I really have to watch what I say, how I say it, because they will take it very literally and it's almost like a dad talking to them. It's like there's a lot of military guys and former military that work for me, so using the Lord's name in vain, I think it's just vocabulary that the military uses, but everybody knows that "GD" comes out of their mouth during roll call or something. Now I don't even have to say anything. The other guys will say, "Hey, hey, Lieutenant doesn't like that!." Or sometimes, mid-sentence, they'll stop and go 'gosh darnit', and so, that little bit is me sharing my faith. It's sort of tough. With my co-workers it's a little easier because I can't really share it with the public. I can't prophesy to them on a traffic stop. Other officers around the country have been fired for doing that, but if the public opens that window, then I'm much more apt to jump right in and share my faith.

Steve: Like pray with them, or what?

Adam: I haven't actually prayed with people at the scene, but when somebody has asked for help or if someone is in a bad situation, I'll say to them, "Do you mind if I say a prayer for you?" Especially if I know they're a person of faith, they love it, but it's not always when I'm able to do it right then and there, sometimes it's after the fact. A lot of times, I've left the scene, I'll pull my car down the street, stop and pray; for healing, for strength, for whatever it may be for that family, that person.

<u>Steve</u>: To recover from the trauma or whatever it might be?

<u>Adam</u>: Yeah, exactly.

<u>Steve</u>: In thinking this through, we're called to be disciples first - then we're called to make disciples, and to share the Good News, to share our faith with others. In your professional world, you kind of have to pick and choose, when is an appropriate time for that. As a public servant, obviously, there's probably lots of rules and regulations, but when do you feel comfortable, like with work colleagues, or if it's off duty, or if you're just having dinner or just having coffee, or you're on break….how do you know when the time is right to share your faith with somebody? Is it just offering to pray for people or how do you normally do that?

<u>Adam</u>: So, with the public we spend a lot of time being social workers, counselors, so a lot of the time it's just being open, loving, listening… I can still model being a disciple without sharing my faith with them in words.

<u>Steve</u>: Sure.

<u>Adam</u>: If they respond back and I can tell they have faith, or sometimes they've got no faith at all - but they're open to it - then I just have to watch for those doors to open up, and once they do, then I step in and ask if they go to church? Do they have people they get together with? If they

don't go to church, do they hang out with people who go to church? So, I can sort of ease into it that way without saying, "You need to be saved." There are ways to do that. My co-workers; I pay attention to their conversations, especially around the holidays. You'll find out where they go to church or I'll see them on Facebook or Instagram and you'll see, everyone is going to Easter service, so obviously, if they're church going, I'll notice that. To some other guys, apparently, I exude that I've got some faith, because one of them said, "I'm not really a spiritual person like you, but…"

Steve: Your work colleagues?

Adam: Yeah, one of the other supervisors, because he was going to have surgery and I said, "Well, I'll say a prayer for you that it goes well". He was very accepting of it.

Steve: Sure.

Adam: But some things get a little tough. I'm a little guarded in my words, so I don't offend anybody, yet I don't hide my faith either. So, they know where I stand. I think people see it in a good light, especially the one colleague who's "not spiritual". He appreciated my support and consolation and telling him "things are going to be better".

Steve: That makes sense. I heard you tell a story at the banquet about how you used to view people…or how you have a lot of friends and family on the police department and fire department and that you tend to get a little bit jaded, or calloused…

Adam: Cynical.

Steve: Just because of all the stuff around you, but how has the Lord spoke to you through that? As you became a Christian, how did you change?

Adam: Well, it used to be real simple: there's good guys and there's bad guys.

Steve: *Black and white? (figuratively)*

Adam: Black and white. And there's even some good bad guys. So, there's good people in bad situations, but I just viewed them as broken, you need to go to jail, I have no use for you. Here we go. Now even with the bad guys, while I want to be condemning of them, I also see a softer side - sometimes there's a reason for that situation.

Steve: Right...

Adam: So, I try to see the *person*. The biggest thing I try to keep in mind is: I've obviously sinned; they've sinned. I'm not here to condemn them, just like I don't want to be condemned either. So, I try to keep that in mind. I have to do my job, but I can still be compassionate toward them. Now, there are some people who don't deserve my compassion; child molesters, stuff like that. It's tough.

Steve: It's hard to be compassionate...

Adam: It's not up to me to condemn them, but I'm also not trying to save them. They've got a little more work to do on their end. Before I saw good guys and bad guys; now I see *opportunities for people to be saved*. So, there's the good people in the bad situation that need some hope. I've taken people to jail, and on the ride up there, by the time we get there, I've shared a message of hope with them: "Things can get better. This isn't the bottom. You can bounce back from this!". If nothing else, it seems to change their attitude a little bit.

Steve: Don't give up hope.

Adam: Exactly. I sort of give them the talk that I would hope Jesus would give me if I were in that spot. To "don't give up. Have faith". I can't always have the time or even get into a deep conversation to find out if they're followers of Christ.

Steve: Sure.

Adam: Not losing hope and keeping faith, anyway. I don't really care if they're Jewish, if they're Muslim, they've got a God to pray to. You can still have faith. It's non-denominational to have that love, that faith, to share with each other. But yeah, the way I look at people is very different now.

Steve: So, I think I remember you saying something at one point about dedicating life to the Lord, dedicating what you do to the Lord, as the Bible talks about; 'whatever you do, do it for God'.

Adam: Do it unto the Lord.

Steve: So, how does that play out in your professional world?

Adam: So, years ago, I was a lot more selfish. Very ambitious. Self-promoting, wanted to move up the chain. Just like the corporate world, we have the same stuff. 'I want to get promoted, be in charge of stuff,' and this was probably ten years ago. Looking back, I had no business being where I thought I needed to be, because God wasn't done with me yet. God hadn't prepared me. I didn't know that at the time. Now, looking back on my life, the 'no's' I was getting...If I had someone standing in my way, making sure I didn't get a certain position or promotion, now I see it was God making sure I didn't get too far ahead. He had me exactly where I needed to be at that time. And I share that message with other guys who don't get positions they want at the right time or a specialty, 'Don't lose faith. Don't give up.' You're just not ready yet. If I know they have faith, I'll even share with them, 'God's not done with you yet.' And I'll share my story with them. I do this with my kids, too, because it's a youthful thing. You think you're ready and want to push ahead. And I share with them my setbacks, where, if it was always left up to me, where I was, I would mess it up. God tells us 'no' sometimes to make us think: "What am I missing? What are you trying to teach me? What are you trying to show me?" So, now I look at my job and that I have been saved about ten years...So, I'm an infant still. But to look back over those ten years and think, 'okay, if I hear a no...'; First I ask, "What am I supposed to be learning now? What are you sharpening me for later?" If it really hurts, I say: "You put me in the fire for a reason, I'd love to know where I need to be". But, you have be patient. So, I come to work every day, and I just want to do a great job because God has given me so many opportunities, and *do-overs*, that I want to make it worth it. Jesus died for me. If I gave up my life for somebody on duty, I would hope they would spend the rest of their life trying to make it up...you can't earn it, necessarily, but you sort of *want to try to earn it*. Christ died to save us. I want to live up to it... I want to do right by Him. So, that's the way I see my job now; just coming to work every day. I want to make somebody else's life better. I've got that opportunity to make somebody's life…or the police department…better. I just want to make sure when I leave, they will forget me…a week after I retire, I will be forgotten. But if I know I touched somebody's life, or made that place a little bit better somehow, I've done my job.

Steve: How many years have you been on the police force?

Adam: 24 years.

Steve: 24 years on the police force - Wow.

Adam: That's the gray hair.

Steve: Yeah, so you look back over your whole career, and you just say: "Yeah, I've impacted people, I've helped keep our community safe, and then I've also been able to bless people through sharing my faith. And whenever God presented that opportunity…"

Adam: I just try to lead a good example. The guys who work for me, I try to be a good example for them. And the bad part is, and it's not just us in the police world, but anybody, you may never know who you touched. And that's why we always have to go out there, every single day, trying to make a difference, and not get frustrated by not seeing the fruits of our labor. Sometimes we're not intended to see who we touched. But if you've done your job, you've planted the seeds. Somebody's going to plant the seeds. Somebody else is going to water them. It's sort of cliché', but it's so true. Maybe I planted that seed, somebody else ten years from now is going to water it, and then it may be 20 years from now before it really sprouts and they do what God intended them do.

Steve: I'm thinking I remember you saying you had a life verse. Is there a verse that's kind of your main verse right now? One that really speaks to you the most?

Adam: Well, my biggest is John 15:13. *"Greater love has no man than this, that a man lay down his life for his friends."* Because I go to work every day, prepared to die for somebody I don't even really know, and not think twice about it. I don't want to die, but I think what I used in my talk is: "Before, I was afraid to die, because of selfish reasons. Once I was saved, I don't want to die, but I'm not afraid to die, because I know where I'm going, and I know I'm not going to die until God's ready to take me home. So, I have a confidence, not to be reckless, but not to be in fear either."

> *"Before, I was afraid to die, because of selfish reasons. Once I was saved, I don't want to die, but I'm not afraid to die, because I know where I'm going, and I know I'm not going to die until God's ready to take me home. So, I have a confidence, not to be reckless, but not to be in fear either."*
>
> *-Adam M, Police Officer*

Steve: I love that. As a leader in the police force, as an officer and a leader, what would you say are the main leadership principles that God's Word has shown you, that are important to you in your role, as a leader of men?

Adam: It's kind of funny. So, in Bible Study Fellowship this year, we were studying people of the Promised Land, so a lot of the prophets, but really, we focused on Saul on to David, and into Solomon. Those are God's chosen people, and to see, by their own devices, they were messed up individuals. They made some seriously bad mistakes. Yet, God was never going to give up on them. He had a plan for them, even in their turmoil, God did great things with them. And each generation got better. But the biggest thing is how, really with David and into Solomon, despite their shortcomings, how they treated their people. Whether it be their soldiers, even the people that they conquered, because God would spare a third of all the lands that David conquered. We talked about why God would do that. Partly to show His grace and mercy, and partly to have people to testify to that grace and mercy. When they go on to their kids, and their generations, these conquered people are going to go forth and tell them: "He's not their God" - hopefully they convert, but they're going to tell the good news of how great God is, even though they were conquered people.

Steve: So, there's a big difference between Saul and David?

Adam: Oh, huge! Well…

Steve: Not completely, but in a lot of ways.

Adam: Saul never saw the big picture. David - it took him awhile, but he finally caught on. It took that promise that, 'David, you're not going to be the one to build the temple. You're not going to be the one to see this through; your son is. And even Solomon who was...that was a whole other story, how David's first child, obviously, out of adultery…

Steve: With Bathsheba…

Adam: Yep...died. But Solomon, because, after Uriah was actually dead, he married Bathsheba, so Solomon was born, and God blessed that one. So, those stories right there, one, give me a lot of hope and promise because when God wants it done, it's going to get done. We have to trust God's will and be very patient. What I've learned from those is patience, dealing with anybody, but when they've got out of their own ambitious ways, and were patient on what God's plan was, they were successful. When they showed love. And what really struck me was Solomon, when in His dream, God asked, "What do you want?" And Solomon says: 'I just want wisdom'. And God said, 'since you asked for wisdom, I'm going to give you wealth and power too', because you weren't as concerned with that. Whereas, Saul was all about the power. David was more of the hybrid. Solomon, just to be wise. And when I think about wisdom and what that really means, or if I think about the truly wise people, they're the ones that are really in tune with God's will. They listen.

Steve: I love that.

Adam: They listen. There's a double-edged sword though, with being wise, it is now you know what God is all about and what God can do, you're expected to uphold that. So, be careful what you ask for. If you're truly wise, you're held that much more accountable. But as leaders, I really see that's how I'm really going to change the culture of our department, the future officers, is by teaching them compassion for people early on. I was taught by old school guys. It's black and white. Sometimes you are the judge, the jury, the executioner, etc. Well, now, times are different, but if I'm going to teach these new guys, even though you see nails everywhere, you don't always have to use the hammer. The old adage, where, 'when all you have is a hammer, everyone is a nail'. You don't always need that. So, teaching them compassion. To be loving. To be helpful. To do the right thing. To be bigger than thinking "we want to punish people". It's in our nature. It's not our job to punish. So, I'm trying to teach our young guys, not knowingly on their end, but how to be compassionate and loving, but yet still take somebody to jail. We still have to do our job, but you can affect some change. It's not just putting the cuffs on them and running them to jail. Spend some time with them. Sometimes the best thing to do is not arrest somebody or not give them a ticket - to be able to touch somebody's life. So, that's the biggest thing. I wish I had bosses that taught me that. I think it's getting a little bit easier. I don't know if it's because of me and the other people that are in leadership that want to share our faith or are more open to it, or if things are changing and we are trying to be more compassionate in our job.

Steve: From your experience, having been on the force 24 years, what percent do you see that grew up in church? Is it 50%, or is it 20% or 30%? If you had to guess....

Adam: That's a good question. People in general, or people I work with?

Steve: People on the force...if you just had to take a wild guess.

Adam: I think it's a much higher percentage now. The only reason I know that is, I've noticed more people more open to letting their faith be known. Not hiding the fact that they go to church. In the past, at least, with our job, nobody talked about it. I was shocked by how many people were in Bible studies or did go to church. You would never know about it because they wouldn't talk about it. It was very guarded. Now it's not.

Steve: Is it guarded because professional life and personal life are totally separate?

Adam: Part of that and the mystique of what a Police Officer should look like. And I think our profession is changing because it needs to. We're not just *the law enforcers*, we're people of the community. To some degree, it's going back to how police or *cops* were back in the old days, when policing first started. We are, 'of the people'. We have to keep that in mind. We're not above everyone else, we're a part of the populous. So, we should be caring...that has started to change. A lot of that has to do with being more aware of mental health issues with other people, as well as with us. So, we've made it easier for guys to feel comfortable talking about their feelings and what's going on. So, I think they're more comfortable talking about that they go to church or that they grew up in the church. Which, I think is outstanding!

Steve: They're good citizens.

Adam: Yeah, absolutely. It's sort of how they've taken prayer out of the schools, or even the Pledge of Allegiance in some places. When we were growing up, we unknowingly knew that was a good thing, because it bonded a lot of people together. Being able to say, 'God,' or know what God is, even if you didn't go to church. That was a good thing.

Steve: Absolutely.

Adam: But times, I think, are slowly changing. We still fight with that in the government realm. You can't talk about God, but you can. You just have to find better ways to do it. You have to be careful how you do it, too. There are certain people that have been disciplined for it. Well, they go out of their way, to almost make people feel bad if they don't go to church or that they're not saved. I don't think we're supposed to ram it down people's throats.

Steve: But if they give you the open door?

Adam: But if they give you the open door... I told a story in one of my devotions. I've done a couple different teams, so you've probably heard it, a call I was on, it was a 12- or 13-year-old little girl. She had a lot of mental and family issues going on. But we were talking about healthier ways for her to deal with anger, or when she's upset, and she had a friend over at her house with her that's the same age, and the 13-year-old friend of hers said: "Well, when I don't know what else to do, I just pray." And you talk about the skies parting and opening up! So, we had adults in there. I had other officers, and you talk about that open window, and I thought, 'perfect' because the other girl goes, "Well, I don't know how to pray." And so, first of all, this 13-year-old girl who opened the window for everybody, she and I just fed off of that. It was great, because I knew my other younger officers were listening ...the mom, the aunt, the uncle, who were in the room, they were listening. It was as simple as that. So, that 13-year-old girl made it that simple: "When I don't know what else to do, I pray." And when someone else says, 'I don't know how to pray'. "It's simple, you just tell God what's on your mind, what's hurting you, and offer it up. And that's prayer. It doesn't have to be eloquent. It doesn't have to be ten minutes long. It's just between you and God". Every prayer is different.

That was just a really cool thing that I saw happen, so, that's how I know *when windows are open.*

Steve: And by you supporting that and encouraging that, and being there to support her young friend, praying with her, and being there and just talking, you showed your witness. You didn't crush it, but you didn't instigate it?

Adam: Yeah, someone else already opened it up, it was just up to me to support it. Because I think if that opportunity is there, and we avoid that opportunity, that's just about as bad as persecuting. So, if the opportunity is there, I don't necessarily feel the need to go be the preacher on it, but I need to support it. And I think people seeing those of us in uniform having faith and not afraid to share it is a very powerful and positive thing. They need to see we're human, they need to see the people we deal with. They may go to church and be strong in the faith, but they see us in uniform - we look like robots, they think we're like that. But for them to see that we have police officers who grew up in the church – that we know who Christ is - I think to make that bond, it makes us a little more human to them. It just really helps. Because I will stop being a cop in a few years. I will not stop being a Christian. That's the most important thing. I'm never going to sacrifice my faith for my job. I'm not going to deny Christ, so to speak, and if the opportunity is there… I'm not going to shy away from it. I did early on, because I wasn't quite sure how to jump in, but now I know …

Steve: It's who you are.

Adam: Maybe I'm older and wiser now or I just don't care as much what happens to me. I'm not going to deny it or hold back.

Steve: Alright. Good. Okay, last question. So, the fruits of the spirit are: love, joy, peace, patience, kindness, goodness, faithfulness, gentleness and self-control. How do you see them manifest in your work, in your professional life?

Adam: Some of these, quite a bit. The joy, love, peace, kindness...well, kindness, usually, when I'm not stressed out, low blood sugar, or tired. The self-control and patience go first.

Steve: Just from stress?

Adam: Well, I hadn't eaten all day and last night, and I was at Costco with my wife and it had been a long shopping trip. And I got a little frustrated with her on what line to pick to get out, and I finally just said, "Just pick a line!" and the problem was, I said it a little bit louder, and I think maybe in my *cop voice,* because I walked away because I had to go to the customer service counter, and unbeknownst to me, some guy opened up a checkout line for her, because he felt bad for her.

Steve: Oh wow.

Adam: So then, I felt bad, so I humbled myself on the way out, when I met up with her, and I said, "I'm sorry, I did not mean to embarrass you or yell at you. So, there's the difference, too: technically, I was right, 'Go find a line; just get it', but the *way* I did it...So, that's where my faith has changed me, I'm still impatient, I still lose self-control, but I recognize it right away... and seek forgiveness.

Steve: So, you're not perfect? (laugh)

Adam: No, I play *perfect* on TV, but not in real life. So, most of those... the love, the kindness, like I was talking about, trying to say, 'hi' to people and just to smile; it helps me come out of my shell a little bit, but I'm exuding the love, the joy, the peace...because that's how I feel. I mean, the fact that I'm saved makes me happy, even when I'm having a bad day. It could be a whole lot worse.

<u>Steve</u>: Take joy in it, even if you're having a bad day, right?

<u>Adam</u>: Absolutely.

<u>Steve</u>: Very cool. Any final words? Any final thoughts?

<u>Adam</u>: You know, this endeavor, the whole *'showing faith at home versus showing faith at work,'* the closer I get to Christ, I don't see a difference between the two. It's an internal change. It's a heart change. It's a mind change. I think the more Christ-like we get, we're going to be that way no matter what we do. And I think the more we focus on making that a personality change of our own, it's going to come through both places. I'm not afraid to share it at work. Part of it is because my faith is strong enough now that if somebody is going to come down on me for sharing my faith at work,

> *"You know, this endeavor, the whole 'showing faith at home versus showing faith at work,' the closer I get to Christ, I don't see a difference between the two. It's an internal change. It's a heart change. It's a mind change. I think the more Christ-like we get, we're going to be that way no matter what we do.*
>
> *- Adam M*

even though I know I'm not ramming it down anyone's throat, I'm not going to apologize for it either. I would apologize if I offended someone, I'm not going to apologize for being... (pause)

Steve: For being you?

Adam: ... for being me, or sharing the fact that I'm saved through Christ.

Steve: That's awesome.

Adam: In fact, the more persecuted, Paul says, the more persecuted we are, take joy in it...because that allows us to be closer to Christ.

Observations, Lessons, Application:

- What were your key Observations from Adam's life and faith journey?

- Are there any parts of Adam's journey and story that you can relate to personally?

- How do you think God wants you to apply these principles in **your** life moving forward?

Chapter 2

Andrew
Senior Director, Consultant
Disciple of Jesus Christ

Andrew is an extremely thoughtful, strategic, and cerebral thinker. He is a chess player. Analytical and articulate in his work life, spiritual life, and personal life. With a quick wit, and a very approachable demeanor, Andrew is a comfortable and inviting person to talk with – about business, family, or the Lord and His Word. And, He is a Disciple of Jesus Christ – a follower, a student, a learner, and our interview was very insightful. Enjoy.

Interview with Andrew, May 6th, 2019

Steve: So, Andrew, tell me about how you came to faith in Christ?

Andrew: It was actually a process. It was not one moment in time. I had been raised Catholic, but coming out of college I was pretty much more of an atheist. Actually, thinking back, I had become a hardcore atheist. I don't even remember praying or even giving a thought to pray when I was bedside when my mother passed. I remained in that atheist state until someone in the workplace approached me. He was new to the team and I was getting them introduced to what we were doing on the engagement. They said "that's interesting and all, but have you accepted Christ?" I was shocked by how bold they were, so it got me thinking. It started with being in the Word. I was given the challenge to go off and read the Gospel of John. I did that. It raised a ton of questions. And I just dove in.

I remember when I started to raise these questions, my co-worker would say very confidently, "Look, I don't care what questions or doubt you have about the Bible. It's Truth with a capital T. It will hold up to whatever you've got, so, why don't you just outline for me what your questions and points of doubt are, and let's just walk through the Word and address them one-by-one. He was so confident and so bold. I was, if nothing else, intellectually curious enough. And they say, 'Faith comes through hearing', but it was a process over time of just being in the Word.

Steve: I love that. Three key words came out of that: PROCESS, and you were CHALLENGED, and I'd say you were challenged by a BOLD disciple.

Andrew: Bold. And *doubt's not a bad thing.* Look into your doubt - It makes you even stronger.

Steve: Exactly. How many years ago was that?

Andrew: I'd say, a ballpark of ten or eleven years ago. Something like that.

Steve: Okay. Very good. So, how do you, and we'll get into it…how you do it in the workplace…here in a minute, but how do you live out your faith in your personal life? What does that look like? You and your family, obviously, you go to our church, but how do you live out your faith? What kind of things do you like to do to build the Kingdom?

Andrew: I'm challenging myself to figure it out…to grow that responsibility. To figure out being trusted with a little, do something with it. Hopefully the opportunity comes to be given more. So, it's mostly around leadership in the family, of course.

Steve: Your close circle of family or your larger family in context?

Andrew: Well, both. I am challenged both to be a leader, while encouraging my family to apply scripture to the challenges that we face. We're going to encounter all kinds of challenges and various trials as part of being Christian. We never know what's going to be thrown our way. Having Scripture to fall back on is critical. When we start operating out of fear, uncertainty, doubt, we can all go there, but really trying to understand that it all comes back to love; what does that really look like? Looking at roles; what's the actual role of a father look like? What does the role of a husband look like? And drawing on Scripture for that. And, also, then teaching that too. It's my responsibility to teach my family. So, it's one thing for me to go off and take on a Bible study… but if I'm not helping that to grow my family and help them in their knowledge and understanding of the Word of Christ, then that's on me. I take that responsibility very seriously. So, day to day, as I 'm studying, I study daily, a couple hours a day, typically, I'm sharing that with them, trying to share that around the table.

Steve: So, is that two hours personal study every day? Or is that two hours with family?

Andrew: Two hours personal study, every day, at a minimum. And then I'll apply that both to our study at work, to the family itself, but most importantly, there's times where you don't have access to the Word. This does happen sometimes. It's going to come down to what's in your heart; do you have enough scripture in your heart to share with others and continue to disciple, when you don't have a copy of the Bible in front of you? To me that's really important.

Steve: Do you do family devotionals?

Andrew: We've tried some different things. It's really less formal than that, honestly.

Steve: So, how many people are in your immediate family?

Andrew: So, it's just my wife, my daughter, and I. And she's thirteen.

Steve: Ok, gotcha. So, she's starting to run around and do her girl stuff? Sports? And things like that?

Andrew: Exactly. Yeah, pretty busy that way. We actually started her, actually at Lifepointe, some years ago, when she was five, I think, in an *AWANA* program there. Still trying to get her introduced to the Word early in that context too.

Steve: What about your prayer life? What's your prayer life look like?

Andrew: So, I try to really pull from how Christ talked about prayer, which was not to be a lot of words. Don't go on and on like the gentiles do. I try to do it more in private. I try to take advantage of this whole concept of, 'Be still'. So, when you get in your car...I've got to commute every day, right? So, I've got guaranteed 15-20 minutes, where I can just turn the radio off entirely. When you wake up and go to sleep, your commute time, and lunch, you're guaranteed five times, so you want to be continuously in prayer. I don't try to pray selfishly. I truly try to pray for Kingdom work being exposed and being wise enough to see opportunities to do things. So, it's all about, 'Thy will be done, on earth as it is in Heaven'. So, what are you doing on earth now? So, I pray for opportunities to either glorify God or be given more challenges. Or I heard this Sunday, this idea that, 'Your test becomes your testimony'. I try to pray properly around trials. It seems like over the last ten years, I've had a lot of challenges, really pushing...

Steve: So, you had a *test* that became your *testimony*?

Andrew: Several. Just a lot of deaths. Working through marital issues to the point of coming right up to that precipice of divorce. Wife and daughter were almost killed a couple years ago in a car accident. So, praying our way back through that. Just a lot of things. Again, praying that you handle things in a way that's going to show that you are a *Christian*. And not let other things motivate you. But overall, to me it's the Lord's prayer, over and over a lot. And thinking about that and being very intentional, about every word in there, but really focusing on His will and His kingdom.

Steve: I love that. You were telling me a little bit about this Bible study that you've been running now for three years at your office. But it's with consultants that are spread all over the country and you're doing it via telephone, right?

Andrew: Right.

Steve: So, how did that start? And what does that look like?

<u>Andrew</u>: So, it's really another gentleman and myself that have really driven that. We've had people fall in and out, but basically, it's consistently finding a time and making it a priority. It's a weekly cadence. And it's about an hour long. And we ask for folks to spend some hours researching and studying and looking at commentary, or listening to sermons. And obviously reading the Word in the first place. And those kinds of things. But we've found that a couple folks have naturally emerged as leaders that really get into that. And then we have some younger folks that rotate in too. So, the idea is to, where we can, pass the baton. Try to enforce some kind of accountability. Every week we have someone that should be leading it.

<u>Steve</u>: It sounds like, from seeing your notes right there, this is real solid Bible study, kind of expository - get the Word out, read it, talk about, 'What's it mean?' 'How to be quiet?' I mean, real expository style Bible studies.

<u>Andrew</u>: Yes. Absolutely. This is tying, backward and forward, into other scriptures, exploring larger themes, getting into application. It's really meant to be a nice expository discussion, followed up by application. And then we bookend it with prayer. We open up in prayer and we close in prayer, and that prayer is going to be tied to, 'What did we learn?' We can apply this. We can share this. It's become its own little small group, in a way too, because we expose any kind of prayer considerations for, if someone's going through a surgery that week, or pray for this or that.

<u>Steve</u>: It's a small group. It's just done via technology.

<u>Andrew</u>: Yep, that's right.

Steve: Do you ever all get together… all in the same building, like once a year for business meetings? Or is it still scattered?

Andrew: No, we do. Like over Christmas, we all made a priority to all physically get together over a nice long lunch. We had the study right there in the restaurant. It was obvious to all those around us what we were doing.

Steve: Is this a multi-state study or is this people just gather all around the city?

Andrew: Most are in the city, but there are some, depending on where we're at, and we've got offices in three different states.

Steve: This can be in your personal life as well, but just from talking with you, I get the feeling that you're not afraid of sharing your faith in Christ; that you'll publicly share that. People at work know that. Obviously, you don't rub their nose in it, but how do you typically share your faith? What does that look like?

Andrew: I think it's a couple of things. Again, going back to scripture, we're called to be *salt and light*. I know that sounds cliché' to answer, but it's true. People should be wanting some of whatever you have, so I think there's a joy aspect. So, when people see you going through trials and yet, you have a smile on your face, you're high energy, and that kind of thing. There's plenty of things in my office. If you looked around, there are a lot of notes, and a Bible that can open up discussion sometimes. But I think it's…one, I think there is a 'bold' aspect to it. But there's also an understanding when people are in pain or having challenges and sharing with them how there are things that have helped you in your life. So, there's opportunities there to really help. As an example, we recently had a death in the family that was very... all deaths are substantial, but some... you feel the hurt more. It was my daughter's first family death that she had to deal with.

Steve: Was it a close family member?

Andrew: Grandfather.

Steve: Grandfather. Okay.

Andrew: And so, very close. So, how do you provide a framework for handling and coping with death? And thinking through that and talking through that, and then seeing how she reacted and responded and applied that, was incredible. And then feeling the need to say, 'You know what? I have a lot of friends that have daughters around this age, or sons around this age; they're going to be going through this soon'. So then using this as an opportunity to say, 'Hey, I know that we just went through this and I think it's something that could really help your kids.' And whether they're believers or not, there's other sources that they can read, a book they could pick up, and it can give them some of this frame, it exposes them to some truth, and the Gospel in a different way.

Steve: Okay. How often would you say that you are blessed to actually share the Gospel of Jesus Christ with others?

Andrew: So, this is an interesting question. First answer is not often enough. But I also think this answer is about being *at the right spot on the chess board*. In a fairly conservative Christian community, in the middle of Indiana, those opportunities are going to be less frequent... they're there, but consider if you were to plop yourself in the middle of a prison ministry or a rehab ministry, those kind of things, where you've just got, if you chose to, you'd have a lot more opportunities. It's about how you prioritize and where do you spend your time on the chess board. So, the answer is, it depends on the season and where I'm at. There are times when I've been able to have a huge impact and talk to dozens of people all at the same time. There are times in my day to day life, where I may not see anybody; on a Saturday, I may not leave the house. [Laughter] But there are times where you're just surrounded by people that need the Gospel and you can share it with them. But you can't do that unless you've got the Word in your heart.

Steve: I love that: *right spot on the Chess board.* That is brilliant.

Andrew: There's a concept of being *activated* in Chess. Think about this: If you're a bishop, you're working on a diagonal. But if you're trapped behind a row of pawns, you can't do anything; completely *inactivated.* If you're free to move, you're *activated.* If you're on the longest diagonal, you're fully activated. Right? So, you think about given your spiritual gifts, where do you need to be? And that will impact what kind of influence you can have around you, based on being the same Chess piece you are, where do you need to be?

Steve: I love that. Very good. And if you're a knight, you can jump over the pawns. Right?

Andrew: That's right. [Laughter] If you've got a spiritual gift, just go for it. [Laughs]

Steve: So, have you ever felt the Lord's leading in your business life...Do you see your business life as a ministry platform? Or have you ever felt that way?

Andrew: Yeah, it's a mixed bag for me. I think there are different dimensions of it. One of it is just doing the best you can at everything. So, the idea that you're doing this for the Lord. And bringing glory that way. And there's a certain amount of energy you need to bring. I think there's a certain amount of growth you need to demonstrate. And it seems that gives you more opportunity for people that want to hear more about things you may want to share with them. I know that our company, as a whole, puts faith as a priority. The idea is that if you walk into a sales meeting on Monday mornings, underneath every single person's notebook or laptop is a Bible. And that's because they pray first. When you go into a meeting and someone looks like they're in trouble, we pause right there, before we start, 'Are you doing okay? Let's say a prayer right now'. So, it's a very unique...I don't think that's very common.

Steve: No, that's not common.

Andrew: So, it's interesting to see, having worked on the coasts and working here, it seems like there are different priorities about what's more protected, and what you do and can and can't talk about. And I think it's more distinctly unique midwestern phenomenon. So, I don't know if that answers your question.

Steve: Yes, I think so. In a previous interview, my brother, David, who is an amazing disciple, said something… he lives by himself, and he said: "but I spend more time with the people in my workplace than I do with anyone else on the planet, and not only with them in their office, but maybe at lunch, outside the office." He said, "Those are the people I'm around all the time. And then all the people that are on the bus, riding in the city". And that IS his ministry field. That's the space he moves and the people he interacts with. And so, for him, that is his mission. I've talked to other people, from different walks of life, that see that their workspace is definitely opens them up to conversations with people. And sometimes it presents themselves and sometimes they don't. It's one of those circles that we travel in.

Andrew: I tend to plant seeds a lot. I think there's a lot to that.

Steve: What's that look like?

Andrew: Not shying away from how you would talk about things with your, quote unquote, Christian friends. 'I'm going to pray for you about that.' Or I walk in and I've got a Bible with me... and someone asks 'What's that?', 'Oh, it's my Bible'. 'Oh, wow, look at that'. 'Oh, yeah.' 'How was your weekend?' 'Oh, it was great! I went to a new church. And went through this. And the sermon was about this.' When people ask, 'How was your weekend?', if you can share something about the sermon that you heard that day...

Steve: That opens a door...

Andrew: It may. And either they're going to be 'Uhuh, uhuh' and can't wait for you to stop talking... [Laughter]... or you share something that's really applicable to their lives. And that's the idea, right? You have to lead with the application or something that's going to entice them to want to hear more. To me, that Monday morning, 'How was your weekend?' question, is an awesome opportunity to bring that up.

Steve: I love that. Last question: The fruits of the spirit: love, joy, peace, patience, kindness, gentleness, self -

control. How would you say that you see those manifest in your life? Both personally and professionally?

Andrew: I think I do a lot better with these in my professional life. Because there's a certain amount of controls that are in place. You know your purpose. You know why you're all there. There are some set boundaries. You have a basic understanding of the things that are going to come your way. And if you love what you do and you love the people around you, these will just flow out, period. It should actually come from within. But I feel like the challenge for us sometimes, is these are probably easier to express at the workplace than at home. Just because there's....

Steve: I was going to ask you: Why do you think that is?

Andrew: I don't know what it is about family, but... maybe it's because you want the best for them, especially for your kids, and you can see the end. And with the end in mind you can say, 'Hey, this right now is not going to bear great fruit, and you are my fruit, to a degree, so I need to make sure you turn out the way you're supposed to.' But I think part of it's just the challenge of living with someone for many years. The idea that it's... people at work see you at your best, typically, and you see them at their best. And when you're at home, it's not that way. They get the version of you that's been working for ten hours and may be tired. You've used up a lot of your goodwill and energy during the day, leaving them what's leftover. And so, really kind of sorting that out, and making sure you're getting your priorities right, is a big deal. So, how do you spend your time? How do you spend your money? And where do you spend that energy?

Steve: Yep. Exactly. I love those three questions: What do you do with your time? What do you do with your money? What do you think about? How do you spend your energy? Very good. Any final thoughts?

Andrew: Well, I think the more things you're involved in, that you can invite people to...I think that's a great way...to your point, when you have all those folks you're surrounded by at work, you do have a lot of opportunity to say, 'Hey, what are you doing this weekend?'. 'Oh, we're going to an airshow'. 'That sounds really cool.' For instance, the one thing I think we talked about briefly was, the Indianapolis *Great Banquet*. It's a 72-hour retreat for men and for women. And once you've been through it, you can sponsor others. As you look at folks that have not done that, you can talk about, 'Hey, how was your weekend?' 'Oh, it was great. There was a *Great Banquet* this weekend. So, I got to go and help support that. Have you ever heard of that?' 'No, what's that about?' Explain. 'Is that something you think you'd ever be interested in?' Or something your wife, or husband, or whatever it might be. Being involved in different ministries allows you to talk about... 'Hey, what are you doing this weekend?' 'I'm doing this.' 'How was last weekend?' 'I did that.' 'Have you ever heard of that? Do you want to?' So, I think just the more activities you're involved in; the more ministries you're involved in, the more you can talk about them. I think the more you're inundated with Kingdom work; if that's what you do and that's what you focus on...it's kind of like if you watch the NFL all day on Sunday, guess what you're probably going to talk about on Monday. But if this is all you do, all you think about, if this is your true priority, people are going to get THIS, just because you're just dripping in it. Right? You just need to be so...

Steve: It's who you are, right?

Andrew: Yeah, you can't help but get some on you...
[Laughter] ...if they hang out with you. It's that kind of
thing. It means it has to be a priority. You have to look at
yourself and say, 'Am I dripping in this stuff? Am I
covered in it? Am I so immersed that if somebody gets
anywhere near me, this is what they're going to get, not
something else"?

Steve: It's not just that you went to a building with a
steeple on top, on Sunday, it's part of who you are, so it
comes out. Is that what you're saying?

Andrew: That's exactly it. In fact, I think the problem is,
kind of like this idea of yeast that's dormant until you wake
it up - yeah, it's technically yeast, but it's not active.

Steve: Yeah, tell that little story you said over lunch. That
was really good.

Andrew: The sermon this Sunday was talking about this
idea of yeast and the fact that you have starter loaves. And
basically, those characteristics are carried through the
loaves that are descended from that starter. But yeast has to
be active; it has to be living to have an effect. So, there's
this idea of dormant yeast, which is what you get in the
little packets, something needs to wake it up. The idea of
Christian within the four walls of the church, and that's
where they exist, you're not really having a leavening
effect on anything else around you, if that's the only time
that you're hanging out... is in your 'yeast packet'.

Steve: You're *in the packet*... [Laughter]

Andrew: So, what are you going to do? Again, going back
to the idea of where you are on the Chess board: If you go

and get filled somewhere; let's say you have an incredible message at whatever local church you're at, hear an incredible sermon, you can go and hang out right there and everyone agrees it was a great sermon. That's one thing. If you can take it, just like you and I are talking right now, and share it somewhere else, you can be *leavening*, or have a *leavening-effect* elsewhere, by sharing that; by becoming that active yeast somewhere else. I think that goes back to the idea of salt. It goes back to the idea of, 'How do you take that and keep it?' So, the problem is, if you just go to church, depending on what that body looks like, it may be dormant. How do you inject new life? How do you become the... the water, the flour, the sugar, the things you need to get it reactivated? How do you become those things to that body, because it may be that that church itself may be very dormant, based on the looks of it?

Steve: Very cool. I love that. That analogy, it's like the sign at a church that, as you're walking out the door, says, "You are now entering the mission field". Because we're in the *yeast packet* when we're inside the church, but it's when we walk out where we are actually opening up the packet and spreading the Good News? I love that. Thanks for sharing. It's been awesome getting to know you, brother.

Andrew: You too. I appreciate it. Thank you.

Observations, Lessons, Application:

- What were your key Observations from Andrew's life and faith journey?

- Are there any parts of Andrew's journey and story that you can relate to personally?

- How do you think God wants you to apply these principles in **your** life moving forward?

Chapter 3

Dr. Barbara Haehner
Medical Doctor, Medical Director
Disciple of Jesus Christ

Dr. Barb is a dear personal friend. She is also one of the most amazing people I have ever had the pleasure of knowing personally. Anyone who knows Barb would tell you that she is super-friendly, energetic, caring, compassionate, and exudes the Love of Christ in all that she does. She is very active in our church, coordinating and organizing functions, events, Bible studies, training events, church decorations… or, anything else that needs done. Barb's enthusiasm and passion for the Lord is inspiring and contagious – and it's a great joy to have her in our church-family. Her story, witness, and how God has shown up in powerful ways in her life is exciting and encouraging – here's her story:

Interview with Barb Haehner, May 10th, 2019

Steve: Why don't you tell me your story. How did you come to faith in Christ as your Lord and Savior? How did that happen?

Barb: Okay. Well, I was fortunate enough to grow up in a great family. And my parents dragged us kids to church every week. And so that was good. I grew up in a Presbyterian church. Interestingly enough, like many Presbyterian churches, there was a lot of teaching, but really not telling you that you had to make a personal choice for Christ. It was more like, 'It's time for you to join a church, so you go through the class and then you join a church and then you're fine'. But it wasn't really about a personal relationship with Christ. Our church really didn't have a very strong youth group. And I started going to this other youth group with a friend, and one night at a youth group meeting, it was this epiphany that you really have to make this *choice* for Christ. You really have to accept Him as your personal Savior to be saved and have eternal security. And that was the night - I was about 13 or 14. Even though I had been going to church...

Steve: So, 8th or 9th grade...something like that?

Barb: Yeah, and it was crazy, because my first thought was, 'Oh no! Is my mother saved? Does she know she has to make a personal choice?' And my father had already passed away, so it was just her and I. That was my immediate thought. And right after that meeting, I went home and I said, "Mom! Mom! Sit down, I have to tell you something." And I said, "Did you know that to go to Heaven, you really kind of have to make a personal choice?" And I was talking to her, and as all moms are, I could not tell whether she knew that she had to make a personal choice for Christ or whether she didn't know that. I never knew, however, not long after that, she told me that she had sat down with her mother, my grandmother, and had that conversation with her. But it was just crazy that when it finally dawned on me, the Gospel message actually came to me personally. The first thing I had to do was make sure my mom knew it too!

Steve: Okay. Very cool.

Barb: So, that's kind of my story.

Steve: Very good. So, how do you live that out? And I know you personally. So, obviously, I see it every week, but in general, how would you say you live your faith out in your personal life?

Barb: The biggest thing, and this of course, has been a matter of growing in my faith over time. When I was focused on getting my career in line and school and training and everything, honestly, I was pretty focused on that. There wasn't much else I could do. I knew that I was saved. I always knew that I had my salvation, but I was not living every day, for Christ, per se. I was kind of self-centered, really focused on my career.

Steve: *Career-mode*, right?

Barb: And I think a lot of young people are there. And my schedule being what it was, when I was training, I really couldn't even go to church or anything. I mean, there was no time. On Saturday nights when I was Resident training, I would start watching Charles Stanley. And I'm telling you, that's when Charles Stanley was on fire. I mean, he's kind of older now…he still has great messages, but he's not as *pounding* as he used to be when he was younger. He convicted me in the sense that I knew that I had my salvation, but I wasn't living with the Kingdom mindset at all. I had no spiritual focus. And even though the Holy Spirit was in me, I was living pretty in my own power; very secular. And I wasn't doing anything bad, but I wasn't living for the Kingdom, for sure. He convicted me. When I became a Fellow, I had a little more time; I could go to church. I started going to a large church on the north side of Indianapolis in the 1990's, when I re-submitted to God, and I rededicated my life to serving Christ. And I went to church as much as I could and I got involved in a lay-counseling ministry there. That was sort of my reintroduction back to getting the spiritual part of my life back on track. So, fast-forward, and then I married into a family that was Pentecostal. But unfortunately, my marriage was quite bad - it was a very bad situation. I was married for nine years. It was the faith mixed with all this other bad stuff. I struggled with my faith. After I finally got divorced, it took me some time to decide that I needed to go back to church. My ex-husband was a Gospel artist, and everything was *supposedly* centered on Christ. He was very manipulative and he had a very electric, attractive personality, but that wasn't what he really was. It took me awhile after my divorce to decide *okay, now I have to go back to church, AGAIN.* I had a lot of emotional damage. I would say, up to that point, I was just so blessed my entire life. Everything I set out my mind to do, I was successful. Everything was good. Everything always turned out well for me. This was the first thing that totally just took my legs out from under me, in every way. Going through this gave me a lot more empathy and compassion for people that were going through lots of personal pain. And so, I think God has really used that nine years of my life to put me on the Kingdom path, and to know that's really the only path that ever leads anywhere. And that purpose, that you're serving the Kingdom, in everything you do, and the way you live...everything has to be Christ-centered! The way you spend your quiet time to grow personally, so that you can not only grow in your vertical relationship with God, but love other people - some people that are really hard to love. And as you mature, and become more Christ-centered, that's sort of the litmus test, in my opinion. It's not, 'Oh, I have such a wonderful relationship with Christ' when I own my quiet-time, but what happens when a person that really has a difficult personality is really irritating you, and you want to lash out at them but you can't. You have to love them instead. So, that is the litmus test of living a Christ-centered life.

The more you can relate to your family, friends, and co-workers in a Christ-centered way, this reflects the strength of your vertical relationship with God. You must keep feeding your spirit with regular Bible study, meditation, and quiet time. That keeps the Truth coming in to your spirit, so you can live it out. If you start slipping on that part, you immediately notice the way you conduct yourself (i.e. you get more irritated quicker) when you're working, when you're doing anything. So, how do I live my faith personally? Well, completely submitting myself, to the best of my ability, every second of everyday, to what the Holy Spirit would have me to do. Your quiet time puts you in touch with that *still small voice*, so you can live outside of your own flesh. It's always being sensitive, and being so in-tune, that the minute you step out of what Jesus would have you doing, into your fleshly behavior, (like reacting impatiently or angrily - or saying something quickly that you should have not said) - that conviction is right there and you have to respond to it and admit that you are wrong. And somehow either say, "I'm sorry", or say, "Okay, next time I can't let myself do that." God is forgiving. You must keep that relationship so close that you're immediately convicted and you change quickly. Because the longer it goes before you change your behavior, we all know, God will chasten you harder.

Steve: I know you're real active in our church - you've been a director and you're very involved in many ways. So, as a doctor, and now in your current role as a medical director for not-for-profit...how do you live out your faith in that professional space?

Barb: Well, I'm going to have to give a little more background. I'll try to be short, but God really has had His hand on me the whole time. I worked in private practice nephrology for almost 20 years. It's high pressure. Lots of sick patients. Many, many hours.

Steve: In small clinic? Or in big hospitals?

Barb: All of the above. We worked in three or four major hospitals. And then we had 23 dialysis units. We were a huge nephrology practice. Many patients. We went many places. I rounded in the hospitals. Saw patients in the office. Rounded in dialysis units. I mean, I did pretty much everything a nephrologist does. And I did that for about 20 years. About the last five years of my practice, I was getting older. I was less able to take the hours, call and sleep deprivation. The call was really getting me. But God gave me a word, about five years before I retired. It was kind of this thing where He said to me, "You know, I'm not going to have you do this for very much longer." I received it and just waited and trusted.

Steve: So, you heard that? Nice.

Barb: Yeah, I said 'Okay'. I was just trusting that I would know when the time was that I was supposed to stop. Because, again, God has blessed me dramatically in my finances, so whenever He was going to ask me to leave, I could leave. And I would be able to support myself. That's a blessing in itself. Our practice was set up to where if you knew you were probably going to leave in a year, we agreed to tell the others so they could get somebody else in - you can't just hire a Nephrologist in a day. It was so strange, and I won't go into the details, but it was one day that things happened, in a sense, and I just got the definite word that I was supposed to give my year's notice. And it was just that! It all happened in one day. I gave my notice in 2014, and I retired in 2015. And so, then I thought: 'What are you going to have me do? What are you going to have me do?' I was thinking of becoming a Certified Biblical Counselor. I thought, well, that's my plan.

Steve: right... [laugh]

Barb: I thought, 'I could start taking classes and become a counselor', so I set my mind toward that. I also thought I could *fill-in* with international medical missions. I had signed up for some of the counseling classes, was ready to go. I retired in July of 2015 and the Jamaica trip was coming up. When I go on mission trips, I must have the Holy Spirit say: "I want you go to on this mission trip". Otherwise, it's not for me. I was getting a lot of pressure from friends - I said "No, no, I've not been called to go". I did not go. When that week came around that the group went to Jamaica, a couple who ran a local food-pantry-ministry came to our church to talk about their ministry. She was talking about how it was her dream to have a mobile health clinic. Right then, as I was sitting there, the Holy Spirit spoke to me so loudly, it just took my breath away. He said, "That's you". I was like, "What?". "The mobile clinic - that's you!!" I was back-pedaling and thinking what it would take to start a free clinic. And I felt the Spirit tell me, "I want you to do that". That week was when our church group went to Jamaica – so I was supposed to hear that. I immediately began looking online at all the free-clinics in Hamilton county, which was Trinity, and Hope, and the Heart & Soul clinic. I sent emails to the executive directors of all of them and introduced myself. I said, "I'd just like some more information and would be glad to serve." And not ten minutes after I sent those emails out, I got a phone call from Heather, who had just moved into the executive director spot.

Steve: At Heart & Soul?

Barb: Yes, of Heart & Soul. She said, "You know, we need a medical director and I'm the new executive director. We really need to move this place somewhere." And the rest was history.

Steve: It happened so fast…

Barb: …and the fact that I said "No" to the Jamaica trip. That's what gets me. I said no, because He wasn't asking me to go. Because He had His plan for me. If I had not been sitting there, that day, in the congregation, listening to the couple talking about their ministry the Holy Spirit couldn't have spoken directly to me. The Heart and Soul clinic was in a position that they were going to either fail or grow. Things had to be moved forward in reorganization and a positive direction. They needed a full-time medical director.

Steve: So, it needed a push?

Barb: The Heart and Soul Clinic provides healthcare and dental care to the uninsured. We are funded by grants and donations. All of our health care and administrative workers are volunteers. In 2015, we had a total of 170 patient visits. God has blessed our growth so greatly in the last 3 ½ years. To make a long story short, we have been blessed with a beautiful new clinic space…we have a 38-

foot RV which operates as a mobile medical unit… and we have greatly expanded our dental services. God promised me He would grow us, and He has brought us the funding and volunteers that we need to grow at an explosive rate. At the end of 2019, we had greater than 1200 patient visits! When I took this on, I knew it was my calling. He gave me the gift of a ministry. We are openly operating as the hands and feet of Jesus! When I was in my Nephrology practice, I could witness, but had to walk a line.

Steve: You had to wait for patients to open the door for that conversation?

Barb: Correct. And I prayed with people. Every now and again I would have a spiritual conversation with someone or be able to pray with someone. But think about how amazing this is that God wasn't done with my abilities as a physician! He took me from the place I was professionally, to this place now, where I can be a doctor… but also pray with patients on a regular basis. So, I'm delivering healthcare, like I was before…practicing medicine. But I'm also delivering Spiritual care, hand-in-hand, with no limits. I don't have to be afraid that I will get reprimanded for sharing my faith.

Steve: So, He used your passion for Biblical counseling. It's just in a different capacity than you thought it was going to be.

Barb: That's right! I thought I was burnt out and done with the whole doctor-thing. "I want to leave this behind and I want to go to something else!" God wanted to still use my skills as a physician, but allow me to b His direct hands and feet and say it freely and widely!

Steve: That's awesome. Love it.

Barb: I can say it! We're open. It's all over our waiting room. It's all over the walls in our waiting room. And no one has any doubt as to *why* they're getting free healthcare.

Steve: You're doing it in Jesus' name.

Barb: Yes.

Steve: That's beautiful.

Barb: God was so amazing. He allowed this profession of mine, that I trained all these years for and worked so hard for, and turned it over and used it for His glory 100%. Not that it wasn't for His glory before, but it's *un-masked* now!

Steve: You couldn't have made this happen if you tried…

Barb: No. [laughter] No. No. When I just think about how He promised me, that if I took this on, and did my part, that I wouldn't have to worry about it growing and doing what it's doing now. Right before my very eyes! It's such a blessing that this is in God's hands, and I just have to be faithful to work.

Steve: It's kind of like we talked about with the old tractor… you can't steer them sitting still. You just have to get it moving and then let God do His thing… let Him steer.

Barb: That's right.

Steve: What is the stated mission and purpose of the Heart & Soul Clinic?

Barb: It's to provide free healthcare to uninsured and underinsured in Hamilton and surrounding counties, in the name of Jesus. It's a faith-based mission.

Steve: That's beautiful. I have just one more question: The fruits of the Spirit are: love, joy, peace, patience, kindness, goodness, faithfulness, gentleness, and self-control - How do you see those manifest in your work?

Barb: I was reading a book by Bill Johnson, *The Way of Life, Experiencing the Culture of Heaven on Earth.* He coined a phrase and it stuck in my mind - that I couldn't put into words until he did. He said, *"Religiosity is perfectionism, and man can never reach perfection."* And, he said "When you have a healthy relationship with Christ and you're working in tandem with the Holy Spirit, you seek excellence in everything you do, which is a lot different than perfection". Every single thing that you do, and you say, 'Okay, I'll take this on - I'm going to do it'. You do it with excellence, as if you were doing it for Christ. If I really can make this the focus of my life, anything I choose to do is going to be excellent. Not perfect, but excellent. Whether that is working as a medical director at the Heart and Soul Clinic, planning a chili-cook-off at church, or greeting people at church – it's excellent. It's personal excellence for the right reasons. When you do anything, do it for the Kingdom and put your all into the effort. When you do that you can come away with that feeling inside that you're serving the Kingdom in a real way. I try to live, and it's taken my almost 60 years to finally know that that's the key to keeping His peace and His joy in your life. And you're not doing it to make somebody else see how good you can do it. Or you're not doing for someone else; you're doing it for the Kingdom.

Steve: You're doing it for the right reasons, right motives, for God's glory.

Barb: That's right. Remember when I said at the beginning? - 'You know your relationship with Christ is right when you can treat others right, even under circumstances that are not easy.' Using our gifts in a way that help other people enhance their gifts, building others up. This person has their gifts and I have my gifts. When we combine them, the result for the Kingdom is amazing. You don't just get the addition of two people's gifts together, we get 50-fold, 100-fold, or a million-fold! Everybody glorifies God and everybody gets personal satisfaction from knowing they're doing this thing for the right reason. It's finding God's purpose for your life and helping others find their purpose.

Steve: You can really feel it too. 'I'm doing what God called me to do.' It feels like you're doing exactly what God made you to do. And it just feels so right.

Barb: That's right. And there's so much about what I actually do at the Heart & Soul that I could see in my practice, that God was grooming me for. Healthcare is becoming so *non-patient oriented*. That is my style of practicing medicine… *patient-centered*. It was becoming outdated and I did not want to change.

Steve: And that's why you were burning out?

Barb: Yes, and that's why I was burning out. I was trying so hard to maintain the quality of every patient one-on-one with me and it was becoming impossible. The system was changing. Even my younger partners were looking at me like 'You do way too much for people. You can't do that anymore.' I would say 'What do you mean I can't do it anymore? This is the right way to take care of patients!' So, now I'm at the Heart & Soul Clinic. Number one: I run it.

So, I can structure patient care and see those patients exactly how I know is the right way to practice medicine. So, how amazing is that?

Steve: And do it in Christ's name...

Barb: God gave me a *forum* that doesn't exist anymore in today's world of medicine. The Heart and Soul Clinic is flying under the radar. We use paper charts, but guess what? I can sit in a room, take as much time as I want listening to a patient. I don't have my nose in a computer. I'm listening. I can pray with a patient. I can do whatever I deem is good patient care. And most importantly, loving that person, maybe on a lot more levels than just serving their physical needs. That is an amazing gift to me from God, because He knew that was an incredible frustration for me in my career as a nephrologist. when I was just getting so crazy at the end of my career as a nephrologist. And now God gave me this forum that doesn't exist anywhere except at the Heart & Soul clinic! Only God could give a gift like that!

Steve: That's amazing. Beautiful.

Barb: God has just given me this privilege. And that's the way I look at it. It's a privilege. He values my heart to want to give to people like that. And He has given me a forum that I can do that. It's sort of like fairy land, because it doesn't exist in the real world of medicine anymore. It used to. 20 years ago, 15 years ago, it used to. But it doesn't anymore.

Steve: So, God's fingerprints are all over it.

Barb: It's all Him.

Steve: So, any final comments about being a disciple, making disciples? Either in the personal life or the professional life. Or any final thoughts?

Barb: I think everything goes back to prioritizing things in your life - in a time when life is so crazy. Everybody is pulling at you from all directions. It's that learning how to hear the voice of God. Keeping enough time and doing what you personally need to do in your prayer life, in your Bible study, in your quiet time. Quiet time to me isn't always opening the Word. It is sometimes. But sometimes it's being in a very quiet place and opening my heart and my mind and saying, 'What do you have for me today? What is your Word for me today?' It's learning how to hear from the Holy Spirit and letting His word and His influence be the number one driver of your actions, as opposed to your flesh. That war between the Holy Spirit and your flesh - It's a constant war. Fortunately, when we receive our glorified bodies and are with Christ, there won't be any more tears! That fight will no longer exist! That will be amazing!

Steve: Amen to that.

Barb: But taking the time you need to, in a crazy life, to make sure that you can hear the still small voice and pick that direction, and not your flesh. That is the key to living a Kingdom centered life. It's not about dividing my professional life, my family life, my friend life, my whatever life. It's one life, and It's Christ-centered. And everything you do and every action you make is being directed by the Holy Spirit.

Steve: I love that.

Barb: And so, separating your life in all these different categories, makes you not understand that it really is just all about the one focus. And everything else will follow, if you keep that focus. And it takes time and devotion. I know immediately when I get so *busy* doing things... even if it's for the Kingdom, and ignore my personal time with the Lord, my responses drift towards the flesh.

Steve: What you've said reminds me of that Psalm, 'Be still, and know that I am God'.

Barb: Yes, it is a Psalm. 'Be still and know that I am God'.

Barb: Another thing I want to say is: I feel one of my gifts is praying and interceding for people. And the definition of prophecy is not always *'Thus sayeth the Lord'* - but the prophecy in encouraging people; speaking into their lives. I believe that gift is in me, that He is developing that gift in me. He has shown that, recently, through some interventions. For instance, if you feel like God is urging you to pray for someone, and even though you might not have any idea what that person is doing at this moment, that you're supposed to share that with that person, even though you have no idea... but it's a specific word. I feel like He's grooming me to do it more. Like, 'Okay God, you're asking me to pray this and share it with the person'. It's always an uplifting thing, or an encouraging thing. It's "I know you're hurting, and this is the word God has for you". Sometimes I know what's going on in their life, when no one has told me! Just recently, there was an issue where God told me exactly what to pray and I felt Him say: 'You need to tell that person this...'.   And I said to God, 'What do you mean? Can't I just pray?' and He said, 'No, you have to tell that person'. It had some details and I'm like, I don't know where I'm getting these details, but I needed to share with the person. I pray for people all the time, but normally I know exactly what I'm praying for. And you know, it was amazing that I found out, in a backdoor way, even though that person did not really reveal that they needed that word and prayer right at the time God sent it! Wow! Wow! God, you trust me that much to say "Pray this specific thing for this person and I want you to tell them. And no matter how they react, know that I told you to tell them and don't worry about it…"

Steve: What their reaction is?

Barb: Or you going into some personal realm area…. how would I know that and why would I say that? But God is moving me more and more into a place where He's giving me things and He's trusting me with some personal information. He's trusting me to do with it what He's asking me to do. But it's always encouraging. It's not like a, 'Don't do this, don't do that'.

Steve: It's not condemning, it's encouraging…

Barb: Yes, encouraging and instructing. For example, 'Don't worry, God is with you and He knows where you are. And it's going to be okay. And He's just telling you this….'

Steve: That's amazing.

Barb: So, God is moving me into that. It's exciting. It's a little intimidating, but that's my willingness to step out and immediately pray for people, or ask people pretty boldly like, 'Let's pray for that' or 'Is there anything you want me to pray for?' And right there saying 'let's pray right now!' God has moved me into that gradually and more progressively over the last two or three years.

Steve: Love that…

Barb: Again, it's just kind of overwhelming. But that relationship with Him has to be so clear for Him to use you like that. You have to have no unforgiveness, with no anger or irritation. Fleshly emotions can block a word completely. So, it's all the more important that you keep yourself clean, if that makes sense. You keep that open, and He can use you in amazing ways. That's just kind of a newer thing for me that He opened my eyes to and said, 'Hey, you know, if you allow me to, I would like to use you like this'.

Steve: Beautiful…

Barb: It's humbling, because….be it far from me to think that He could just use me in that way to help other people know that God is there for them.

Steve: Yeah, that's so neat. And your story of how He's taken you from professional, traditional medicine, into this special thing He called you to do. It's amazing.

Barb: It is.

Steve: Well, that's wonderful. Thanks for sharing all this. It's been an incredible interview. So, thank you.

Barb: Well, no, thank you for allowing me to say it, because when I get frustrated, it's tough. There are certain aspects of the Heart and Soul Clinic where the pressure can build… you know, I'm feeling some pressures because we're growing so fast, and there's just so much going on.

Steve: Does this rejuvenate you?

Barb: Yeah, it does, because it makes me understand that God gave me this and I just need to be obedient and do what I can do, and He'll take care of the rest because He wants this to be. I just have to be as faithful as I can as a human, I just have to do that. I just have to not get crazy about things, and He'll take care of the rest!

Observations, Lessons, Application:

- What were your key Observations from Barb's life and faith journey?

- Are there any parts of Barb's journey and story that you can relate to personally?

- How do you think God wants you to apply these principles in **your** life moving forward?

Chapter 4

David Harbaugh
U.S. Government Employee
Disciple of Jesus Christ

David is one of my younger brothers – and one of the most amazing people I have ever been blessed to know. He is a friend to everyone… loving, kind, gentle. He serves food to the down-trodden at missions, he serves the homeless at shelters, and delivers toys or food to charity events. He is often interviewed by news stations covering various community activities. He is unique, a very memorable man. David also is an amazing mental-toughness giant, who has overcome so much in his life. He is a cancer survivor. He has undergone numerous surgeries on his legs since childhood. He battled things in life that would have made most people fall to the ground and cry out: "I quit!" and never get back up. But David continues to persevere through the trials and challenges that life throws his way. He also gets on a bus four days a week and rides approximately an hour, each way, into the city to work his 10-hour shifts at the organization he has been with most of his adult life. Did I mention that he laboriously walks on a cane or a walker? Did I mention that David has struggled with the effects of Cerebral Palsy since birth as a premature baby in 1967, and that his doctors at the University Hospital are amazed - and have said "David, we've never seen someone like you over 50-years-old. We just don't know what to expect". David also earned a Bachelor's degree in Spanish at Indiana State University and speaks fluent Spanish - often serving as an interpreter at his job. He is also a prayer warrior, constantly praying for friends, family, and people he meets in his travels. And, I do mean travels – David has travelled to all 50 of the United States, Puerto Rico, Canada, Mexico, the Bahamas - and Guatemala, Costa Rica, and Nicaragua on mission trips. He is an evangelist – or as his Spanish-speaking friends call him, *David Evangelista*. David the Evangelist. He is a devoted Bible reader, and earned a Master's Degree in Biblical Studies. He was the presiding minister at my daughter Dani's wedding – one of our family's most memorable moments. David loves Jesus Christ, and he is an ambassador for Christ wherever he goes. It's who he is, and what characterizes his life in a profound way. David is a Christ-follower, a *Christian*. And of all the people I have ever known, David is at the top of my list of people that I admire and look up to the most. David is a Disciple of Jesus Christ, and I praise God that he is my Brother.

Interview with David Harbaugh - April 27th, 2019

Steve: David, why don't you tell me a little bit about how you live out your faith in Jesus Christ, in your personal life? What does that look like, just going to church, working with family and friends, just in your personal life? How do you live out your faith in your personal life?

David: Well, I look very unique, walking on a cane or the walker. So, it's very easy for me to stick out in a crowd, and very hard to blend in. If I want to blend in, it's difficult. So, I try to be a friendly face. I try to let the Holy Spirit guide me on what to say or what to do; how to approach certain situations and certain people. It's not always the same. I try to seek the Lord's guidance.

Steve: And I know you talk about Christ all the time, especially, "Thank you Jesus" and I know you do that just to make sure people know that you're a believer. What are your thoughts or your prayers about that when you know you're going to be communicating with people? Do you pray about it beforehand? How do you normally do that?

David: A lot of times I pray about it. A lot of times I adlib. And most of the time, that goes well. And I like to say "Hi". And sometimes people react very differently, most of the time positive... but most of the positive reactions, I think, have a lot to do with whether people are used to having someone say *hi* to them or whether they're not used to it.

Steve: I know, Dave, from Facebook and from just being your brother, you get interviewed a lot of times on television, when you go to those charity toy drives, or meeting the Mayor of towns, or for events for homeless shelters, etc.... tell me a little bit about that.

David: Facebook live, You-tube; it's wonderful! The reach of Facebook Live and You-tube; I can have my family and friends see me across the country and across the world much greater than the range of Seattle Television. It was always exciting to be interviewed on a traditional Seattle TV or radio station, but it's much greater when you can put it on Facebook Live or You-tube and those files that I make public, then Facebook friends and the public can see it too. I'm getting a lot of reaction, mostly positive, but getting a lot of reaction from people I never heard of before.

Steve: Yeah, friends of friends, and it can be more viral, right?

David: And the public... you can usually get some information from people who are responding to you when it's public, like where they are. It's like, "Cool. I'm getting hits from all over the world!"

Steve: Right. That's awesome.

David: Thank you Jesus!

Steve: Amen. Amen. You were the minister at Dani's wedding, and I know that in your personal life, in your apartment complex, and when you ride the bus into work, do you take your Bible with you when you're riding the bus, so people seeing you reading the Bible... and maybe it opens conversation... how do you open conversations with people that are on the busses and things like that?

David: Oh, that's awesome. With my iPhone I don't have as many excuses anymore, because my English Bible and my Spanish Bible are always with me, because my iPhone is always with me.

Steve: Right. Okay. So, how do you strike up conversations?

David: Well.... (pause)... It's different with the situations, which is why I had to think about it a little bit. It starts up with "Hello" a lot of times, and then a lot of people compliment me on just the fact of going to work, that it's kind of a big struggle, whether it's on the bus or walking from the bus stop to a building. That's one of the biggest starters. And then of course, walking from the building to the bus stop, a lot of questions I get are "What are you doing down here?" and a lot of people with the city's homeless crisis, with my being downtown with a walker a lot of people see me, and without saying much, will point me in the direction of the nearest food bank or homeless shelter... because I own a walker and walking a little crooked - to many people I look like one of the homeless, and I'll say something like, "Oh yeah, I *give* a lot to those organizations."

Steve: [Laughter] Yeah, you do...

David: And they have to do a double take on that, because, 'Oh yeah, I'm a *donor*. I don't take food or I don't sleep at those places. I don't take food; I donate to them. And I work in that building right over there'. It may sound like something that wouldn't happen very often, but in our city's time of crisis, it happens a lot.

Steve: Okay. Let's shift a little bit to your professional life. You work for a government agency and you've worked there, 24 years? Something like that?

David: 28 Years. It will be 29 years. This winter it will be 29.

Steve: Okay. So, you've worked for this government agency for 28/29 years, and obviously with the government... in working for the government, do you feel free to share your faith with people, the fact that you're a believer, or do you feel like you have to be careful? Tell me a little bit about that.

David: Well, we all have to use some common sense, but I've found that, as long as the purpose is to share the happiness of my own faith, and not to tear down anybody else's...as long as I don't tear down anybody else's, I feel very free. And as long as I do my actual job, to a high standard, when you couple that with my witness, me actually talking about Jesus, when I do my actual job to a high standard, then they know that I have the work ethic, and ethics in general, and government ethics. I have the work ethic that is supposed to be associated with Christians, that I'm not lazy. So, a big part of that is sharing my faith, but it's also doing my actual job to a very high standard.

Steve: Beautiful. Beautiful. So, in the workplace environment, you have been able to make friends, and develop relationships, and ultimately lead people to faith in Christ; tell me about that. How does that normally unpack itself?

David: Well, in the Christian world, we call it discipleship. In the workplace world, we call it mentoring. And my two biggest areas of mentoring, are: 1. Being there for so long, for going on 29 years, so that whenever we do have new hires, when people look to me. I'm the senior person they're depending on, and also, not only the amount of years I've been there, but my particular specialty and inventory. There are very few people who spend much time working the inventories that I work, and nobody spends as much time working on them as I do. And there's only one other person that spends close to the amount of time that I spend on them. So, when my specialty comes up, I really enjoy being the person that they come to. And another way of mentoring is other people with disabilities in the workplace. Whether it's the person with a disability or the frontline employee with a disability, who's seeking the mentor. Or, when it's management, that comes to me and says....when management is working on reasonable accommodations, for a certain employee. There have been several times when management has come to me and I've been a consultant on which forms of reasonable accommodations would help an employee to do their job. And in some cases, to come to the conclusion of what the reasonable accommodation is, and help them transition to it. In some cases, I was a consultant, to make it a much smoother transition for the newer employees, than, in some cases, it was for me.

Steve: Yeah, that makes sense.

David: So, that gives it some purpose, for the real rough patches I went through years and years ago, and it's like, "Oh, I have a purpose now. I'll make it a much smoother process for the disabled employees who are coming in next".

Steve: Okay, that makes total sense.

David: And as people involved, whether it be the management, or the front-line employee, get to know me, through that process, they also get to know me on a more personal level, and it provides an opportunity to share my faith.

Steve: You know, with all the growing Christian persecution in our nation, do you ever feel like your voice is ever squelched, you know, turned off, like you can't talk about that? Do you ever get that kind of messaging from senior management or anything?

David: I used to. I think that's why I appreciate the management that I have now, because I've been there almost 29 years and the trouble that you're referring to, was most prevalent in the first five years. So, it seems like that as long as I use common sense, and don't go overboard, but as long as I use what I know is common sense, it seems like the last 24 years, it's kind of like a reward for enduring the first five years of persecution for being a Christian.

Steve: So, right now, you don't really feel it as long as you say, "use common sense". Okay. So, if you are talking with somebody and the conversation turns to Christ, do you normally do that at lunch breaks, before work or after work, or as the day kind of unfolds? Do people ask you questions? Is there any particular time that those kinds of conversations tend to happen the most?

David: If the conversation gets too deep, and we need a little more time, then we need to set a time on our break or our lunch, or before or after work, but typically it lasts a short enough amount of time, throughout the day, and if we need to, we can set a break time.

Steve: And I was thinking one of the things, just from knowing you my whole life, you tend to ask me and our family members, "Is there anything I can pray for you about?" Do you ask people in the workplace environment the same type of questions?

David: Yes, I ask that as a question sometimes, and what happens more often is, they'll tell me what's going on in their life, and I'll say "I'll pray for you". If we have the time and if we can get started quickly, then I pray for them a little bit right then and there, and then I'll say, "I'll pray for you a lot more about it when I have a lot more time than this."

Steve: Very good. I know you have been very active in ministry and church, and stuff like that; do you see your day to day profession as a ministry platform? You've heard the saying, 'The mission field doesn't have to be across the ocean, it can be right in your backyard.' It can be at your bus stop. It can be at your work. Mission fields are everywhere around us. How do you see your profession as a ministry platform?

David: Because the government probably has the most diverse workforce than almost any private sector corporation. When you do the math, obviously large corporations have large diversity too, but when you do the math of how many Christians, how many Muslims, how many Buddhists, how many Hindus, how many people with disabilities, especially, the Federal government is probably the largest employer of people with disabilities; out in the open disabilities, or hidden disabilities, than almost any other private sector company.

Steve: Sure. That makes sense. I know you used to have a website. I think it was "DavidLoveJesus.com" or .net, or something like that.

David: Something like that.

Steve: In it you had written an article that kind of told your story, and you had often said that "God had created you exactly like you are, so that you could minister in ways that nobody else could. And you considered it a blessing!" Because of your disability, and because you get to work with lots of people with disabilities in the government sector, and I'm not trying to put words in your mouth, but tell me about how you see that God has put you in that ministry, around those people, every day, for a purpose. Tell me what your reflection on that is.

David: I think until, or unless, God heals me completely of Cerebral Palsy, then I need to use my unique situation to be a witness for the Lord and to our world. I think a big part of my mentoring at work has been to other employees with disabilities and also as a consultant to management. I think that's been the biggest blessing. And I think as long as I'm the only person that a lot of people see who walks kind of crooked, walks on a walker or a cane, as long as I'm not able to just blend in, then I need to use that to God's glory as much as I'm able and as much as the Lord will use me.

Steve: Amen to that!

David: And then once that usefulness is no more; when the Lord determines that usefulness is no more, or if the pain gets to be too much, and I pray the Lord might heal me, but as long as I have a uniqueness that helps me to bring people to Jesus, then let me bring people to Jesus, as much as He will use me for that.

Steve: Amen. So, how would you say you've felt the Lord's leading in your professional life, for your work stuff... how would you say you've felt the Lord's hand on that?

David: At times when we had a different culture in the office, and different managers, in the offices, and when I felt a little more persecution, for being a Christian, or being a person with a disability, I would put more energy into searching for opportunities elsewhere; opportunities in other states, back in Indiana, or just anywhere. But when I perceived the persecution got really bad, anywhere but here. And when the Lord started to work all these issues out, and when the Lord said, "You're staying," it wasn't a joke. The Lord was, in a lot of ways, rewarding me for going through some persecution, by making things a lot better. Even if you could point to a lot of earthly explanations, as to why things are getting a lot better, or you could say things are getting a lot better because these managers are out and these new managers are in, changing the office culture, even if you could point it to those earthly explanations, I still think the Lord's hand was on it.

Steve: Right. Right. Okay. I love that. Do you ever feel the Lord guiding you to "go talk to this person, or go talk to that person"? Give them a word of encouragement or something like that?

David: Very often.

Steve: What does He normally tell you? How does he normally tell you that?

David: I think that it depends on how well I know the person. If I know the person really well, I know how to approach them and ask... If it's the first contact of the day, like "How are you doing?" or "You don't seem to be feeling well today, is there anything wrong?" If I don't know the person, it just might start off with a, "Hi" or "Hello", and then see if something develops at that time or if something might develop a little later - because maybe I was the only person who reached out with them with a "Hello" when they were going through something, when no one else was reaching out to them. It doesn't always happen as instantaneous as I would like, and it doesn't always mean that it works out perfectly, but the fact that it works out most of the time, is a good indicator that I do well at reading God's timing and I don't mess it up a whole lot. I think that's a good indication that I'm reading God's timing pretty well.

Steve: So, here's the last question, the fruits of the spirit are: love, joy, peace, patience, kindness, gentleness, and self-control; how do you see them manifest in you, and in your work, and in your professional life? How do you respond to that?

David: Even now, I know I don't have a job that puts me on the throne, I have to realize that my organization has to have some level of kindness, because we represent the government to tax payers. And kindness and patience, and a lot of my inventories that I work, even though I'm not talking to them on the phone, I do have to show patience and to use kindness and patience on determining on what action to take. And I also have to use, speaking of diversity, I have to use kindness and patience on some people who...maybe I have to correct their work for them, or maybe I have to do their work for them, while they're still earning a paycheck. It may be because they're having a bad day, or it may be because I can honestly help them to run the test that they are doing. That takes kindness and patience. I have to balance that with not letting my co-workers walk all over me.

Steve: Sure. So, in terms of living out the fruits of the spirits with your co-workers, obviously, with customers, you can't get into the Gospel proclamation and stuff like that, but in terms of working with your co-workers, but just in living out the fruits of the spirit, the love, the joy, the peace, the patience, the kindness, the gentleness, self-control; do you see that happening throughout your day? I know you well, but I'm trying to get your perspectives on it.

David: Right. During the time I was on the phone, I did have a couple customers ask me to pray for them, and I said, "I can't really go into it right now because I'm on the phone, but as soon as I get off the phone, I would love to take a few minutes and pray for you, when I get off the phones." And my customers seemed to like that and my manager even said that was a good way to deal with it. To not do it while I'm on the phones, but to take some free time, like a break or something, when I'm off the phones, to do it then. Now with my co-workers, if it's something that can be done quickly throughout the day, then I'll do that. But then there have been times when I've said, "when I get that lunch time" or "when I get that break," I would love to take some more time and pray for you on that.

Steve: Very good. Last comments…anything else you'd want to make sure you've said about just being a disciple and making disciples? If you had any final closing statement, what would you want it to say?

David: Look for opportunities, because in a ten-hour work day, like mine, or an eight-hour work day, the time you spend with those people are going to add up. There might be more waking hours than you spend with your family at home!

Steve: Oh yeah, no question.

David: So, use common sense, but look for opportunities with those people who you do spend eight or ten hours a day with. Look for those opportunities. They won't always be there. That's where the 'use common sense' comes in, but look for them, because we do spend so many hours with these people.

Steve: That's a great point, David.

David: Now the waking hours at home, with your family, now you might consider those higher quality time, and in many ways they are, but the sheer number of hours that we spend with people we work with... don't let them go to waste!

Steve: Right. That brings to mind that 2nd Peter 3:15 verse, about always be prepared to give reason for the hope that you have. Always be prepared for when opportunities are there, right?

David: Sweet! Thank you, Jesus!

Steve: Amen. Thank you, Brother.

Observations, Lessons, Application:

- What were your key Observations from David's life and faith journey?

- Are there any parts of David's journey and story that you can relate to personally?

- How do you think God wants you to apply these principles in **your** life moving forward?

Chapter 5

Devon McDonald
Businessman, Leader, Linebacker, Missionary
Disciple of Jesus Christ

Devon's story impacts me every time I've been blessed to hear it…from a boy growing up in Jamaica, to moving to America, to Notre Dame football fame, to a professional football player in the NFL. It's a story that people assume is free of worry, sadness, or gut-wrenching trial – but their assumptions would be incorrect. He made it through the trial, and in the process, became a devoted Disciple of Jesus Christ. Devon is a large man – physically towering above most. Big shoulders, huge hands, a bigger smile, and a kind heart. He is a devoted husband, father to his daughters, and I am blessed and honored to call him my friend and brother. Here is Devon's amazing story:

Interview with Devon McDonald, May 20th, 2019:

Steve: I've heard your story from Jamaica to New Jersey and then high school football and then off to Notre Dame and then the Colts, but I guess tell me about your faith journey. How did you come to faith in Christ? I know that happened over a long period of time, but how did that happen?

Devon: Right. Right. Well, like anything, seeds are planted. As a young boy, growing up in Jamaica, my

Granny was just a strong believer. She wasn't overbearing, it was just love! And she would go around the house and be humming. And one song...

Steve: Singing hymns?

Devon: Yeah. I'll never forget it. *How Great Thou Art.* The only reason I knew it is because she sang it so much. And I love my grandmother, even as much, if not more than, my mother because my mom wasn't around; my grandma was. And so, I just got an affinity to her. So, she, just her having a love for God had me questioning like, 'Who is this God?' So, I believe it started then. I remember one time when I was in Jamaica, there was an earthquake. And when the earth shook, it's like, 'Woah! Okay God. Who are you? What are you? You know what I mean? Where did you come from? Where you going?' All of this. And then obviously, who I'm around was godless.

Steve: Did your grandma keep you in church?

Devon: Yes, she did. Yes, she did. And then also...

Steve: Church on Sundays?

Devon: And then also, she couldn't go to church. So, she went to one, the church that she went to, Emmanuel Baptist, by downtown Port Maria, close to Ocho Rios - the rest of the family went to Free Hill Baptist Church. I love my grandmother so much, that I would walk. When I went back to Jamaica this past year, we tracked the miles, and it was like three or four miles, of walking by myself at six years old. Five or six years old...[laugh]... to go to my grandma's church to give the tithe and offering to represent her. That's how much I love my grandmother. With my brothers, sisters, cousins, everybody went one direction.

And in some ways, that kind of left myself to me... I'm not afraid to be alone. I love being with people, but I am fine by myself. Because those early times in my life, walking three miles, going to church by myself, coming back. The only reason I did that was my love for my grandmother.

Steve: That's amazing. She had an amazing influence on you and your faith and planted those seeds.

Devon: Big time, big time, big time. Big Time. Even today, I sing around the house, and my children be like, "Daddy, can you shut up?" [Laugh] But that's a tribute to my grandmother. That's literally a tribute to her, because that's the impact she had.

Steve: What's your grandmother's name?

Devon: Her name was Mercilina

Steve: Mercilina...

Devon: *"Miss Merci"!* I had an aunt named Grace. My mother was named Gloria. So, Gloria, Grace, and Merci.

Steve: That's awesome. And you grew up in Free Hill.

Devon: I grew up in Free Hill, Jamaica.

Steve: Is that in Saint Mary Parish?

Devon: Yes. Yeah. Yeah.

Steve: I've seen it on a map. I've never been through the Free Hill area. I've been to Guys Hill and all up in through Wallingford? Now, when you were in Jamaica on the mission trip, did you go through Wallingford, or were you at Mango Valley?

Devon: Mango Valley. Yeah. Yeah.

Steve: Close to home.

Devon: Very close to home! So close, I mean, it was ridiculous man.

Steve: Did you go to Free Hill?

Devon: Yeah, I went to Free Hill. My brother still lives there. Yeah, my oldest brother is living in the house, well, he's rebuilding the house we grew up in because of the hurricane, Gloria…one of those hurricanes hit it a few years back.

Steve: In your journey through, coming to America, and high school, and then college sports, and professional sports, and now in the business world, in the ministry too, and *Sports World*, now in the professional space…how do you live out your faith in your personal life? How do you see that playing out in your personal life?

Devon: You want to go here first? Or do you want to bridge the gap first?

Steve: Whatever you want.

Devon: Let's bridge the gap from Jamaica coming to America. My mother, when she came to America…she wasn't a believer in Jamaica. She was wild. My daddy was a Policeman, my mother was a nurse. So, when they came to America, it was a different family dynamic. Because in Jamaica, we weren't really a family. Daddy was doing Police duty. He would come back home with bullet holes in his car and I thought I was so cool, man. 'My daddy's car got shot up!' But when we came to America for the first time, we lived as a family. That showed what we were not. Because of the fighting, just a lot of animosity. But I remember my mother came home one night and said, "I want all my children to receive Jesus Christ". When she came to America, her sister-in-law, my Uncle's wife, was in church, and she was living with them and she got a *drug problem*... "drug her to church"... and she got saved. So, when we came over here, one of the first things we did after the plane landed, is we went to church. But that night she came home and she said, "I want all my children to receive Jesus Christ". And I just remember my older brother said, "No". So, I said, "No". My twin brother said, "No" because I said no. My younger brother and sister went and got baptized. I believe they made confessions. I didn't go with them. And so, I really believe, man, that there is a point in our life where we reject Him or we accept Him, at a young age, from the heart. Now we can act what we want to act. And I believe when I rejected Him that night, man, I had a desire for a lot of things in my life: sex, and hanging out, and all that, but now it's a full-bore thing; it's what I really, really want to do now.

Steve: How old were you then?

Devon: I was about eleven... no, probably twelve, thirteen.

Steve: Twelve, thirteen...got it.

Devon: Yes, yes. But then masturbation started coming in. One night I'm flipping through the TV and I saw, you could see just enough of the pornography. And I was hooked. And then, again, going against Christ, I put that before everything else. Football was that avenue that was going to give me my desire: give me money, give me fame, give me notoriety.

Steve: Girls.

Devon: All that. So, part of my push to be successful in football was...I'm a driven guy. I like to be good at what I'm doing. But then also the benefits that come from it. You make a play, everybody starts cheering. That's intoxicating...you know what I'm saying? Who doesn't like that? Well, you make a bad play and they *boo*. Well, I don't want *boo*, I want cheers! So, I'm going to do my best. Then, I was fortunate to get a scholarship to Notre Dame. But still, even in high school, man... because after you make this good play, you're still you. We won a championship, okay, great. Guess what? I'm still me. I don't feel good about me. So, I thought going to a Division-One college like Notre Dame would do it. It's like, 'Yes! You're at a top school'. And it's like, "okay". It's a lot of hard work. Lou Holtz was a very driven, hard working...

Steve: Oh, that's right. Yeah. You got to play for Lou.

Devon: Yeah. Everything I thought was going to, 'Do it', didn't do it. Going to a Division One college. Okay. Okay, I'm still me. Hello. Okay, starting. Sophomore year, I started. Okay, I'm still me. 'Oh, I know what it is, Player of the Game'. Didn't do it. National Championship. Didn't do it. So, my fifth year. My last year. I was MVP of the Cotton Bowl. I think it's always good to finish strong. I was MVP of my last game.

Steve: MVP. Cotton Bowl...

Devon: MVP. That was it. That was my crescendo - that's it. I'm gone. Got drafted by the Colts. I was like, 'Okay, it's money now. It's money. If I get money. If I started making money.' And when I signed on the dotted line and started making and spending money, I was like, 'Huh. I'm the same person.' I hear what they're saying, "You're going to feel good." No. I feel bad about myself, now just with a lot of money. Now I can medicate myself at a higher level. You know, whatever drugs, alcohol, whatever I want. And the women and all that. I'm just dealing with my inner self; that turmoil. As I'm sharing today. The drive was to succeed, because I thought if I succeeded more, and for me it worked in reverse, because the harder I tried, was the worse I did. So, the Colts cut me after three years and it devastated me, man. I blamed them. Hated them. But then I got picked up by the Cardinals. And I believe God did that providentially. He took me away. Because as long as I'm around what's familiar, it's hard. That's why you look at a lot of great men in the Scriptures, God takes them away: Moses, David...he was out there. You have to deal with it by yourself. And so, Arizona was like that for me. I remember flying home on an airplane one night and I was contemplating ending my life. I was like, 'This is it. You know what, I'm done with all of this'.

Steve: That's amazing! That really is amazing that you can have what most people would consider to be *everything*... that some young man would want, you're an NFL Player, and you've got the money, and you've got the fame...that you would consider suicide. I mean, that's amazing.

Devon: Deion Sanders did after two Super Bowls, because what you have and what you do is not who you are. You know what I'm saying? It's like wearing clothes. You take it off and put it on. It's not you. It cannot get inside that place that you need to get. There's only one thing, that we're going to talk about, that can do that, that's it. And the world is trying. I mean, you name it. I got cut from the

Colts, I got picked up by the cardinals. I'm flying on the airplane one night say, 'This is it, man. I'm done'. We won the game in dramatic fashion, against the New Orleans Saints, so we should be happy, right? I'm sitting there next to my seat mate, a guy named, linebacker, Seth Joyner. He should be All-Pro. Because of the era he was in...

<u>Steve</u>: Seth Joyner?

<u>Devon</u>: He was like Lawrence Taylor. I mean the dude was *smooth!* Not as aggressive like, "Grrrr", but a great player. He looked at me and said, "You alright man?" I said, "Yeah". I lied, like most people. He sensed something wasn't right, you know what I'm saying? I put my head down - I was writing or whatever I was doing. And I just got to the airport, got into my SUV. I'm driving home and this voice just said, 'Just run this vehicle over this hill, man'.

<u>Steve</u>: Oh wow...

<u>Devon</u>: It would just be quick. I was like, 'No'. I got to my apartment, opened the front door, threw my luggage on the ground and just began to cry. I had prayed, but never thought any of my prayers were answered. I just prayed because my momma told me to pray. But that night I prayed and a peace came upon me like never before. Then I felt HOPE for the first time in my life! I felt like *tomorrow going to be better than today!* Never felt like that before. Then I felt joy. I felt happy. 'I've won Championships. I've got money. But I've never felt like I feel right now.' And then I felt loved. I know my mother loved me. I think my siblings tolerated me.

<u>Steve</u>: And you know your grandma loved you.

Devon: I know my grandma loved me. But, I felt loved. And I knew there was something different. And the next thing that happened. I quoted the book of Isaiah, because I love it. Because I believe when you really experience God, the next thing happens to all of us: you see you for who you really are. I began to see the sins that I committed. I told you that I used to bring the tithes for my grandma. Well, sometimes I would not always put all the tithe in there, you know? Sometimes I got hungry and there was this one ice cream place, it's the best ice cream I've ever had in my life, and sometimes I would take that money and do some ice cream, you know? That was wrong. That's the Lord's money. I knew it. All these things come up; the pornography, the women I was with. I mean, all those things. I thank God for forgiving me because I saw myself from His perspective. Crying that night, I just felt, it wasn't crying of sorrow, it was crying of joy! I remember going to the mirror and looking at myself, for the first time, I liked who I saw seeing looking back at me.

Steve: And that was like in your late twenties?

Devon: This would have been twenty-six. Twenty-six. 1996. Twenty-six years old. Because every year, I am that year. So, this is 2020 coming up. I'm fifty. I'll be fifty next year. I'm forty-nine. 1990. 2019. And so, I got up the next morning and I got Aeneas Williams. Aeneas Williams is… I've been exchanging stories and he should be in the Hall of Fame. Because the man *lived* the Word.

Steve: I want to make sure we capture the name. Who is this?

Devon: Aeneas Williams. He played at a school in New Orleans – Southern University.

Steve: And you played with him with the Cardinals?

Devon: I played with him with the Cardinals. And he finished up with the Rams. He won a couple Super Bowls with Curt Warner and all of them. But he is in the Hall of Fame. All-Pro.

Steve: So, he was playing with you in Phoenix?

Devon: Yeah. But he would invite me to his house, Bible study, and I would say, "No" with my mouth, but, 'Yes', in my heart. I really wanted to go, but I said, 'No' at the Colts and I was like, I said no then and I'm going to say no now. But the next day, I got with Aeneas and I said, "I want to get baptized, man". He said, "You alright?" I said, "Yeah". I said, "I met the Lord last night". So, he called his pastor real quick. He couldn't do it at the church, for whatever reason. I look back now and say, 'What's more important than someone getting baptized?' So, I got baptized in this pool, at his house. And this is what they told me, because in Arizona, especially in October, it's getting cooler. Once the sun gets right below the mountains, that's when the sun goes down. Down here, it's when the sun goes down, no. Because we're flat. But down there, once the sun hits below the mountains; it's three o'clock, four o'clock, it's pretty much dark. It also takes about twenty degrees with it too. It's dry heat. It's not humid that sticks around. It's dry. Once the sun is gone… They said once they put me under the water, the water became like twenty degrees warmer! [Laughter] At that point, I remember them saying that, but I didn't feel anything. I was just happy that I did something that I know definitely needed to be done. I know it made my mom happy. So, I got baptized and confessed Christ. In Romans 10:9, "If you confess with your mouth, the Lord

Jesus, and believe in your heart that God raised Him from the dead...

Steve: You will be saved.

Devon: And that began my walk with Christ.

Steve: Very good. And that was? What year would that have been?

Devon: 1996.

Steve: 1996. Okay. So, flash forward, how do you, here, now the more mature Devon...how do you live out your faith in your personal life?

Devon: Well, I think it starts at home. I tell people this. There are three lives that we live: We live a public life. We live a private life. And we live a secret life. The devil will fight you in your secret life, because if he can corrupt your secret life, the other life is fake; it's a fraud. And we see it every day. We see all these people that we thought in public were sort of dynamic. We find out in secret, they're hellish. So, what I do, I pay particular attention to my secret life.

Steve: I like that.

Devon: My devoted life. So, I don't care what you think about me out here, because my concern is what God knows about me. And if I'm being authentic and real there, because then I won't worry about the public and the private, because they take care of themselves. If I'm taking care of the secret time. So, my devotional time, my time in prayer, when I'm alone in my car, I can't wait to be alone sometimes, because that's my time with the Lord. And for me, it's growing. As soon as I'm alone, that's what I do;

it's me and Him. Because there are times when I was alone, that's not what I did. I couldn't wait to get alone because I wanted to please my flesh. Now, my time alone, and I'm just seeing the fruits and benefits of that, then it's shown in my private life. So, now my family loves me. My family respects me. The more authentic you are in your private, in your secret life, in your private life with your family, they'll respect you more. And then it goes out into the public, you know what I'm saying? Where people, the world teaches you to go the opposite way. Show a *good front*. Put your best foot forward in public. And then whatever you do in private, in secret, that's your business. No.

Steve: I agree. I love that. I love that. What about in the professional space? When you're out there? When you were the President and CEO of Sports World or in your new role, in this new opportunity that God's given you? In the *bigger fish tank*. I love that metaphor. More in your public space, or more in your professional space, how do you see that as a ministry platform or just an opportunity to live out your faith?

Devon: Well, I believe the world is searching. God has put eternity in everybody's heart. Whether you acknowledge it or not, it's in your heart to seek for God. Now, how do people do that? In different ways. You know there's peace, there's joy, there's hope, there's all the good things. How do I get to that? Give me that question again.

Steve: How do we...

Devon: Walk it out?

Steve: Yeah, how do you just walk it out?

Devon: So, for me, I seek to be an example, because people are watching. They watch your actions. They watch what you do in situations. So, for example, at my job, we had an account with 9,000 people. It was all set up. T-ed up. The lady quit.

Steve: Oh, your key contact quit?

Devon: Yeah, the key contact. Yeah, our Plan Administrator. The owner...we started making calls to the people, to the regional people...when he heard that, he did a cease and desist. No more communication. 'Da, da, da da." And it was an embarrassment. Because it was set up, this was going to be IT for the company.

Steve: It was going to be huge.

Devon: Corporate got involved and everything. And it was a sad situation. How do you deal with that? So...I did the best I could. I didn't make excuses. I didn't run from it. Didn't become less visible, because if it did happen, 'look at me'. But no. And the example, it's still not a done deal, a dead deal, there's still some life to it, but in it, I'm sharing with the people, 'You know, God is in total control. If it's His will for this to happen, it will happen. I know it doesn't look like it right now, but God has amazed me so many times'. So, here is an opportunity for me to testify.

Steve: Share your faith. Yeah.

Devon: I was going to be affected BIG time. Everybody would be, but me directly. And how do I deal with that? I think for me, it's moments like those, and then there are people there, I know their lifestyle; instead of coming in and pointing that out, no, I've learned to love them first. You earn a right to be heard. You present your life in such a way, that when you now are talking, you have...because you loved them first. And isn't that what Jesus did? He loved them first, before He judged them. Because He earned the right to be heard.

Steve: I love that. And like you say, people are watching all the time and they saw how you responded to that bad situation and you showed your faith. You showed...you know, you gave glory to God. But you showed your faith in that. That was a great testimony right there. That's a beautiful illustration. You showed integrity, character. And you could've reacted totally the opposite. I'm sure your human side wanted to probably...

Devon: You know what, it kind of went there a little bit, but I have to remind myself that God is TOTAL control. Not some. Not most. Not almost. Not 99.9%. He's in TOTAL, 100%, control. And if He is, *He knows*. And really, and I was working with a partner, and what I told him was this man, what happened was, we started talking more about that than we were about the Lord. So, if He would have given us that desire...we would have made a quarter of a million dollars, easily. I would have been serving that instead of serving the Lord, so with that, I just said, 'Do I want that or do I want the Lord?' At the end of the day, it is about the Lord.

Steve: Now, I know you coached high school football for a while...

Devon: For a few years. For three years.

Steve: And so, between your professional role with Sports World and just in terms of being a disciple, we've talked a little bit about that, but also sharing your faith, making disciples. You gave glory to God there, but in terms of...do you ever share your faith to new people? Or, how do you share your faith to new people that you run across?

Devon: Well, they 'overcome by the blood of the lamb and by the word of their testimony'. Not loving their life until their death. I believe Revelation 12:10. Before I came here this morning, I rehearsed my testimony.

Steve: You did?

Devon: Yes. Because what God is telling me is, and I believe He's telling me to tell other believers, 'it's like anything else, the more you rehearse it, the more you become sharp and clean and crisp, the more I give opportunities for you to share it. But if you don't practice it, why would I bring these opportunities because you're not ready to do it'. You see what I'm saying? I prepare myself and as far as discipling, I have about five men in my life that I communicate with on a monthly basis.

Steve: That you're pouring into?

Devon: That I'm pouring into. I'm doing life with them. And then I have a pastor, I have my main pastor, but then I also have a pastor, Doctor Charles Ware. We used to do Crossroad Bible College. He's the President Emeritus now.

Steve: Yeah, yeah... I've heard him on the radio.

Devon: Yeah. Yeah. Moody Radio. So now he is my "Paul". So, I believe you've got to have, obviously you'll be looking up to God, but then God will always put somebody that you look up to, so like for Timothy, Timothy looked up to Paul. And then there's always a Barnabas encouragement. People on your same level. Well, let's do the instance for Paul. So, Paul was looking up to God. Paul had Barnabas. Then he had Timothy. What does that form? A cross. Above you. The same level. Beneath you. And that's the cross. And everyday He said we need to pick up our cross and follow Him. So, we should be hearing from God, have someone that's discipling us, have people on the same level…iron sharpens iron…and we should always have people that we're pouring into. And if you don't have that order, then you don't have the flow of God moving in your life. I'm conscious of that and I believe in that.

Steve: So, Dr. Ware is your "Paul" and you've got lots of other brothers that you surround yourself with and then you're pouring into five gentlemen.

Devon: Yes.

Steve: Very good. So, you're talking to them monthly? Just reaching out to them? Are they scattered throughout the US?

Devon: Yes.

Steve: So, when you're reaching out to them and touching base with them, what's that look like? Is it mentorship?

Devon: It's mentorship. It's finding out where they are. It's speaking Scripture into their lives. Some personal, because that's how you make it more relevant. 'How does the Scripture minister to me?' And get correlation. Correlate situations from my life to their life and what does that look like. But yeah, it's loving on people. It's meeting people where they are.

Steve: I love that.

Devon: Now, then encourage them to go do the same. So, it's not a one stop shop. It's giving them a bigger vision. A bigger picture. It's like, 'Yes, I'm pouring into you, but my hope is to see you now pouring into other people'. So, that's my approach.

Steve: So, being a disciple, making disciples, and teaching them to do the same, basically.

Devon: Yes. And that's what it has to be.

Steve: That's why you and I are sitting here today, having this conversation, is because men, like Paul and Timothy, they did that same model.

Devon: Yeah, yeah. Right, Right!

Steve: That was a couple thousand years ago, and today, that's why we're sitting here talking about this.

Devon: And well, I think the church...I don't see it in enough churches. We're pouring into, especially the leaders; there's a real emphasis on that. I think some announcements need to be made when we lead a church. Some constant directive. Study your Word. Because it's amazing. If the last thing they hear is some direction, and they keep hearing it and they keep hearing it and they keep hearing it, then you can follow up on that. Have you been? because I've been telling you to do it. Have you been? And I just think for the church to move forward, on an exponential level, it has to be that we are being discipled, and that we're creating disciples for them to create disciples.

Steve: Absolutely. How have you felt God's leading over the last year, in the professional space? Have you had any, where you really felt God directing you or pushing you in a particular direction? Or this whole fish tank thing that you talked about. I love that metaphor. Well, tell that story.

Devon: Okay. I was in the ministry for eighteen years. I was the president for seven; the CEO. Great ministry, however, my wife came to me and said, because she was in the ministry with me, she said, "I think we should be leaving". And I'm a driven guy. I had a vision for how I see the ministry. Where I believe I could take it. When she said that, I was like, "No, no, not if we bear witness. So, I dug in even deeper. The more I dug in, the harder it became, because I wasn't where God wanted me to be. And so, when God allowed change to happen, and I did not want to go, literally. They gave me a $30,000 raise, but they changed the dynamics. But God just said, 'This is it. You need to go'. And as we left, looking forward to what God had next. It was like, what does that look like?

Steve: Probably a little scary. Right?

Devon: Yes. Yes. Because now, it's trusting God. But over a year now I can say, without a doubt, it's God. I shared the example of when I was in college, my friend bought a fish and he said, with a 20-gallon tank, and he said, "I'm going to go buy a bigger tank". And I said, "For what?" And he said, "I want the fish to grow bigger". And I said: "I've never heard of that. With a fish in a bigger tank, it grows bigger?" And he said, "Yeah, they grow to the size of the tank proportionately". Sure enough, he got a 50 or a 100-gallon tank and the fish, an Oscar, it went from a few inches to a BIG fish. And right then, I never forgot that. And I just believe the transformation, what God has done over the last year. I feel like that because I am able to connect and speak with people I would not have connected with if I was still in the ministry. I work with insurance now. And I sit down one-on-one with people. I'm in their personal life. Really, I can ask almost whatever question I want. And just to be there and care for people. They don't care how much you know until they know how much you care. We only have 15-20 minutes. That is not a long time to have an immediate impact.

Steve: To connect with people.

Devon: Yeah, to connect with people. But I just see the grace of God. And God being there, and how He does stuff is amazing.

Steve: Any last thoughts or points that you would want to make sure….like if you were talking to a group, and I've heard you give talks. You're a great speaker, so if you were talking to a group and you were saying, "To be a disciple and to make disciples with others", what final thoughts would you have?

Devon: When I shared about those three lives… I really believe that's very pivotal and important.

Steve: The secret life. The private life. And the public life?

Devon: Yeah. I think the secret life is big. Because, one of the worst things you don't want to be called is a *hypocrite*. So, in your secret life as a disciple, that's why all these great men, they spend time alone with God. The public life is great, because you get all the accolades and people are able to see you and things like that. But if you look at even sports, Muhammad Ali said, "Long before the winner is declared in the ring, the winner is declared in secret". It's that person way back there, three o'clock in the morning that is running, that is training, that is believing they can win that. That's a secret. Nobody's going to see that. That's dark areas. That's where you're made. And I would just encourage anybody that's looking to disciple, make sure that your secret life is intact, because it's like, *'Your gift will you take you places, but it's your character that will keep you there'*. If you want to build something high, you have to build it deep.

Steve: Good foundation, right?

Devon: Look at a tree, a tree looks the same way beneath as it does above. If you have a tall tree, more than likely it's tall beneath. And I just think the world is saying, with this microwave thing, come up quick. I'll share this last story: So, these scientists wanted to reproduce these threes from down at the Amazon Rainforest. They went into their lab and they were thinking they could manufacture these trees. They started to grow the trees in their big green houses. So, the trees are growing and growing. "That is nice!" When the trees got to a certain height, they fell down. And they couldn't figure out...as they began to investigate, they figured out the problem. The problem was this: they didn't have the root. And what they found out was that the root grows based upon the adversity.

Steve: The wind and the storm?

Devon: The wind and the storm to strengthen it in secret. So, that would be my encouragement to people is, as you seek to be a disciple, make sure you're being discipled. Make sure you're being fed. Because 'a lot of output and not a lot of input equals caput'!!

Steve: I like that. Say that one more time.

Devon: 'A lot of output and not a lot of input equals caput!'

Steve: That's funny. [Laughter]

Devon: And I see it time and time again. Make sure you're being fed. Make sure you're spending that alone time with God and so that when you open up your mouth and you speak, and then God will tell you who to speak to, when to speak to, how to speak to them. Because He knows.

Steve: That's good. Thank you, Brother.

2020 Update: In February of 2020 Devon joined *Athletes in Action*, a ministry of CRU, as Pro NFL Director to the Chaplains. Devon had explained it as:

> *"We Strive to Help Athletes, coaches and their wives become devoted followers of Jesus Christ for their whole lives, so that together, we can be positive influencers everywhere we go. Our goal is to WIN non-believers to Christ, BUILD them up by applying the Holy Bible to the unique problems, challenges and temptations they face so they can understand their God given purpose and then SEND them out to do the same with others on their teams and in their communities.*

Observations, Lessons, Application:

- What were your key Observations from Devon's life and faith journey?

- Are there any parts of Devon's journey and story that you can relate to personally?

- How do you think God wants you to apply these principles in **your** life moving forward?

Chapter 6

Don & Karol
Career Military Officer (Retired) & School Teachers
Disciples of Jesus Christ

Don and Karol are a delightful couple in our community, and also close friends. Don is a retired career military officer, who in his second career taught high school to troubled, incarcerated, at-risk teenagers. Don is a quiet, thoughtful, and extremely polite and reflective gentleman, and the embodiment of the old sentiment that "still waters run deep". Karol is an energetic, lively, and very purposeful woman, with strength of character, a big heart, a big, bright smile, and an inner joy that is contagious to everyone around her. Having met in Germany where they were both working at the time (Don in military, Karol as a teacher), they fell in love, married, and lived a story-book romance in Europe and the United States, as they moved around for the military. They are the parents of three beautiful children, one son and two daughters. They are, also, both very devoted Disciples of Jesus Christ. Prayerful, kind, loving, studious, and generous with their efforts, time, and resources to serve God in their daily walks. You will love hearing their story of navigating life as Disciples of Jesus – often in areas that are not friendly to the Christian Gospel.

Interview with Don & Karol - June 26th, 2019

Steve: First, I like to start with this question: How did you come to faith in Christ? Did you grow up in the church? Is that something that happened as an adult? How did that come about?

Don: I came up in the church. I was born and raised into a Christian family. Then about...well, it was my senior year in high school, the understanding of what following Christ and a life in Christ really was, and the issue of salvation or what it means to me, became real.

Steve: Was that through your youth group in church?

Don: As a matter of fact, it was. I was in Okinawa and my dad was stationed there. There was a group of missionaries who ministered to the local community there. But they also had local churches and their kids were magnificent kids. And we bound together. We just had a terrific relationship. And through that environment, through that relationship, I began to realize what life in Christ was all about.

Steve: And how old were you then?

Don: About seventeen.

Steve: Oh, okay. High school.

Don: Yeah, my senior year.

Steve: And you were in Okinawa, Japan. Your dad was serving in the military. And this was through missionaries?

Don: Yeah.

Steve: Very cool. Was there any particular person? Was it the youth pastor? Or who was it that discipled you?

Don: There was no one in particular. We had a magnificent preacher. The pastor was really great and our youth leader, I guess, was probably the mentor. With that relationship, I probably came to the best realization. But more than that, it was the conversations, the one-on-one time with other students who were very devout Christians. And kind of getting down on my teenage level with me.

Steve: Peers of yours…

Don: Yes. So, it was probably more that… than an adult mentor.

Steve: How about you Karol?

Karol: Well, I grew up in the church as a child. But never understood the Holy Spirit. Never had a personal relationship. I had a job interview at Heritage Christian and the question was, "Are you going to heaven?" And I said, "I hope." And she said, "Do you believe in Jesus?" And I said, "Well yes, of course." Well, at that time, I didn't get the job at Heritage Christian, for obvious reasons, and I stayed at Hebrew Academy. I was teaching with an Israeli teacher after, I think it was my third year. And it was an extremely rough year. He didn't know how to discipline. It was an active class. And a lot of the responsibility fell on me. And I was taking a class at Northside called *Master-Life*. I completed the second section and as we were sitting there, and I felt God say, "You don't have a personal relationship with me."

Steve: Oh, wow.

Karol: And I didn't realize I didn't have a personal relationship. And so, I was rebaptized at the age of 40, on Mother's Day.

Steve: Wow. That's exciting!

Karol: And people at school said, "You're not the same person you were. You've changed." And so, Jewish people noticed.

Steve: They saw it, huh?

Karol: My whole countenance had changed. Because I was very down. And it was just a very hard time. And very exhausting. And so, at the age of 40, I was baptized.

Steve: Okay. So, you were teaching at the Hebrew school?

Karol: Yes, I had been there for three or four years.

Steve: Okay. And when was your first...you said you grew up around the Christian church...

Karol: I grew up in a Presbyterian Church.

Steve: Okay, but you were teaching at the Hebrew school and then at age 40, you came to know Jesus Christ personally and it was life changing.

Karol: And have a personal relationship with Him.

Steve: Okay.

Karol: Very much so.

Steve: What was the setting when you felt the Lord speak to you saying, "You don't have a personal relationship with me"?

Karol: I was sitting at a long table on a hard chair.

Steve: Was it at the school?

Karol: No, it was at the Master-Life Class.

Steve: at the class...

Karol: And God just very clearly said to me: "You need a personal relationship." I always prayed. I believed. But I didn't dedicate myself that way. I didn't live for the Lord. I didn't start my day with the Lord. It just came on me. And that's often the way that God talks to me.

Steve: Oh, that's neat!

Karol: So, when I did go to Heritage Christian, eventually, I was praying. I was asking the children to pray and I said, "See if God just puts a thought in your mind." And the next word that came up was 'trust'. And it was very loud. So, God talks that way through me.

Steve: Very cool. So, both of you are teachers. And Don, you're retired army. And then you started teaching at the high school level. And you do a lot with kids that are troubled kids, going through the legal system.

Don: Oh yeah.

Steve: But you're helping them continue their high school education.

Don: Right. First of all, we're a detention facility. So, we get a lot of turnover. Like in a given year, I'll have 300 and 400 kids. Some of them stay for a few days. Some of them for weeks. But rarely more than a couple of months. So, the time that we have to actually build a relationship with them is precious…because it's not that much. So, our kids are there for a very short duration. And you're right, they're very troubled kids. Obviously, they've done something to put them in the position they're in now. And they come to us with a lot of baggage. Not only the fact that they're there, but more often than not, the circumstances they bring with them from their home life, life on the street, and life

DISCIPLE-ing

with their friends. So yeah, they come to us with a lot of trouble.

Steve: And Carol, you did teach in the Hebrew school for many, many years, right?

Karol: 22.

Steve: 22 years. And now you're a...

Karol: I work as an interpreter at Conner Prairie.

Steve: Oh yeah. That's right. That's right. As an interpreter. Now, what language?

Karol: I'm an interpreter in costume…. [Laughter]

Steve: Oh!

Karol: In 1836. So, I interpret history.

Steve: Oh, you interpret *history*… I get it! So, in your personal life, obviously, you guys are active in church and you have raised your family, but how would you say you see your faith being lived out in your personal life?

Karol: I give every day to God and I let Him open doors. And He often will give me a thought. And I'll make a call to a friend. Opening doors is the best way, I think, in my own personal life, that I start everyday asking God where He wants to take me. What He would like me to do that day? And to be my words and my thoughts and my actions. And so, as in my own personal life, I think building relationships has been a very intricate part of what God has done in my life - building trust with others, through kindness, through care. And I think that's taking a personal interest in people. And praying with them. And talking to them. And getting to know them. That has been a really big part of my own personal life. Having trusted friends. Which that just started recently. Having really trusted friends. And God has put those people in my life in unusual ways.

Steve: Very good. How about you Don? How would you say you live your faith out in your personal life?

Don: Well, God burdens my heart with certain students and I don't know why I feel burdened more with certain students than I do with others. Maybe it's because the need there is greater and there needs to be more of a personal contact and a personal relationship with a Christian. But even with someone who is an adult who cares, an adult role model in their life. So, I spend time working with the students working with them one-on-one, and to the best that I can, understand what their circumstances are and where I can minister to those circumstances and meet them at the point of their need.

Steve: Absolutely. Just meeting them where they're at just being the hands and feet of Christ. To support them and love on them. Pray with them.

Don: Yes. Exactly.

Steve: Do you ever get a chance to pray with them?

Don: I have on rare occasions. It doesn't happen often because it's still a public school. But our limitation, well, our *opportunity* is, that if a student comes to us with spiritual questions, and I say this as 'us' because my entire three person staff is Christian, but if they come to us with a specific question or a specific desire for prayer, we can and we do.

Steve: But they have to come to you?

Don: That's right. It's interesting. There are a lot of students who go through, let's call it a 'Jail House Conversion'. They know they're in trouble. Their heart is really burdened for the pain that they've caused their family. The circumstances that they now find themselves in and they're primed to come to a ministry and to find Christ. And these kids do have people that come in after school hours and talk to them also. So, there are occasions when a student will come to Christ in the facility and is really anxious to know more about what's going on. But those opportunities aren't often, but it's significant enough that it's a real blessing!

Steve: Were you allowed to let them know, "Hey, if I can ever pray for you, please just come tell me."

Don: Oh yeah, absolutely. Absolutely.

Steve: They just don't want you trying to force your thoughts on people, but if they come to you and say, "Hey Don, will you pray with me?"

Don: Absolutely. And it's a delicate balance, too, because our primary reason for being there is to ensure that they stay on track with their school - and if they get released, they go back to their school and they're on par with their classmates, so they don't fall behind. Because falling behind generally leads to more trouble and recidivism. It's becomes a real problem when that happens. But when they do come to us with those kinds of prayer concerns, we can certainly spend time with them.

Steve: Karol you can speak to both in your current role in your historic role at Conner Prairie and I'd love to hear from you from the perspective of teacher, especially since you were working at the Hebrew school, both of those.

How have you been able to be a disciple of Jesus in the workspace? In the professional space? Even though it was pretty sensitive, did the kids know you were a Christian?

Karol: I never prayed with children. I did pray with other staff members, quite often. In fact, the principal called me an *ambassador* and said I was 'all heart'.

Steve: That's nice!

Karol: So, just out of sheer concern for people and as the years passed, people were able to see my actions and how I lived my life. Did I talk about Jesus at the table? No. But I could talk about God. I could live out my convictions, which I did through the children and though the staff. And then, as I got to know people and I saw that they were hurting, I would say, "Would you like me to pray with you? Is there anything I can pray about?" With Rabbis, with Israelis. And people, most often, said yes. So, I made it a personal prayer, leaving Jesus out, in my words, but not in my head, and I could say, *Lord* or *God*...so I believe that prayer, that concern, being steady, caring and loving people, was very catching.

Steve: It built bridges of relationships?

Karol: It built relationships. Now at Conner Prairie, I've only been there a year, but I'm starting to get to know people and gaining trust. And it's intentional on my part. At Conner Prairie, on Friday, nobody was coming through and we were porch sitting. We sit out in the prairie and sit on the porch. And two ladies who work in agriculture said, "We never porch sit with anyone, but we like you." But to build that kind of relationship and that trust is how God uses ministry through me. I don't hit people on the head with Jesus. That just turns people away. But I think through proof and action and kindness and concern, that builds a lot of the ministry God has built through me. Both jobs. How I got both jobs were all God. It was nothing I had done and God opened those doors for that.

Steve: Do people know you're a Christian? Even if you're not praying in Jesus name at the Hebrew school, obviously, that was a challenge, but did your children know you were a Christian?

Karol: I wore a cross. My cross would come out and one little girl said, "She wears a cross because she loves Jesus."

Steve: Awww...

Karol: So, yes, everyone knows.

Steve: So, it was sensitive. You just had to be *appropriate*?

Karol: Well, it's not even appropriate. It's just that to me, it was God-led. He put circumstances in my path. I would pray for, "Who can I minister to today, Lord, in your name?" So, God would put people in my path and it was pretty magnificent over the 21 years how being a Christian wasn't an evil thing, but looked on with great compassion, for a friend.

Steve: Any particular stories that really stand out for you in that?

Karol: Oh, I prayed with a Rabbi last year. His son was going in for open heart surgery. And he was my teaching partner. Very young. And I said, "Might I pray with you?" and he said, "Oh yes, please." So, those opportunities came up quite often where people would cry in my arms. I couldn't hug a Rabbi obviously, but I could hug other women. So, just that steadiness of, 'I care and I love people and you can talk to me'; so, building that trust, and that isn't something that happens immediately.

Steve: Okay. You were praying for open doors and where you felt the Lord lead you, and obviously you would see open doors for opportunity and you would follow that. How about you Don, have you ever really felt the Lord's guidance in any particular situations? Are there any stories you can think of like that?

Don: Well, the one that comes to mind most, was in the beginning I began praying for students. In the morning I would get up and do my devotions and in my prayer time, I would go individually, one-by-one to every student, putting them in that seat they're sitting in, recall their face, and pray for them.

Steve: Pray for them by name?

Don: Yeah. And there were three students who really stood out. God burdened my heart that these students need prayer. Above and beyond. One of them was one of the children who had a jailhouse conversion. Based on his circumstances, he began asking a lot of questions about Christ. Another student, his brother had just been in a very tragic car crash. The brother was a real mess. And here's this student now, who's in jail and can't really be a part of comforting his family and being a part of his brother. And, hopefully, in some kind of recovery. God really put that student on my heart. And the other student, nothing really stood out about him, other than he was just a really troubled student. But God really placed him on my heart; to pray for each one of those three students. And I still recall their faces now. I think about those students and still pray for them. That's probably the story that stands out most in my mind.

Steve: A general theme is, relationship, love on them, just show them that you care. And that you're there for them.

Karol: Building trust.

Steve: Build the trust. You're approachable. And then just pray for them. And then if they come to you or if you see an opportunity, "Oh hey, can I pray for you about that?" or "Would you like to pray?"

Karol: God always puts that on my heart. That's not something I usually do.

Steve: You feel it.

Karol: If God puts it on my heart, He won't leave me alone. He bothers me. And I'll say, "Okay, okay." [Laugh] And that's happened in stores, where I'll tell someone, "God just told me I need to tell you: you are a wonderful person." And I'll say, "You think I'm crazy, but God will not leave me alone. And I can walk right out those doors, but He's going to make me come right back in, so I might as well just tell you right now." So, I feel that burden to ask people if they need prayer. And, "Can I pray with you?" But that's when God has put that on my heart. I don't use that lightly. I figure He has His moments when He needs things, but as you were talking about certain students, I had a troubling class, maybe three years ago. Fourth graders - troubled group of fourth graders, who just had horrible reputations from when they were little preschoolers. I built these personal connections with kids and they found that they had abilities to do things, they'd been told they were so naughty for so many years. They had no idea. They had no confidence in what they could do. And I started to see these little lives change. In fact, there was an essay written about me, by a seventh grader, that I had changed her life. And sadly, it was one of the most miserable, angry little girls I had ever met, but I somehow touched her life by being steady there and not showing that emotion against her as she ran out of a classroom crying. And at the time, I didn't even realize I was that steady because it was really quite a horrible year.

Steve: So, the thing she commented about was that you were the most help to her was just the consistency and steadiness?

Karol: And caring.

Steve: And caring…ok…

Karol: And caring and loving her, in spite of herself.

Steve: So, loving her in spite of her behavioral challenges.

Karol: Yes, which she was very fearful. She was very afraid of not succeeding. She has overcome that now. She wrote this beautiful essay.

Steve: I hope you have a copy.

Karol: I do. I just got it about a week ago. Her mother gave it to me.

Steve: So, if you were going to give advice to future teachers, who are Christians, who are going to be in public space, the public sector - what advice would you give to teachers about how to be a disciple in your professional space?

Karol: Give God each day.

Steve: Give God each day...

Karol: And let Him guide you. Let Him be your every thought and every word. It's so surprising how many times He has shut my mouth from saying something in my own spirit when I was irritated with a child. That nothing comes out. He has shut my mouth more often than not during those years, of something that wasn't appropriate to say. That wasn't always the case. I've certainly tripped quite a few times. However, as I started to pray over my classroom, to anoint the classroom, and to ask for opportunities in ministry, God was very, very steady in that. And that was about the last five years at the Hebrew Academy. But He built me up to building relationships and trust with families and respect. And caring and kindness.

Steve: Caring. Kindness. Love.

Karol: In fact, one of the students last year, it was a parent conference - his father came in, kind of spur of the moment, and I said, "Do you know what a gift from God your son is?" And I had this personal connection with the child. Really personal connection. He and I shared this love for adventure. And he said, basically, "No." And I said, "But he is such a gift. And I know how much you love him." And he and I both started to cry. Well, he died of a heart attack this year; the father.

Steve: Oh, my...

Karol: But I was able to minister to him in that way. It was said of him that he really started to focus on his family. Now, I don't know if I was part of that or not, but he shifted in the way he cared for people. So, I don't know if I had any part of that, but it was just loving him, which he needed.

Steve: Very good. How about you Don, what advice would you give to a new up and coming teacher or somebody that was going to be working and helping out with kids, troubled teens?

Don: Well, my advice would be, don't discount the power of prayer. And consistent prayer. Prayer with focus. And then to be receptive to the fact that doors will open and opportunities will present. And in my case certainly, there's the opportunity to be one-on-one with students in their quest for Christ. But I think even in a non-jail environment, public school, my understanding is, even in those situations, if a student approaches a teacher in private, one-on-one, there can be that kind of ministry. I think the difficulty in a public school would be if that teacher were to do something in front of the class. But if you pray earnestly for students and students come to you with a desire to know more, there's certainly that opportunity, one-on-one, to be a great minister.

Steve: Very good. Any final thoughts? Observations you've had or other wisdom you want to share?

Karol: For me, it has been God putting me where He needs me. And sometimes shutting doors in a very ugly way. But I had no idea I was applying at a Jewish day school when I got the job. It just said 5th Grade Teacher. And I applied and got the job within a day. And then when I had left Heritage Christian, I had called the Rabbi that was the principal and I told him what had happened and he said, "Is three hours enough for you tomorrow?" And they had just had a first-grade opening. So, I stayed in first grade for ten years. And then at Conner Prairie, we were on a field trip last year. I had called and written a thank you note and got a call to meet with the senior educational director and before I knew it, I had a job at Conner Prairie. So, God has made those circumstances, where He puts me, rather interesting.

Steve: One thing I was going to ask you, you said you like to give each day to God and Don I know you've talked about praying for the kids by name and you see them in their seats, but when you say, "Give the day to God", what does that look like? How do you do that?

Karol: I start with, "This day is yours. Every thought. Every word. Every action. Every reaction. Let it all be yours. And lead me to where You want me to be and who you want me to talk to." And I've done that for many, many years, every day.

Steve: That's beautiful. Well, thank you both! I really appreciate you.

Observations, Lessons, Application:

- What were your key Observations from Don and Karol's life and faith journey?

- Are there any parts of Don and Karol's journey and story that you can relate to personally?

- How do you think God wants you to apply these principles in **your** life moving forward?

Chapter 7

Jeff Carson
Barbeque Master, Entrepreneur
Disciple of Jesus Christ

Jeff Carson's story is a beautiful example of the transformational power of the Lord Jesus Christ. A story of Redemption. A story of God's Grace and forgiveness, and how God calls us out of spiritual darkness into relationship with Him. We all, in one way or another, can relate with Jeff's story because all believers experience redemption and transformation through Christ. Jeff and I went to high school and played football together in Terre Haute, Indiana. Though it seems like a thousand years ago, talking with Jeff was so warm and comfortable, and I praise God for his life, his family, his heart for God and the ministry of the Gospel. He is, truly, a Disciple of Jesus Christ.

Interview with Jeff Carson, May 22nd, 2019

Steve: Jeff! It's been a long time! We grew up in Terre Haute...high school... but, such a long time ago! Thanks for taking the time to talk. So, Jeff, I know you own that business, *Carson's Barbeque*, down in Bloomington, Indiana. You have another job too, right?

Jeff: Yes, I do. Yes, I do. I work for a pharmaceutical company in town.

Steve: Ok, excellent. I really appreciate you helping me with this project. As I said, the purpose of this is just to learn about different disciples out there in the world and how they share their faith and how they live out their faith. As we get started here, let me just ask you, how did you come to have faith in Jesus Christ as your personal Lord and Savior? Tell me about how that happened in your life.

Jeff: Well, Steve, back, we went to school together, like I said...we went to college, got out of college, started working in the world. Just working and just an average life. Had kids at 24 years old. My first son was my 24th birthday present... [Laughs]

Steve: [Laughs] Very good...

Jeff: So, life was going on. Things were happening. I started working for the High Community Center as a project manager, program director for the youth and kids. Got up there. There were some worldly influences that crept into my life, in the sense of doing drugs. So, the drug situation was 'fine'. I'm thinking I'm okay. Everything was fine. But then it started leading to me doing more drugs. Nothing to hurt nobody. Just hurt my family and hurt myself... not using my time wisely. We graduated in 85. In 1995, started doing cocaine. That led to more drinking and carousing. And a lot of worldly things that shouldn't be indulged in while you're being married. So, as this took place, that lasted for several years, then as I was going through life, as things were just happening, 1998, with my wife, she was saying, "Well, Jeff, things ain't working right. You're not spending enough time...". So, anyway, the drugs started taking over. I didn't work for like two years after that.1998-1999, didn't work. Then in August of 1999, my sister came to me and said, "Jeff"... We're really close. She's the oldest, I'm the youngest. So, she said, "Jeff, you've tried everything else. You know, you've tried the women. You tried the drugs. You tried everything. Why don't you give Jesus Christ a chance?". So, we're close and I'm listening to her. You know how it is after you...You may not know, but what I'm saying is, what takes place is, you're listening, and you're like, 'What else can I do in life?' I should have been dead. And in hell, but by the grace of God, He started working on me. So, during the fall months of 1998, Christ started working in my heart. I was out doing more drugs, doing everything else. Ended up going to jail. My wife came home from work one day and she's like, "I'm just tired of it, Jeff". I was babysitting. Didn't do anything bad, but I was like, "I just need some money". She said, "No". She said, "I'm not going to give it to you". And I said, "Hon, I'll be right back". So, she gave me some money. And she said, "But I'm leaving". And I said, "Don't leave. Don't leave". So, anyway, I ended up grabbing her by the arm, nothing bad, but it was bad enough where she pulled away, and slipped and fell and broke her arm.

Steve: Oh, boy.

Jeff: Yeah, that night, in 1999... I went to jail that night, because it was domestic battery, you know. I've never been in trouble before. So then, it was that Friday night, so God said, "I'm going to show you what's going on". I look back and see how He works. So, I was in jail all that weekend. So, that lasted up until December - I didn't come back home. December 25th, I remember her taking the kids to her parents' house. For Christmas. So, I'm at home. I'm lonely, but I didn't feel alone. I didn't feel alone, because there was something that was there. And I think it was the

Holy Spirit, Jesus started to work in me. So, I started cleaning my life up. God doesn't need me to clean my own life up - He cleans it up Himself. But not knowing, I said, "I'm going to do this and I'm going to do that"...I started trying to get myself clean. Trying to do what I thought I could do. That's when we got a bad winter, in 1999. When January came, the first two weeks, we had a bad storm. The first week, my daughter said, "Daddy, will you go to church with me?" I said, "Yeah." I said, "When the weather gets better, I'll come. I'll come." So, we had a blizzard and really bad weather. So, the following week, it was January 17th, 1999, I went to the church I was kind of raised in. The same people, the older people, people got older. They were still praying. They were happy to see me. So, my pastor ended up preaching the Gospel of Jesus Christ that day. So, at 12:30, when the service was out, you know how you give the invitation, I came forward and gave my life to Jesus Christ as my personal Lord and Savior.

Steve: And when was that again? That was January ...

Jeff: January 17th, 1999. Right around 12:20-12:30.

Steve: Okay, very good.

Jeff: Yeah. Because I always remember because that was the end of the service. So, I gave myself to Christ. So, after that point, Steve, I just felt a whole relief. Like everything in my life...once I gave my life to Him, it was just a relief. Of everything I was holding onto. Of everything I was doing. I'm thinking, "something's different". My mom got to see me in Christ. She just got out of the hospital. She got to see me be in Christ for a couple months, probably about six months, and then she passed in June of 2000. But during that duration, my first prison ministry...my first ministry was at the Rockville Women's Prison. I had a mentor... his name was Mr. Hershel Pumphrey. Our first ministry, that he and his wife had, was at the Rockville Women's Prison. So, I go to Rockville Women's Prison. That was one of my problems. In life before, before I came to Christ, before He drew me to Himself, I had a *women-problem*. So, He said, "I'm going to take you to the women prison". So, I go there. Ministry was good. God was working on me. Inside our church, grounding and rooting me as a solid foundation and having a personal relationship with Him. So, I was really on fire for the Lord, because I had seen what He did in my life. And a lot of people don't understand, when God releases you of your past sins, no matter what you've done, and gives you a new lease on life, you want to go share the Gospel. I was on fire, like I said, we went to Rockville, So, the Pumphreys had that ministry, and he went to Dallas Theological Seminary; grounded and rooted. Solid. So, God brought me around a lot of men in my church. It was a small church. I went to Terre Haute Gospel Chapel. It was a small church, yet again, my pastor was from Indianapolis. That was his second or third year there, at Terre Haute Gospel Chapel. Ray Russell was the pastor all of his life, until he passed. And my pastor, he was solid. He was a Greek scholar. He had a passion for us to know the Bible and give us all kinds of study work. You name it, we'd be ten or twelve of us; my sister and some other families, Wednesday night, we'd be in the pews. We'd have six to twelve books out, just studying. From that point on, the hunger kept on going. The desires kept on getting better. And I saw, as I was sharing the Gospel, you'd hear the negativity in a sense, 'Oh, it's just those church things. You're going to fall off. You're going to do this, do that.' So, after that night, January 17th... I'm a

Vikings fan, and they played in the Championship. They were going to play in the Super Bowl if they won, but the kicker missed the Field Goal. The first one he missed in four years.

Steve: Wow.

Jeff: So, from that night on, that was the last time I cussed, Steve. I cussed because the Field Goal kicker missed. In the city, the life I lived before Christ drew me to Himself, was to go to the bootlegging house. That's how stuff happened. So, I went to the bootlegging house that night and had a beer. I drank a beer, man, and it made me sick. Didn't want to do anything. That's when He started working and taking stuff away. The cussing, the alcohol. Then the next day, I thought, 'Well, okay', I still had a craving, because everything's like cold turkey. He just took it all away. He said, "I've got your back, but I'm not going to let you do what you think you need to do". So, the next morning, I go to the dope house to try and get me some dope. Because I'm just thinking, that was just a fluke. So, God says to me "I'm going to show you a fluke". As I'm approaching the dope house, as I'm coming around the corner, I look at the front of the house, the front and back was surrounded by State Police. So, that was another opening that God said, "I'm cutting this off!". 'I done cut off the women. I done cut off the drinking. I done cut off the cussing. I done cut off the drugs. Now, you're going to serve me one way or another.' So, I'm like, 'Okay, God'. And that was in my heart. And I was thinking, 'He really does love me!'. From that point on, we started doing the ministry, after that stuff, after Christ came to me. Some of the men in my church had a Vigo County Jail Ministry. And then we did the Vigo County Juvenile Center Ministry. So, after church, I was single then, so I had the opportunity to go share the Gospel with those inmates, who I knew on the streets, but then again, when I went to the Juvenile Center, I got to see some of the kids that I had dealt with before. And I got a chance to minister to them. All in the meantime, I had an opportunity and chance to share the Gospel with my kids! With my daughter, with my younger kids. I would take them to church with me. I would just go and wherever I went to, it was just about Jesus Christ, my Lord and Savior. From that point on, after all those little, small door closures in life... that God who opens up and closes doors, so during all that time, He allowed me to grow in the wisdom and knowledge of Him, being humble about it, because it's all about Him. It wasn't about me - I can see Him at work. God is at work, even when we don't see it. He was opening up doors and doing some wonderful things. So, from that point on, I just started serving Him. Started doing ministry. I met my wife here. She was going to a church. I met her before I started up here at work. So, I've been there at work... it will be 12-½ years. I commuted to work my first two years and then we started dating. And we got married in 2008. So, from that point on, I was looking for a church. Still the hunger was there. Still sharing the Gospel of Jesus Christ. I would look at ten different churches. And in Bloomington, there's a church called Sherwood Oaks. And there's an Evangelical Community Church. These are big churches. So, I looked at ten or twelve different churches. And the Holy Spirit wasn't leading me to any of them. Not that the Gospel's not there, because they're good churches. It was just the spirit of God didn't want me there. So, my wife said, "There's another church my pastor who taught me at Indiana Wesleyan told me about". He said, 'If you were ever looking for a church, come and visit'. Maple

Grove Christian Church. I said, "Okay, let's go check it out". So, when we pulled up, we were looking for something for kids, because we had like eight kids in the house, because I had three or four and then she had some. So, when I walked up on the porch, Steve, the pastor was outside, greeting me, like how we do in the Gospel. And he, "Welcome Brother!" And from that point on, we've been attending Maple Grove. And I meet with my pastor every week. Every Tuesday we meet, as long as the schedule permits. Sometimes he goes to his Mom's, but 90% of the time we meet once a week. Like I said, I do deacon duties. But before, when I was at Terre Haute Gospel Chapel, my pastor taught at Crossroads Bible College.

Steve: Okay...

Jeff: So, I went there. I started going and he said: "To save you gas and money", he said, "God has blessed me". He said, "You don't really need to go to Bible college. You don't need a degree, because the Holy Spirit leads you". He said, "You know, the disciples didn't have a degree. Paul did, but in general, He chose twelve ordinary people".

Steve: Right...

Jeff: So, he just uses ordinary people to do extraordinary things. So, like I said, that was a point where He started working in my life. Started to take stage, like I said. That was in 2001. It was neat, Steve. My mom passed in June 2000. My pastor gave me an opportunity to do some of the benediction for her funeral. It was a good opportunity and I just knew I would see her again. I didn't cry like I thought I would. Life wasn't what I thought it would be. Because I've been to so many funerals and I've seen so many people go drink and go cuss and do whatever. But no, God was real. He was real in my life. Because I got an opportunity to share the Gospel with my family members who didn't know and all those who got a chance to come to my mom's funeral. My pastor did the eulogy. But I got an opportunity to share the gospel, so that was a blessing.

Steve: Excellent.

Jeff: And like I said, from that point on… I've got different ministries going on now. I do Kairos Prison Ministries…

Steve: Oh cool. You do Kairos? Very good.

Jeff: Yep. And then I got a chance to go on an Emmaus walk. Walk '77.

Steve: Excellent. I've done Great Banquet weekends, many times. Love those weekends. I have a lot of friends who do Kairos up at Pendleton Prison.

Jeff: Right. It's a blessing. That's where the discipleship comes in. We are to be making disciples continuously, Steve, like I said. And that's Matthew 28, the *Great Commission* to go make disciples. And it's a humbling experience, whenever you get a chance to share the Gospel of Jesus Christ with someone, and get a chance to share your testimony about what Christ has done in the midst of your life and how He's working and how He's dealing with you on your job. People didn't like Jesus and they're not going to like us, especially if we are boldly proclaiming the Gospel of Jesus Christ to a lost and dying and sin-cursed, messed-up world. Because you can see us. We're going, totally, to the other end of the scale.

Steve: Yes...

Jeff: God has brought me around a lot of godly men. I listen to a lot of ministry tools. I have listened to a lot of ministers. I listen to Ravi Zacharias. I saw him... he came to Bloomington last year.

Steve: Oh nice. I love listening to him speak...

Jeff: We do a lot with Lifeway Ministry down in Tennessee. I get a lot of ministry tools. Like I said, God has brought me around a lot of godly men who have been encouraging to me about the Gospel and being a disciple. That's the key, the discipleship that is supposed to happen, we miss out on a lot of times... we're worried about who's looking at us and what we're doing. And it's not about us, it's about Christ. I've always taken the stance that I've got to be about learning myself, but also sharing what I learn, to make individual disciples. And that is the key to our walk. The more we learn, the more we have to go out and tell somebody. Tell them that Christ loves them and share the Gospel in a capacity and in a way that's plain and simple, that they would want to go out and do the same thing. I remember coming to Christ, Steve, and I'd go down to the bookstore, right there in Terre Haute and I'd buy all kinds of tools. I'd buy the little 100-dollar bills, or whatever.

Steve: The Gospel tracks?

Jeff: Yeah, the Gospel tracks. Then I'd go and share them. And the little books...

Steve: Like pocket testaments? The little Gospel of John booklets?

Jeff: Yep. The pocket testaments. I would buy so many of them and go out and share the Gospel with people. Because that's what we're supposed to be doing. We can't save anybody. It's by God's grace that we've been saved, through faith. Not of works. So, there's nothing we can do to add to it or take away, but we can be obedient, in a sense, in sharing the Gospel with those who do not know. And if we love them, we're going to tell them the truth out of love. Then we're going to share the Gospel. And hopefully, the Holy Spirit tugs at their heart, that those who do not know Christ, they will receive Christ and hopefully you will send them to a Bible believing, Bible teaching, living, preaching church where they can grow. Small groups, or whatever they have to help people get close to Christ, that's the key. It's been a blessing. In the ministry, we don't give up. We don't tire. We're all running a race, but it is...we want individuals to have a personal relationship. We want to hear, "Well done, good and faithful servant." But you have to have that discipleship heart. You have to have the discernment for individuals to see where they're at. You have to listen. You have to listen to people. You've got to see where people are at. I'm a foster parent. So, that was another opportunity. We just adopted our son two years ago. We had 80 children we were foster parents for. So, it was an opportunity to take them to church, to try to disciple them and have a relationship with Christ.

Steve: Did you say you have fostered 80 different kids?

Jeff: Yes.

Steve: WOW! That's amazing!

Jeff: Yes. And some of them come back. You still see some now. I still have a passion to do it, so maybe in a couple years, after one of them gets older...my youngest daughter, Bella, she's eleven, and she's got a lot of activities now, but yet again, it's a blessing though, Steve. Last November, I got a chance to baptize her! So, it was an honor.

Steve: That's beautiful...

Jeff: Yeah. And like I said, my other kids, I get a chance to share it with them. I've got some grandkids that came to church back in November or December. Anyway, we were playing the song *Good, Good Father* and they had the chance to hear it and spent time with us... but yet again, you can see the Holy Spirit working on them. So, that's my passion now, sharing the Gospel with them. I've got a new granddaughter... she's about two now. I just got a book. A buddy of mine at work, he just came up with a book that he wrote for his daughter, but I bought it yesterday, because I'm going to give it to my granddaughter.

Steve: Nice.

Jeff: You never stop being concerned about a lost soul, especially now. I think it's more prevalent and more important that we share the Gospel more now than ever. Before, I used to go knocking on doors. There are different ways that we should do it. But as time has changed, people have hardened hearts. People want to hear, but yet again, Satan and his tactics are keeping people with a closed ear. We never know who's going to be saved, that's why we have to always continue to share the Gospel. There's no, "I quit. I'm going to quit sharing Jesus." No, you never quit, because you remember He loved you so much that whatever state that we were in, He saved us. He chose. And He knew that before the foundation of the Earth when He was going to save me. What path my life was going to take.

And what is going to be taking place now. He's got some things planned. I'm just looking forward to what He has planned. I don't know. But yet again, I know He's in control.

Steve: Amen to that. Amen. Well, hey, quick question - what about...in your personal life, you're on fire for the Lord. I love that! You're active in your family, in your church, in doing outreaches, and prison ministries, and Kairos and Emmaus walks, and ministering to your children and foster kids; I mean, that's just beautiful. What about in your professional life as an entrepreneur, as somebody that owns a barbeque restaurant, but also as someone working in the Pharmaceutical area, in your professional life, what's that look like in your professional life? How are you able to live out your faith in your professional life? You know, Paul was a tentmaker. We come across people all the time in our professional life; how are you able to share your faith in that part of your life?

Jeff: You know, Steve, it's been a blessing because I've been working my job for twelve and a half years.

Steve: Right...

Jeff: I've always had an opportunity to share the Gospel, in a sense, with individuals or people who can tell something is different...not by me beating them down with the Gospel. I've prayed with coworkers. If a certain situation or circumstance goes on, because I'm always inquisitive about what goes on. People say, "You know everybody. How do you know them?" First of all, we as believers, we have to be friendly. We have to have an opportunity for the door to be opened up. So, when that door opens up, by knowing people… Just like I was telling somebody today, one of my favorite Greek words is *ginosko*. It's the Greek word 'to know', 'to experience', to have that relationship. So, I try to get to know individuals, just like Jesus wants us to get to know Him. Just like He knows us. He wants us to experience. And He wants us to do those things that He called us to do. To submit to Him. Through obedience. But the long story short, as I'm sharing the Gospel with people, they see Christ in me. I see if they're crying or if they're hurting, or whatever, and then I get to know them. And at that time, you can work your way in. "Look, you don't mind if I pray with you, do you?" They see something different about you, but yet again, you have to earn that right to share the Gospel with them.

Steve: Right.

Jeff: You can't beat it down. In the business world, sometimes, it's a no-no. You can't share the Gospel in some places. I've seen places at work, where I work at now, some people have t-shirts on. Some people have opportunities to do stuff, and it's like, they say, "Jeff, they made me take my shirt off." But yet again, I tell them all the time, I've never had that problem. If we're in the cafeteria and somebody's talking about drinking or if a female, they're around other females, but if they're talking about going to bar this weekend and I'm going to do this, you can say, "Well, I don't really think you need to do that." Some of the women around them, which are Christian ladies, they listen up. I've had them, when I'm walking down the hallway back to where I'm going, by myself, I've had them say: "Hey, I really appreciate you really bringing that out. Because I didn't know how to do that." The key to this is getting to know people. So, you have to know them. If their kids play sports, find out how they play sports? If something's going on with them, find out what's going on with them. So, that way you have a right, that way you have an opportunity to share the Gospel with them.

Steve: You have to be their friend first, that's basically what you're saying?

Jeff: Yeah, you've got to be their friend. You've got to know the right time to approach them. You have to *BE* there. You have to listen. You have to have discernment. You've got to always be aware of your surroundings and what's going on. So, it's a blessing for me to be in the Pharmaceutical business and individuals knowing, I'll tell them where I go to church. I'll invite individuals to church with me.

> *"You've got to be their friend. You've got to know the right time to approach them. You have to BE there. You have to listen. You have to have discernment. You've got to always be aware of your surroundings and what's going on..."*
>
> *Jeff Carson*

Whatever I can do to get them to understand; if not, I can send them to other friends. As you get a chance to meet people, I've been around other churches now. Me and my coworker, we'll pray together. One of my close friends who works in the First Aid or health department, me and him used to have Bible Studies in the morning. We would invite individuals, and one of my close friends here, his name's Derek, me and him started our first Bible study at work. We've been doing that - and then about a year ago, a young man came to me. Somebody pointed him in my direction about starting another Bible study. It's neat that people kind of know what I do and who I am. And it's an opportunity for me to share the Gospel. To let them feel secure and relaxed about who they are in Christ. Christ is the one opening doors up. So, that's one of the best things, to share the Gospel at where I work, because we went public...we've got a lot of new people - 500 or 600 new people in the last year, probably. That's crazy.

Steve: What about at your barbeque business?

Jeff: So, I advertise as a Christian-run business... when people come in, I have a cross there...and people see the cross. I get believers in...as you get to know people. So, they know it's a Christian-run business, in a sense, because they know something different when they come in. I'm just a people-person. If I get a chance to know them the same way I know my coworkers, then they open up. They start talking. I have customers come back and say, "The reason we come back is because you come out from behind your counter. You come from cooking. You play with the kids." You have to win people over. In that capacity, as my customers come in, they see it. My brothers and sisters in Christ, they come. And then, sometimes, I get churches that want the opportunity to come and do business with me. I have one brother that goes to my church and he gave his testimony. He came in maybe two months ago and he said, "I was watching you, Jeff. Everybody that came in, you shared the Gospel with them. Or you prayed with them. Or you got to know them. Whatever it took. You took the time to talk to them and see how the family was. To see how church was if they were church-going. You found that niche with those individuals." And I think that's what Jesus Christ does. He comes alongside people. He picks ordinary people to do extraordinary things. We are Christians. We're like little Christs. We're to do the same things He did, with humbleness, with love, and knowing that He is one hundred percent behind us, and as we're obedient and do what He calls us to do.

Steve: That's beautiful.

Jeff: I wouldn't have anything else. I tell people all the time, "Man, I wish I had a ministry." It's not always about being in front of people. People say, "Well, your business is your ministry!" And that's so true. But people I talk to say, "Jeff, your ministry, your business. You talk to people. You do this." I feel like there's something else. I was thinking earlier, I need to go to...right here there's a lot of meth going on and heroin. I need to go to the jail, like I did in Vigo County or down to Lawrence County, because they have a lot of stuff going on.

Steve: Sure.

Jeff: There's a church around here, a guy I used to work with… it's called *The House of Prayer*. He goes and they go down to the Monroe County Jail. He said, "Well, come on by and check it out, Jeff." But I haven't a chance to go with him yet, or the Chaplain. So, with my business and other things, it just went to the wayside.

Steve: Sure. I get it. This has been fascinating to hear. I love it. What final thoughts do you have at this point?

Jeff: I think that individuals need to be discipled once they come to Jesus Christ as their Lord and Savior. Because it's a struggle. If you're a Christian, you're struggling. If you're grounded and rooted in the Gospel, the more that you learn about Him, the more you read the Bible, the more that you share the Gospel, the more that you pray, the more things that you do for Christ, the more He opens up opportunities for you and a chance to be a disciple - but also to disciple one another. We are to disciple. We are to teach those who do not know. So, once Christ and the Holy Spirit gets ahold of you, then there are opportunities. If you don't know, ask. If you need a church to go to, ask around. Find believers who are solid in the Word. There's so much going on now. You've got to make sure people are grounded. You've got to make sure people know Christ. I was talking to somebody yesterday, for example. They were talking about a lady; I was having a Bible study. And it was because I was running behind. Long story short, it was one of the ladies who was in my class. She had a friend who was 40 years old, going to church, going through the motions, but never had the personal relationship with Christ. She said she came to her because Jesus Christ drew her through the Holy Spirit when she was 62. But those 40 years before that, she was just going through the motions. Doing the right things. Saying the right things. So, the key to it is always trying to allow God to work in and through you. But yet again, it's through humbleness. It's through obedience. And just letting God work in and through you as a vessel and a conduit.

Steve: I love that.

Jeff: And then as you humble yourself, people will see it in you. And then you'll have that passion. You'll have that desire to go out and share the Gospel with others.

Steve: Amen. Amen. I love that! That was awesome. Jeff, I really appreciate you really giving me your thoughts. And I look forward to coming down and having some good food at *Carson's Barbeque!!* God bless you, my friend.

<u>Jeff</u>: Sounds great! God bless you, too.

Observations, Lessons, Application:

- What were your key Observations from Jeff's life and
  faith journey?

- Are there any parts of Jeff's journey and story that you
  can relate to personally?

- How do you think God wants you to apply these
  principles in **your** life moving forward?

Chapter 8

Jim Laidlaw
Carpenter, Contractor, "Sawdust"
Disciple of Jesus Christ

Jim is a passionate, energetic, and fun person to be around. He loves being around his friends and he loves serving the Lord through serving others. That passion has been expressed through many different outreaches, men's ministries, prison ministries, and personal care. Whether he is standing outside in the cold tending the smoker for a large men's retreat, or sharing his passionate testimony in front of a group – Jim's transparent energy is apparent. He is also a man fighting a health battle, but his faith in the Lord is unwavering, and his commitment to live his faith out loud is inspirational. I hope you are blessed through this interview, and through hearing some of Jim's story. He is a disciple of the Lord Jesus Christ.

Interview with Jim Laidlaw – November 25, 2020
Originally on video podcast recording

<u>Steve</u>: Hello everyone! Glad today to have my longtime friend, Jim Laidlaw, joining me. We're going to be talking about being a disciple of Jesus Christ, and making disciples. Jim and I have served together on some ministry teams over the years, and worked in the kitchen together, and served a lot of people a lot of great food….and Jim is quite the chef! Jim, this is just a chance to pick your brain

a little bit, Jim…so, I really appreciate you being here today.

Jim: Thank you, Steve…it's my honor.

Steve: Last time I saw you it was at that barbeque that Brian Emmons and others organized, and I got thinking afterwards "man, I need to talk to Jim!". You have a really cool story, and I wanted to capture that… so, why don't you tell me about your personal journey… when did you become a Christian? When did you become a follower of the Lord?

Jim: Well, I grew up as a catholic, going to St. Joan of Arc grade school. So, we went to church all the time. So, I knew *of* Jesus, but not really connected *to* Him. It wasn't until the year…2000 or so that Ron Blancaneaux, a buddy of mine from Christ the Savior church invited me to a *Via de Cristo* weekend. That's when the lid came off, and I was exposed to what being a Christian was, and all of the heart-felt giving. I've always done these things, but I never had an outlet or an understanding of these things. So, that's when I really became connected to Jesus.

Steve: Okay. So, around 2000, so approximately 20 years ago. Beautiful. I know that you have served in a lot of different roles over the years, helping out at Great Banquet, etc….. and I know that you have also done a lot with Kairos prison ministry…. why don't you tell us about that, and how that has been an impact on your life.

Jim: Well, it's been a GREAT impact on my life. I'm going to back up a little bit… (Jim holds up a framed painting of an African-American young man) …see the date on that? 1996. So, that is Antwon Whitney… I was in the Big Brothers and Big Sisters program back then, and

Antwon was my little brother. He was 14 years old. And, again, I knew that I wanted to give and do things way back when, but I didn't know how to punch through that. He taught me more…[laugh]… than I taught him! As far as picking him up from his home, seeing his home, understanding about simple things in life, that I took for granted. I can't recall any one particular conversation, but I can tell you that those conversations were impactful and powerful to me…because that made me understand that…I'm a blessed man. We're all blessed men. He came from a different place, and he taught me a lot. So, him and his mom wanting him to get into the Big Brothers program…and I've unfortunately lost track of him over the years… but it probably saved his life. And I say that, because now I'm going to talk about Kairos. So, I have done 14 Kairos in 7 years, that's two a year.

Steve: Wow. That's a lot.

Jim: …and there's 42 offenders…there's always a full team and a complement of 42 offenders each time. And I've been honored…I have served in every position inside of Kairos, including leading one.

Steve: excellent

Jim: to an offender, it is a male role-model, father-figure. They got into gangs because they didn't have a father-figure, so they wanted to get attached to something…

Steve: Right…

Jim: So, once I got in there and understood that, it brought me back to Antwon…and the impact I had there. And so, Kairos has had an impact on me because we go into there to minister to them…but they are ministering to us…just like

Antwon did to me. Just to listen to these men talk about their lives, how blessed they are, and how thankful they are… the offenders are not a homogenous group of Christians…

Steve: Right

Jim: …they are Buddhists, atheists, American Indians, Vikings… you name it, and it's in there, in that weekend! And it's very interesting to note that we are in there…and the team coming in, we're like lost cousins. We only see each other at team meetings and on the weekend…

Steve: And you meet for several weeks leading up to that weekend, right?

Jim: Yes, eight weeks… eight team meetings coming into that. Yes, that builds us into our team. So, the offenders think we all know each other and see each other all the time and going to the same church…in fact, we're not.

Steve: Right…

Jim: And when we go in there, we don't care what these guys have done. All we care about is what's in their heart. A lot of these guys come into a weekend with a lot of hate…lot of hatred, a lot of bigotry…racism in their hearts. All that stuff is *taught* to them…it's a learned behavior. And by the time the weekend is over…again, *Christ shows up, He shows out…* these guys are Aryan Brotherhood, and Muslims… are hugging it out!

Steve: Really? Wow…

Jim: It's powerful! And that sends ripples and shockwaves through the camp. Because that gets known very quickly out there…and that's very tough for them, for one of the talks we have in Great Banquet and Kairos is *Environment*...

Steve: Right...

Jim: ...these guys are in an enclosed environment, and they cannot escape it. They cannot get away. So, if these guys change their ways, they are changing their ways knowing that the repercussions of this could be serious! And they do it anyway. That is powerful to me.

Steve: Transformation...

Jim: Transformation, that's right... and all we did was show up and give them X-number of talks and let them do their deal, right?

Steve: And for those who may not be familiar with that kind of model, it's...done over the course of a few days, and there are speakers throughout the day that share their story, and share their heart, and point people to Christ...and are vulnerable, and take the mask off, and share what's really going on. So, why do you think that model is so powerful in the prison? Why does it work so well?

Jim: We disarm them. It's *Love, Love, Listen, Listen.* These guys on the first day are coming down with their scowls, and their arms crossed... we just walk them through the process. There are talks, just like any other weekend. And after a talk they have table discussions. There are six offenders and three team at a table...and then they'll do a poster. And then they'll do another talk. We have fifteen talks throughout the weekend, and each one builds on the one prior. And, like every weekend of a *Via de Cristo* or *Great Banquet*... rarely will you remember the outline of the talk being given, but you remember the content of the human giving his talk, his personal testimony. That is what sticks with these guys!

Steve: Yes…

Jim: **A lot of these guys have never understood or been taught or been exposed to some very simple concepts of *responding* to something…versus *reacting*.** So, these guys would *react!* to things, verses *responding*…

Steve: right…

Jim: so, we would talk about those things, and you would see them melt over time. The next day they would come in they were a little more friendly, and jovial, and talking…by the time Saturday comes around, in the gymnasium at Pendleton where I go… we're high fiving each other, and we're hugging each other, and these guys are starting to each other! They even say by the third day…which would be Saturday…they know they're in prison, but they are not in prison! They are understanding this is a different environment all together. The entire camp knows that we're there.

Steve: It's kind of an oasis of love, and brotherhood, and friendship inside…. You know, they are behind walls… but it's kind of an oasis where people can be themselves and develop friendships and love that…out there in the yard, they can't do that.

Jim: That's correct! Crying or hugging is seen as a sign of weakness. I'm telling you, these guys are balling their eyes out! And hugging on each other. It's quite the transformation, and you're correct in that. Once we're done with the weekend, they have a *Prayer and Share* on Saturdays, and the Kairos alumni can go to chapel and reunite, and reunion together and pray and do all these things…and stay connected.

Steve: that's awesome…

Jim: it's beautiful…

Steve: and if you think about the Gospel and throughout the New Testament, with Jesus saying "they will know that you are my disciples if you love one another". And being able to share the love of God and share the love of each other… people can feel that! And it's sometimes so revolutionarily different…it's like "Wow!… mind-blowing. Darryl Pitts has told me some stories from serving on Kairos… I've never experienced serving on a Kairos weekend, but maybe someday.

Jim: I hope you get to…

Steve: So, if you're one-on-one with somebody… maybe outside of Kairos (which is a structured weekend designed to share the love of God with people) …. So, if it's just you talking to your neighbor, or… I know that you're a remodeler and a carpenter…if you're working with somebody, how do you typically engage people with your Christian faith? The Gospel? How do you normally do that?

Jim: I was just talking with my great nephew about that today…. I don't force anything. I let the situation present itself. And it does present itself. Whatever that opportunity is… I go with it. Just through conversation and talking with people. I don't want to know what's in their head, I want to know what's in their heart. Then, once I'm there, they will say something…then I'll probe a little, and they'll start opening up. I'm really just rolling up next to them and being quiet. *Being present* for them…

Steve: Right…

Jim: The guys that worked for me clearly understood who I was and what I do and it did have an effect on them… because they told me I did. And I'm thankful, and I'm blessed. Now, with customers… you have to be careful walking into a customer's house and thumping them with the Bible…

Steve: [chuckle] Right…

Jim: You just don't know who they are. I'm the one who went out and did the estimates, and so I purposefully parked my truck in such a manner…straight out in front of their door, they could see the logo on the truck, and I dressed nice, and I looked nice…presented myself nice. When I went inside the house, I would just observe and we would talk…and I would let the situation present itself. If it didn't present itself, I didn't do anything. If it did, I would just start talking with them about that… and eventually we could start talking about the crosses that I make…

Steve: Right…and we will have to talk about that, too!

Jim: Thank you! And so, on the next day…or if we won the job, which we normally did… I would bring them a cross, or crosses for them to have. Eventually I learned just to have crosses in the truck all the time, so I could walk out and get it and bring it back. Once it was laid into their hand, it didn't come back. So, it wasn't anything forced…it was just genuine. Genuine conversation…heart-felt.

Steve: Nice

Jim: You know, I'm not a guy that knows a lot of Bible verses...I just know what the Bible says *to do*...

Steve: Right...

Jim: So, I do those things the best way I know how...

Steve: What would you say are those main things that you know what to do and you do them? What would you say they are?

Jim: Being respectful, kind, empathetic, listening, understanding...you look them in the eye, firm handshake. It's all those things that reassure the customer that you're a good human being. And that comes from the fact that because of Jesus I am a good human being. That's what comes across.

Steve: [looking at bookshelf] I moved recently, and other than in my truck, I don't know where my little cross is.... Do you have one?

Jim: [holds one up to the camera and smiles]

Steve: Oh! There ya go...[laughing]... I remember when Jim gave me my first one of those. Jim is a "Cross-a-holic". Why don't you explain all about that...

Jim: Ok... so, this cross [holds up the small red cross] is different than this cross [holds up the larger, cross on a leaning stand]... so, which one do you want?

Steve: I don't care, you pick...

Jim: Ok...so, this smaller cross is a Kairos cross...and I call it a Kairos cross because Matthew 25:36, and I'll paraphrase... "you came, you saw, you fed, you helped me..." this is how I understand the Bible...how I relate it to me, so I can relate it to others. So, how do I...Jimmy Laidlaw, relate Matthew 25:36 to others in my way? Since I make crosses and I do sawdust... and by the way, I gained that nickname "Sawdust", and I am a *cross-a-holic* [laughter] and I'm not repentant on that!

Steve: [Laughs] right...

Jim: So, it dawned on me one day out in the shop when I was out doodling away that if I take 25 and 36 and divide by 12... I come up with this size [holds up the small cross] and 12 is being the 12 apostles. So, that is how this cross came to this size.

> *"I was naked and you clothed me, I was sick and you visited me, I was in prison and you came to me."*
>
> *Matthew 25:36*

Steve: Okay...

Jim: Palm-sized. The cross is red... Padauk wood, it's naturally red like that...that represents Jesus' blood. The nail through the center right there represents Him taking our hurts, habits, hang-ups, burdens, and sins into his heart. That's what that nail is for. It wasn't the nails that held Him to the cross...it was his heart (Jesus' love for us). This is actually a prayer-cross, and it's not supposed to be comfortable to hold on to....it has sharp corners. There is nothing comfortable about being on the cross...

Steve: this is true...

Jim: In time the wood will round off and become brown, like dried blood...dark brown...but that nail will always be there to remind you that He had done that for you.

Steve: You're right... when holding those, you can always feel the nail pushing into your palm. It's a great prayer cross. Thank you. Share with us about that larger cross...

[Jim then explained the larger, multi-piece leaner cross to the camera. Very difficult to describe... similar overall theme to the smaller prayer cross, with the ADDED focus of praying for other people's hurts, habits, hang-ups, burdens, and sins – represented by the small wood wedges cut out of the base of the cross]

Steve: Thank you for explaining all that Jim. I remember hearing you explain it, and it impacted me, and I know that you have impacted many over the years with that.

Jim: Thank you. If I may... I've made thousands of these crosses in my time. There were some girls from Fort Wayne who have been through a lot of Via de Cristo weekends, and I made a lot for them. Come to find out, the girls *trade wedges*!

Steve: Really?

Jim: Yes, so...they're praying for somebody else...

Steve: Wow...

Jim: Right... it came from God, through me, to do that.

Steve: Beautiful...praying for each other. So, Jim... if you were going to answer this... *"the most important thing about BEING a disciple to the Lord is to _____."* And then *"the most important thing about MAKING disciples would be _____."* I know those are big questions, but what are your initial reactions?

Jim: I'm going to go back to Matthew 25:36 and John 3:16. John 3:16 is *you have to believe*, right? But, Matthew 25:36 is *action* by somebody. So, that's how I do what I do. I go visit people, I roll up next to them, I'll feed them, I'll give money, even if I don't have it... I'll still do that. And I'll listen and be compassionate. Whether I make a disciple out of them or not, that is not my goal... that is up to God to do that. I'm simply there to offer *me*, and what I can do for them. It's the old adage: "You can lead a horse to water, but good luck on trying to drown it!"

> *"Matthew 25:36 is ACTION by somebody. So, that's how I do what I do. I go visit people, I roll up next to them, I'll feed them, I'll give money, even if I don't have it... I'll still do that. And I'll listen and be compassionate."*
>
> - *Jim Laidlaw*

Steve & Jim: [Laughter] That's funny... and it's true

Jim: And the more I get to be around people who *want* me around, then the more they become disciples, if you will. I'm a sinner like anybody else, but I go about my life with Him in my heart the best way I know how. I think of my crosses and things I've done...and I think of things I've done that I *don't* want to do again. I'm more interested of meeting somebody in the valley of what they don't want versus what they want. I can tell you real quickly that I don't want to get hit in the hand with a hammer. The more I learn about what they *don't* want, the more I understand what they *do* want. It pares it down.

Steve: Ok. Very good. Thanks. So, last question... the Fruits of the Spirit are love, joy, peace, patience, kindness, gentleness, faithfulness, and self-control... and knowing you for many years, I see a lot of those fruits exhibited in you in many ways...

Jim: Thank you...

Steve: so, the question becomes: How do you feel that God moves you or speaks to you to exhibit the fruits of the Spirit? Do you have any insights on that?

Jim: [reflects for a moment] I've always been told that I wear my heart on my sleeve. I have a natural empathy for people, and I want to help them. And people may or may not know, I have been diagnosed with prostate cancer, stage 4...so I'm terminal, and the cancer has spread to my bones. So, once I was diagnosed and understood that, my understanding of all those things you rattled off became much clearer. There's an old saying in my family when Mom and Dad were trying to discipline or teach us something "yeah, I know, I know, I know...". So, the day my Mom and Dad passed away, I knew. I had to know, because I couldn't go back to the well. The same thing happened, twice, to me... the day I was diagnosed with all of this...now I know. I can't undo all of that... so now my effort.... I thought I was sincere before... I am MUCH more sincere about things now. I am much more adamant about it now. A lot of things just don't make any difference any more. Perspective.

Steve: Right...kind of helps you put the world in perspective, doesn't it?

Jim: Very quickly, right? Very quickly... a lot of this bologna that's going on now just doesn't make any difference. It does, but it doesn't to me...

Steve: Right, right… you said to me the other day "I'm looking forward to being with the Lord…"

Jim: I am !

Steve: …whenever that happens…whether that's today, or tomorrow, or six months, or a year, or two years…whenever…and everyone of us can say that same thing. I don't know that I'm going to be here tomorrow… I might drop dead of an aneurism in five minutes!

Jim: Exactly right.

Steve: I love your heart, and I love your perspective. Any final thoughts that you want to leave with people that can go in the book, or final thoughts about being a Christian and following the Lord?

Jim: **Get with it!** [laughs] **Get on it! Because this is your one and only opportunity. This is not a *dry run.*** At one point I thought I was invincible. No, this is the *real deal.* [pauses in reflection] And this…Get out of your head, and get into your heart. Let your heart do the driving versus your head. I understand we have to be logical and do certain things, but once you allow your heart to get after it, then you're starting to figure out and understand what Jesus has been talking about all along. Back to Kairos, it's *Listen, Listen, Love, Love.* All we on the Kairos team care about is what's happening in the heart of the offender. We don't care about the head…it's the heart that we're after.

Steve: Right… love that. I've heard it said many times that the longest distance is often between the head and the heart. You may have intellectual understanding, but until it becomes at the core of who you are as a person, and it lives in your inner-most being…it's not just some intellectual concept in your brain, but it actually becomes who you are and how you live that out.

Jim: Yes. I was talking with Simon about this earlier today. It's about God's timing. I don't look for God's timing…it appears. Right? There's my opportunity. Just like we were talking about in discipleship: There's my opportunity! I don't try to force anything. I'm there. I may only say a few words to someone, and make a comment "I'm sorry…what can I do for you?" For some people, no one has ever said that to them before.   When I was married, her son had a bunch of friends who would come over and we would just talk, like we're talking now, and I had a couple guys tell me "no one has ever talked to us like that!... we love it!".   Very straight forward stuff…that affirms to me that He has me on the right track.

Steve: That's one thing I love about you, Jim…you're REAL. I don't like *fake people*…I like real people…

Jim: Yes, yes…

Steve: I know with you, you don't have a mask on, you'll just tell me…

Jim: *Covid-beard* [as Jim played with his super-long beard] [Laughter]

Steve: Thank you so much for doing this interview today, and I'm truly blessed to be your friend. And I look forward to going through all this for the book.

Jim: I'm honored and blessed. Thank you.

Observations, Lessons, Application:

- What were your key Observations from Jim's life and faith journey?

- Are there any parts of Jim's journey and story that you can relate to personally?

- How do you think God wants you to apply these principles in **your** life moving forward?

Chapter 9

Jim & Anita VarnHagen
Rescue Mission Leaders, Engineer, Mother of Nine
Disciples of Jesus Christ

Jim and Anita are a delightful couple – full of stories, and a vast array of experience from their 80-plus years on this planet. Parents, Grandparents, Great-Grandparents, they are the Matriarch and Patriarch of their large family. As well, they are Senior Leaders in our local church. Full of joy, smiles, laughter, and wisdom, the VarnHagens are a huge blessing to our community. With experience in the US Air Force, engineering jobs, and a lifetime spent organizing and leading Rescue-Missions in Chicago, Detroit, and New York City, the VarnHagen's lives are great illustrations of service to mankind in the name of Jesus Christ. Jim is an Elder of our church, and we are blessed to have them in our lives. Here is their story:

Anita and Jim VarnHagen, June 6th, 2019

Steve: Tell me about you, how did you come to faith in Christ? Did you grow up in the church? Did your parents take you to church? How did that happen?

Jim: Well, I didn't go to church hardly at all from the time I was about six years old, and in high school I don't think I darkened the church door once. And so, my background in the church was limited. However, there were some meaningful moments when I was quite young. But it was not until I was 19 years old when I was in the Air Force in Morocco, North Africa that I had a spiritual awakening.

Steve: In the Air Force?

Jim: Yes, In the U. S. Air Force and on an air base in Morocco. Of course, I didn't know this, but Anita was praying for me all the time I was over there. I should have known that.

Anita: You have to realize we were engaged. I was a senior in high school. He had graduated a year earlier and was now stationed in North Africa.

Jim: Our engagement took place just before I left to go to Morocco. During that time, Anita's faith grew and she realized that I probably was not a Christian. Well, she *knew* I was not a Christian.

Anita: I knew you weren't. It's just that I had done some studying and Daddy Van...

Jim: Rev. Orrin Van Loon Sr., affectionately known as Daddy Van, was the senior pastor of the church Anita attended and where we got married. At any rate, she kept praying for me. There were several fellows in the Air Force who said to me, "Jim, you need to know the Lord." And a couple of them said, "You know, we're praying for you". And, I thought about these things especially when one of these men told me, "Jim, you need to go to the Protestant Mission." Well, the Protestant Mission was an evangelistic service; a revival service at the Air Force Base

Chapel. The evangelist who came there, was a Presbyterian minister. He was going from base to base across North Africa preaching the Gospel where we had military installations.

The fellow who told me, "You need to go to the Protestant Mission at the base Chapel." was Floyd "Smokey" Brown. Actually, Smokey was his nickname because he always had a cigarette in his mouth. At any rate, he also played the guitar and rode on a donkey, our squadron mascot. He was an unusual guy. [Laugh]

Smokey had two large tattoos, one on each arm, of a naked girl. He said to me, "Jim, the Lord spoke to me" and said, "I've got to take these tattoos off." Well, I said to him, "Why don't you just put some clothes on them." And he said "No, I can't do that, I've got to get them off my arms because the Lord spoke to me about that." I asked, "How is this going to be done?" And Smokey said, "The base surgeon is going to cut my forearm open about 12 inches long and peel the skin back and scrape the tattoo off on both arms."

I responded and said, "Oh, that's going to be kind of tough." And he said, "Yes, but I've been praying about it and I'm going to do it." Smokey was the first person I knew that his faith actually determined what he should do to change his life. Sure enough, he got those tattoos off and I went to the Protestant Mission, and that's when I heard the Gospel from the Presbyterian preacher. A visiting Methodist Chaplain who was with a newly arrived Bomb Wing was assisting the base Baptist Chaplain during the evangelistic services.

I thought, "Is it possible for a Baptist, a Presbyterian, and a Methodist to sit down together?" I listened to the Presbyterian, and after two to three nights, I decided to trust Christ as my personal Savior. The Methodist Chaplain led several of us to the Lord and the Baptist Chaplain arranged to have us baptized. A short time later we went up to the Atlas Mountains to Khemisset, Morocco where a missionary organization known as the Gospel Missionary Union was located. One of the missionaries who baptized me was Bob Schneider, whom I remained in contact with over the years.

Steve: Excellent...

Jim: And so, I was baptized soon after I was saved.

Steve: And what year would that have been, approximately?

Jim: Oh, that would have been...early 1956.

Steve: Okay. Very good.

Jim: So, I was almost 20 at the time

Steve: And that made Anita happy, I'm sure.

Jim: Well, you know I never....

Anita: I didn't even know.

Steve: Oh, really?

<u>Jim</u>: I didn't tell her about it because I wanted to wait awhile and see, "How is this going to affect my life?" You know, I noticed that the first thing I did was to stop using bad language. I realized that it wasn't good to do that, especially now that I knew the Lord. But it was pretty easy. I just gave it up and that was the end of it.

I didn't stop smoking right away. But I did stop using foul language. And of course, being in the Air Force, you learn this kind of language. As I was planning to leave and go home, my tour was extended an additional three months, which was probably a good thing, because I grew in faith during that time.

We had to delay our marriage until July when I finally got home. As we met, after being away from each other for over 15 months, Anita said, "You know, I have something I've got to tell you." And I said, "Well, I have something I need to tell you as well." And she said, "Well, you go first." So, I told her...

<u>Anita</u>: Yes, because I had bad news.

<u>Jim</u>: She had bad news and I had good news. I told her how I had come to know the Lord and wanted our marriage to be on the right foot as we went forward. I didn't know about her faith, so at this point, she said, "Well, I'm glad that you told me that, because I was going to say if you didn't know the Lord, we should stop right now."

<u>Anita</u>: I didn't even ask "if." I just said, you know, because I was calling it. Because I knew he hadn't been a Christian when he left.

Steve: And you came to faith in Christ while you were in high school?

Anita: No, no, no, no. I went to church with my grandmother when I was really young.

Steve: Oh, okay. So, you grew up around the church. Very good.

Anita: I was saved when I was 11 years old while attending Bible school. And then I always had Christian friends. Throughout my high school years, I attended VCY (Voice of Christian Youth) and was also involved in other church activities.

Steve: Okay. Very good.

Jim: And I have to say that, I heard stories from the Bible when my mother had me go to Vacation Bible School when I was about eight years old. I heard the story about Abraham and Isaac, and it just didn't rest well with me. 'Why would the father want to kill his son?' I couldn't digest that at all. I thought, that's an awful mean thing. I didn't see the full picture at that time.

Steve: The whole ram and the bush? And the whole thing. Right?

Jim: Yes, after that I decided, 'I didn't want to go to Vacation Bible School anymore.' But early on, when I was about five years old, I can remember my grandparents died, all three of them in a row, within about a year's period of time. First my dad's father died, then my mother's mother died about six months later followed by the death of my dad's mother after another six months.

My dad's mother and father had taken care of me up until I was nearly five and a half years old, because my mother worked as a nurse and my dad was working long hours. So, basically, my dad's parents raised me. We all lived in the same house during the depression years when many people at times couldn't afford to have their own private home.

So, my mother and father, my aunt and uncle, and their two children, and my two grandparents; all lived in this big farmhouse. And it was large enough. We had barns out in the back with all the normal farm animals. After my three grandparents died, my mother had to go into the hospital. Well, I didn't know why she was going to the hospital, but learned later that my brother was going to be born. All I knew is that she was going to the hospital and I remembered my grandparents, all went to the hospital and they died. And so, my aunt was there and I said to her, "Who's going to take care of me now since my mother has gone to the hospital?" I thought she would die, also. My aunt said, "Well, I'm here and I'll take care of you."

Steve: Aww…

Jim: So, I went out there by the barn, and I sat down on the grass and I looked up into the sky and I said, "I wish I knew more about God." This may have been my way, as a child, of talking to God, and so I think that was my first prayer.

Steve: About how old were you then?

Jim: I was just a few months past five years old. I started school that fall.

Steve: About five years old. Wow.

Jim: But nothing really took place, until I was 19.

Steve: Very good. I love that. And in North Africa, in Morocco. I love that. So, you came back, you and Anita talked. You ended up getting married. And then, as you went down your life, and I know you've got a long, interesting career, how did you live out your faith in your personal life as you were growing into a being a new Christian?

Jim: Well, we moved. My next assignment was in Greenville, South Carolina.

Steve: In the Air Force still?

Jim: Yes, I was stationed at Donaldson Air Force Base. Right after we got married, we went on our honeymoon to Mackinac Island in Michigan's Upper Peninsula. Then after settling in Greenville, we attended Southside Baptist Church. It was there that I really grew in faith.
Steve: Okay. Good. Was it through somebody discipling you and teaching you? How did that happen?

Jim: I think just the activities of the church and attending the meetings I began to realize the importance of reading the Bible. I hadn't seriously read the Bible; however, I did read some Bible verses shortly after I was saved. I had a little Testament that the Gideon's had distributed when I entered the military.

Steve: With the Psalms in it and the New Testament?

Jim: Yes, but Anita bought me my first real study Bible.

Anita: The Scofield.

Jim: The Scofield Reference Bible.

Anita: That was the thing back then.

Jim: So, I started studying that Bible. We attended an adult Sunday School class.

Anita: Sunday School was very important in teaching adults as well as the kids. But we were also involved in various activities which the church normally would have had. We helped with Youth activities and where ever needed

Steve: Very good. Very good. So, you were taught and trained and could ask questions and learn and just through reading the Word - and also through church and the different activities including Sunday School classes.

Jim: I also developed a friendship with Clayton Hadley. He was very interested in witnessing to anybody that came along. And so, he would take me with him. One of the places we went to was down to near the railroad station where the Greenville Rescue Mission was located. This is where I first got involved in working with down and out people.

Anita: Early on. Early on.

Jim: And, also with an outreach to Servicemen...

Anita: At the Servicemen's Center.

Jim: We wanted to start a Christian Servicemen's Center. This was Clayton's vision and he was very helpful in getting it started. He was Pentecostal but decided that he didn't want to be that...what would you call it...*emotional*. So, he decided to attend a Baptist church. He told me that on one Sunday, "The preacher really preached such a great sermon, and I had to get up out of my seat in the pew and go out on the porch of the church to shout!" [Laugh]

Steve: That's funny. [Laugh]

Jim: He was a great guy.

Steve: So, after the service, I know you worked as an engineer, correct?

Jim: Yes, in the service I learned electronics. I remained in the service for seven years and I went to military technical schools probably half of the time I was in the service and learned all about electronics. So, when I got out of the Air Force, I initially worked as an electronics technician.

But, when I was working in research and development my supervisor, Charlie Sie, said, "Jim, why don't you join the

Institute of Electrical and Electronic Engineers? And I said, "Well, I don't have a degree." He said, "You don't need a degree." He said, "I've got a Ph.D. and I am a member because they have good insurance rates." He said, "Here fill out this application with all your experience and qualifications." "You've had enough experience," he said, "and I'll sign it." And sure enough, after he signed it and then sent it in, I became certified as an electrical and electronics engineer.

Steve: Oh, very good.

Jim: I continued doing engineering work as I had been doing already. The certificate just confirmed that.

Steve: Okay. Very good. And so, in that professional space, were you able to share your faith or witness to people? Share the love of Christ?

Jim: Oh, yes, there was opportunity to do that. I can remember one fellow, Lou Schwartz, in particular. He and his wife suffered a family tragedy. They lost a child. The child was maybe three years old.

Anita: I think she was two.
Jim: Two. Okay, two years old. And Lou was very bitter and angry with God. I think he may have been raised as a Catholic.

Steve: So, he was angry with God?

Jim: Yes, and we shared an office together. I talked to him about the Lord and he told me how he went to church and had done all the right things. I told him, "You know, going to church doesn't make you a Christian." I said alluding to a similar example, "You can go into a bakery and you don't come out as a cream puff!"

Steve: This is true. Very true. [Laugh]

Jim: So, anyway, I had some really good talks with him, yet he still didn't trust the Lord. A short time later he left and got a job somewhere else. Where I was working, the projects were coming to an end. All of a sudden, I got a call from Lou. He said, "Jim, you could get a job over here at Eaton Corporation." So, I went there, and after being interviewed, I was offered a job. We were now working together again. In the meantime, Lou had become a member of the *John Birch Society*. I don't know if you know about the *John Birch Society*.

Steve: I've heard the name, but I'm not familiar with it.

Jim: They were a real right-wing group back in the day. So, I went to a couple meetings with Lou. I gave him a New Testament and told him that he needed to read this and receive Christ into his life. But it didn't happen right away.

Anita: But it was building a relationship with him.

Jim: Yes, building a relationship was the way it happened. Over time, I saw that there was a change in Lou's disposition. I said, "You know, I see a change in you." He said, "Yes Jim, I received Christ into my life."

<u>Steve</u>: Oh, yay!

<u>Jim</u>: That was one of those wonderful opportunities.

<u>Steve</u>: Very good. Very good. So, after working as an electrical engineer and working in industry, at some point, you ended up getting into...God asked you to go into the Rescue Mission business, if you will. How did that happen?

<u>Jim</u>: Well, it happened in spurts. In the Air Force, I was in for seven years. Actually, it was two enlistments. I was out of the service for about four or five months.

<u>Anita</u>: We went to Moody.

<u>Jim</u>: Yes, we went to Moody Bible Institute. We started at Moody and were there for one semester, but it was just financially more than we could handle. So, the decision was to leave and go back in the service. Then when I finally got out of the Air Force after the second enlistment, and after a series of engineering jobs the Lord spoke to me about focusing on Christian work.

It all started with my last engineering job when I decided to take some courses in Linguistics and Phonetics. Actually, these courses were offered at the Detroit Bible College. I needed to take these courses which lasted about a year because I was working on a project in electronics on...

<u>Anita</u>: Voice Synthesis.

Jim: Artificial voice production - Voice Synthesis. We worked on developing Voice Synthesis technology. And, it is used today, everywhere.

Anita: Yes, when you get those *robo-calls*…you can blame him. [Laughs]

Steve: Blame it on Jim. [Laughs]

Jim: So, while I was there, it just spurred me on about going back to Bible College full time. It so happened that the Korean GI Bill, since I was in during the Korean War era, was still available for another two years. And so, Anita and I prayed, "Lord, help us to know what your will is."

I spoke with my supervisor, and said, "You know, I'm thinking of going back to college full time and I may need to terminate my job here." As it happened, he and the vice president got together and just days before I was about to leave, they said, "Jim, we'd like to do this. We understand that your college classes will be on Monday, Wednesday and Friday." They said, "You can work here Tuesdays and Thursdays. And if your college classes are on Tuesday and Thursday you can work here on Monday, Wednesday and Friday."

Well, they already knew my schedule from before when I was going there to study for the Voice Synthesis project. They said, "You can work here the two days or three days in the week when you're not going to college. You will receive full company benefits and your pay will match your former salary, but on an hourly basis."

Steve: You got paid!

Jim: Yes, I got paid. And it was based on...

Anita: Engineers' pay.

Jim: Yes, thank the Lord, I got engineer's pay and then I also received monthly allotments from the GI Bill. So, we were able to make it. We didn't have to go to the food bank after all!

Steve: Very good. And where were you going to school then?

Jim: I was going to what was Detroit Bible College. It later became William Tyndale College. And I received a degree there, Bachelor of Religious Education. After I graduated, I came back to work fulltime for the company and worked there several months, until all of a sudden, their business started to decline. The company I had been working for was Federal Screw Works. Not any part of the government!

Anita: They made nuts and bolts. We had a neighbor, and when he knew who Jim was working for, he became more remote. The neighbor grew marijuana ...

Jim: In his garage.

Anita: Yes, in his garage, at the time when it was illegal, totally. And then he always thought Jim was part of the FBI or something like that. [laughter]

Jim: You see, my brother was a police officer and I was working for a company that had 'Federal' in its name and our neighbor didn't understand it. We just made nuts and bolts and then we had an electronics division where I worked.

Anita: That's funny.

Jim: He simply got my brother and me mixed up.

Steve: That's funny. So, what happened after that?

Jim: The expanding Chinese market played havoc with the U.S. auto industry here in this country. And Federal Screw Works, nut and bolt production diminished such that they had to do away with their electronics division and research department. Since my job was in research and development...

Anita: Bottom line...

Jim: The bottom line was that my job kind of fizzled out at the end. But, by now I had a degree in Religious Education and engineering skills I could count on. What happened next is, I started looking for another job and I was offered an engineering position with another company in Detroit.

Anita: At Stanley Works.

Jim: They needed someone to manage their engineering department and it looked like a real promising job.

Anita: It was!

<u>Jim</u>: But then I also had been interviewed by the Detroit Rescue Mission. They hadn't responded with an offer. So, Anita and I sat down to pray on a Thursday evening, because I told the people at Stanley Works, that I'd give them an answer by Friday. And as we prayed together, we asked the Lord to lead in what our next steps should be and we needed to know by the next day.

About 11 o'clock that evening, we got a knock on the door. It was the director of the Detroit Rescue Mission. He said, "Jim, the mission's board has decided to offer you a position." That was the answer to our prayer and we've been called to serve in that type of ministry for over 35 years. I can tell you, that through prayer, sometimes at the last minute, we've seen God give us a definite answer.

<u>Steve</u>: Definite answer to your prayers?

<u>Jim</u>: Right.

<u>Anita</u>: Well, it's a curious thing. He hasn't brought out a number of things, but even when he was saved in Morocco, he was ultimately a witness for the Lord, because they had a whole convoy of trucks that went up into the Atlas Mountains and watched him be baptized along with some former Muslims.
He also didn't bring up that we had studied with Wycliffe because we were thinking of going to the mission field to serve as Bible translators. But with nine kids, it's a little harder to gain support. So, nonetheless, Wycliffe was a good experience.

Jim: It was a continuation of my study in the area of Linguistics and ...

Anita: Phonetics. Etc...

Jim: and Phonetics. And all the various aspects you would need for Bible translation work. And when we were considering that it was satisfying my study requirements at William Tyndale College.

Steve: Very good. So, when you went to Detroit Rescue Mission, you were there for quite a while before you went to New York?

Jim: We were there for about five years. The executive director moved to another ministry, and the board had a different idea of who might be the new executive director. I had been interviewed, but was not accepted for that position. So, at the same time I had an opportunity to go to...

Anita: Missionary Internship.

Jim: It was an internship program to train people to become missionaries. Originally many came having very little church background. They would be placed in participating churches where they would serve as an intern. I supervised several interns that were placed at the Detroit Rescue Mission.

So, I was familiar with the ministry at Missionary Internship as I began working with them for about a year and a half as Director of Development. Missionary Internship then had a change in their focus. And ...

Anita: They moved to Colorado Springs.

Jim: They moved to another place and they reduced their operations significantly. Missionary Internship started out with *SEND International*, which is a current mission agency. So then, there we were again; what do we do next? I was offered another position in the Detroit area, but then I wasn't sure of that.

We prayed about this, the Lord answered prayer and then we were called to go to Chicago area to work with *The Light Bearers Christian Ministry*, which was a Chaplaincy Ministry. They had Chaplains in different hospitals, jails, nursing homes and halfway houses located in Chicago and its suburbs, Milwaukee Wisconsin and Southwest Michigan.

Steve: The Light Bearers. Okay.

Jim: I was Executive Director of that organization for about seven years.

Steve: So, you up and moved the family from Detroit to Chicago?

Jim: Well, actually our new home and the Light Bearers office was in Wheaton, Illinois which is a short distance west of Chicago.

Not all nine kids came with us. Just the youngest three of our children came with us to live in the Chicago area.

Steve: Because the rest were grown up?

Jim: Yes, the oldest four children were married and the nest two were attending college and came home on breaks.

Steve: So, anyway, you're in the Chicago area. And then, how'd you get to New York?

Jim: Well, like I said we were with the Light Bearers for seven years. We had reorganized the Light Bearers, to the point where each Light Bearer Chapter was independent. When that occurred, they didn't need the central office or an executive director to head up the organization. I kind of worked myself out of a job.

So, then there was another organization that wanted me to join their staff in Chicago, but I wasn't confident that that was where the Lord wanted us. Again, we prayed, "Lord, help us to know your will." I gave them the same answer I said, "I'll let you know by Friday morning."

Steve: Right. You put a deadline … 'Okay, I'll give you an answer.'

Jim: Without any prior knowledge, the Executive Director of the McAuley Mission in New York City, whom I had met and had known his family through church acquaintances, gave me a call on Thursday afternoon. He said, "Jim I'm planning on retiring." "We have a board meeting coming up, and I'd like you to come here for an interview" So, Charlie and Agnes...

Anita: Ross.

Jim: The Ross' were getting ready to retire. He was in his 70's and I was in my 50's at that time. I was just about to turn 54 when I went to interview for the Executive Director position. We looked over the possibility of moving to the New York City area.

Steve: That's my age now...

Anita: There you go.

Jim: So, at any rate. I went and visited with the board. They offered me a position. We had about six months to prepare to get there. And it all worked out. We went to New York, and spent 23 years at that McAuley Mission. That's the longest I've spent at any position.

Steve: I'm sure Anita was glad she didn't have to keep moving around.

Anita: I didn't mind moving. I liked the military moves and being in mission work. It didn't bother me in the least.

Steve: So, I guess, in a lifetime of you working together, a lifetime of being disciples and making disciples, what would you say are the most important things of *being a disciple*? What are the most important things, to you, having grown up, and served in ministry in different capacities over your whole career? What's most important to BE a disciple?

Jim: I'd say, to be a witness, we're all witnesses in a sense. How good are we as a witness? We just let our lives show that we are trusting Christ. And others can see that in us. We are a witness regardless. How effective are we at being a witness? I think being a disciple means that you need to be a witness for the Lord. I think others see Christ in us without the fact that we will even verbally tell them.

They'll notice how we live. But also, we need to speak out.

One fellow in New York I went to lunch with was a man who owned printing business. How I got acquainted with him was through another Christian man who sold printing paper. The man who sold paper, sold it to the guy who was in the printing business. He thought, 'Well, I can sell this paper at a lower cost to the mission because I want them to succeed, and I'll get this printer to help the Mission in some of their printing…'

Steve: Printing needs…

Jim: Yes, so we went to this little Chinese Restaurant and we're sitting around a round table in the restaurant. And you have to realize, the three of us were sitting there, and there were eight seats around the round table. So, there's Chinese people sitting there and they're talking. I don't know what they're saying. But we're talking to each other…and this is New York City's China town. I just happened to say to this printer, "Do you know Jesus Christ as your personal Savior?" And he sort of sat back in his chair. And he said, "Yes."

And so, we just kept eating our soup and I wished him well. And actually, he did do a printing job for us. But two years later, I saw him up at the Harvard Club where there was this weekly Bible study. I happened to go to this early morning Bible study. They regularly had a good speaker. The same guy who owned the printing business was there. I was getting my coffee and everything to go sit down and he said "Why don't you sit down with me."

So, when I sat down there, he said, "Jim, do you remember asking me, 'Do you know Jesus Christ as your personal Savior?'" And I said, "I think I do. In that Chinese restaurant" And he said, "You know, I never knew the Lord, but that just registered in my mind." And he said, "I started reading the Bible and I received Christ in my life. And I'm going to church now." You know, you don't have to say a whole lot sometimes, to a person. But that triggered him to want to…

Steve: Want to learn more?

Jim: Learn more. And he received Christ!

Steve: Very good.

Jim: I can't say that I lead him to Christ, but maybe I planted the seed.

Anita: Planted the seed.
Jim: Yes, absolutely.

Anita: And he had an experience with a Jewish rabbi, who lost his Yeshiva and family, who ultimately became a Christian because he had read a Gideon Bible in a hotel. His name was Herb Opalek. Herb went to the library in New York City. And he said, in his mind, 'I want to go where they're working with people...'

Jim: Where Christianity is active...

Anita: ...and being enacted.

Jim: Yes, being enacted.

Anita: And so, he saw a reference to the *McAuley Water Street Mission*, which was the name of it at the time, before it changed to *New York City Rescue Mission*. So, he came to the mission and was there, and basically was mentored by Jim, because he was a very learned man, of course, and eventually asked to be baptized.

Steve: This is the rabbi?

Anita: Yes, the rabbi had been disowned by his family when he put his trust in Christ. In a sense, Herb went from soup to salvation; and from soup to Superintendent of a California Rescue Mission, after going through some basics. We sent him up to Albany...

Jim: As an intern.

Anita: As an intern. Jim had...
Jim: arranged that.

Anita: And then he went to Bridgeport.

Jim: Connecticut.

Anita: At the Bridgeport Rescue Mission, he served as assistant director. And, Herb ultimately ended up in California to serve as executive director of a relatively large rescue mission. He had remarried a Christian gal, an older woman, because he was older. And so, it was another experience where Jim's witness and discipling had come into play.

Steve: Excellent.

Jim: Yes, that was an interesting thing. Herb had lost his baggage somehow, when he was flying to Boston. He was the head of a Yeshiva. He was well known in Jewish...

Anita: Circles.

Jim: Of course, he was Orthodox. And, as an Orthodox Rabbi, he had his prayer books with him, but had these memorized. Upon arrival at his hotel room he realized he didn't have his other Scriptures which were in the unaccompanied baggage, so he reached in the bedside drawer and found a Gideon Bible. Well he said, "I'll start reading this now." You know, many Orthodox Jews, really know the Bible.

Steve: Old Testament?
Anita and Jim: And they also know the New Testament.

Jim: They've studied the New Testament because they want to know how to react to Christians. But they haven't received Christ. They may know a lot about it, but somehow the Lord spoke to Herb's heart as he read that Gideon Bible. And, he received Christ into his life and it changed his life tremendously to the point that the Orthodox Jewish community considered him to be dead. He had no place to go. When he went to that library he found out about the mission. And well, Anita told the story.

Steve: Very good. That's beautiful. Beautiful. So, in terms of being a disciple and making disciples, what would you say are the most important things? Having worked in rescue missions? What would you say are the most important things in terms of making disciples? Discipling others and making disciples? Sharing the Gospel. Sharing faith. What do you think are the most important elements there?

Jim: I think you just have to make a conscious effort to talk to people about the Lord. And live your life in a way in which they can see Christ in you. I think you have to do both things. If you're honest and faithful to the Lord, I think that people can see that.

We're all sinners. I haven't ceased to be a sinner, but yet I know I'm saved. And I want others to know that too. You can't continue to live like you were a sinner. So, you have to continue to develop and grow in your faith. There's no end to that. So, I think as we continue to develop and grow, other people can see that in us.

Steve: Excellent. How about you Anita? What would you say…?

Anita: Well, let me ask him, don't you think that being open to building relationships with people also? You build relationships with people. I don't mean in a dishonest way. I mean being *real*. You have to be *real*. And become friends with people. Be open with your life. And then they're open with you and that encourages the Lord to work within the hearts of other people.

Jim: We can't isolate ourselves from people. Let's say, we come to know the Lord and now we're identifying with people in the church and we're no longer identifying with people outside the church. I think that we have to be open with other people as well. And be available to interact with them. There are some people that you say, "Well, I'm not going to go there." But I can remember one fellow that came to our work there in Detroit, years ago. We operated a pre-release program at the Detroit Rescue Mission. And I was the director of that program.

Anita: Well, you founded it.

Jim: I was the founding director of the *Christian Guidance Center* in Detroit, which was a pre-release program that was under the auspices of the Detroit Rescue Mission. And so, I had prisoners from Federal prisons, from state prisons, and so on, that came, and also people that came there who were directed to us by the courts.

We had, at one time, five medical doctors that were part of our pre-release program that were sent there by the court. They didn't send them to prison, but they sent them to what we were called, a halfway house.

One prisoner came to us. He was a young fellow from Jackson Prison in Michigan. He got out of prison early, so that he could go through our program and could get out of prison a whole year or even 18 months earlier. While he was there, he was just...you couldn't work with him. You couldn't accommodate him.

They first had to look for a job. They had to open a bank account and then they had to find a suitable address to go to. So, once you meet those three requirements, then after 90 days, you could release them.

Well, this guy could never get off first base. He was incorrigible. But yet he had been here a period of time. I bumped shoulders with him a few times. So, I told the state agent, I said as I left there that Friday afternoon, I said, "I want this guy sent back to prison." I said, "He's incorrigible. We can't do anything with him. Send him back to Jackson." And so, about eight or nine o'clock that evening the State agent called. He said, "Mr. VarnHagen, the prisoner is now back at Jackson Prison. I just want to tell you that." I said, "Thank you so much. I won't have to see him on Monday morning."

So, I forgot about him. I don't know, maybe it was a month and a half later or so, after he was sent back to start all over again at the prison that I got this letter from him. "Dear Mr. VarnHagen." He said, "I'm now back in Jackson. I've been here about six weeks." He said, "I finally was able to get out in the yard and sit on the bench." I sat out on the bench, breathing the air, and so on. While I'm sitting on the bench, someone came along and sat on the other end of the bench. And he sat there and finally he looked at me and I looked at him. Then he said to me, 'Do you know Jesus as your personal Savior?' He said "Mr. V, you've got your people everywhere." [laughter]

Steve: That's funny. [Laughs]

Jim: So, I kind of felt bad sending him back to prison, but after I got that letter, I said, "Yeah, that's where he had to go."

Anita: The Lord works in mysterious ways.

Jim: So, I don't know what happened to this man. But that message that he got there sitting on the bench, I know registered in his mind and in his heart.

Anita: Confirmation.

Jim: So, our witness takes us into different avenues.

Steve: Absolutely. Well, this has been wonderful. I think we could probably go all day. If you were going to give some final thoughts, what would your final thoughts be?

Jim: I'd say, be available to listen to the Lord's call on your life.

Anita: And never stop learning.

Jim: And never stop learning, right? Yeah.

Anita: Never stop learning, being open.

Jim: Earlier I spoke about how the Lord opened the door when I went to William Tyndale College. Then while we were living in Wheaton, Illinois and working in the Chicago area, I took a class in fundraising at Wheaton College. I needed to know more about raising money to keep the Light Bearers going. That wetted my appetite for some other training at Wheaton. So, I registered as a student, and got a Master's degree from Wheaton College Graduate School.

Steve: Very nice. What was your Master's degree in?

Jim: It was in Christian Missions.

Steve: Very good.

Jim: I was in mission work, so I got a Master's Degree in missions. So, then I decided to take some seminary classes at Trinity Evangelical Divinity School (TEDS). And, I started by attending 4 days on campus in class and then turned in a paper by mail afterwards. I got all the way up to the point of submitting my final requirements for…

Anita: a D.Min.

Jim: for a Doctor of Ministries program.

Steve: Right…

Jim: And what happened then was 911. As we were going into the city of New York, we could see…

Anita: The Twin Towers.

Jim: I could see the puff of smoke come out of the first tower. As we drove by a large building, I couldn't see what caused this puff of smoke, but it was obviously the first plane that went in and I said to Anita, "I believe there's a fire up on top of the Trade Center." The traffic was stopped and we couldn't proceed to the Holland Tunnel. After a while we were directed to turn back and when we were doing this Anita was looking out of the window on her side of the car and she saw the second plane hit the other tower.

Steve: Oh, wow. You saw it.

Jim: With that, everything kind of changed in New York City and I couldn't focus on the D.Min. program.

Steve: Yeah. Academics. You were rolling your sleeves up and taking care of business, right?

Jim: Right. Exactly we were in a different state of learning.

Anita: At that time, I guess I was not thinking particularly about the issue of academics...

Jim: But just a constant...

Anita: ...use of Scripture and passing the Scriptures along.

Steve: Very good. Very good. Well, this has been excellent. Thank you both so much! This will be great!

Anita: I'll give you my life verse. "And we know that all things work together for good to those who love God, to those who are the called according to His purpose." Rom. 8:28

Steve: Amen.

Jim: I've got a verse too.

Steve: What's that?

Jim: "Therefore, if anyone is in Christ, he is a new creation; old things have passed away; behold, all things have become new." 2 Cor. 5:17

Steve: Amen. Very good. Thank you.

Observations, Lessons, Application:

- What were your key Observations from Jim and Anita's life and faith journey?

- Are there any parts of Jim and Anita's journey and story that you can relate to personally?

- How do you think God wants you to apply these principles in **your** life moving forward?

Chapter 10

John Gidman
Career Electrician & Devoted Husband to Sandy
Disciple of Jesus Christ

John is an amazingly kind, gentle man, with grey hair and a grey beard showing his 80 years of life. Quiet, soft-spoken, friendly eyes, and a warm countenance, people are drawn to him for calm, sincere conversation. And, just wait until you hear some of his stories! I know John through our church and from our monthly men's ministry group break-fasts. Though John is one of our church's more senior men, he is a tireless work-horse of a man who is constantly volunteering for new projects. Rewiring and updating the church, running electronics for updated sound and technology equipment in the sanctuary, HVAC systems – whatever is needed, John is there. And that includes helping families with electrical needs at their home, helping with remodeling or maintenance projects. His dedication to our church-family is inspiring and admirable – and I consider him an amazing role model. John is married to the love of his life, Sandy, and they have several children and grandchildren. After praying through whom God wanted me to interview for this book, John Gidman immediately came to mind. He is a Disciple of Jesus Christ Following is the interview transcript from our conversation:

Interview with John Gidman, June 3rd, 2019

Steve: Tell me how John came to faith in Christ. How did that happen? What's your story?

John: Well, it was about 1944.

Steve: Wow. Okay. Wow.

John: The war was going on in London. And at some point, my mother was playing the piano. One day she sat me down at the piano bench and talked to me about my soul.

Steve: How old were you then? Roughly?

John: Seven.

Steve: Seven. Seven years old. Okay. Wow.

John: It wouldn't have been '44. It probably would have been '43.

Steve: Okay.

John: I'm not sure. My math is getting really off. Anyway, somewhere around there. I was seven years old. I just knelt at the piano bench and gave my heart to Christ then.

Steve: Nice. So, you grew up in a Christian home? Did your mother take you to church on Sundays?

John: Yeah. Both my parents took me to church. Unless my dad was working during the war. He was in the railroad industry, so he was required to work at the railroad as if he were in the military.

Steve: So, instead of going overseas, he kept the trains running at home?

John: Right.

Steve: Gotcha. So, throughout your life you've been around, blessed with at Christian home and a Christian family. Not that it was perfect, just that you've grown up in that environment and that's a great blessing. How has being a disciple of Christ, in your personal life, what's that look like? What's your Bible study? What's your prayer time look like? Are you a big prayer? Or are you a big Bible study guy? What's that look like?

John: More into Bible Study, but maybe a little bit of background would help. Even though my background was Pentecostalism, it was not what you would see over in the States. It was a very stayed, rigid, type of life.

Steve: Now were you in Europe at the time when you were a kid?

John: Yeah.

Steve: Okay. So, your dad worked in the railroads in Europe.

John: Yeah. Yeah.

Steve: Okay. Gotcha.

John: In England.

Steve: In England. Okay.

John: And so, I never felt the joy of salvation. It was just a duty. And not until, I almost can say, that not until I went to Bible college, did I really become a disciple of Christ. There's a difference between, in a sense, a *follower*, because you know that that's the right thing to do - and having a *relationship with Christ*. I grew up in the era when you were a *Soldier*, and to have a relationship with something, not talk even. So, when I got to Bible college, my whole view of God, of Christ, of the Holy Spirit, all of that changed. And from there on, being a disciple has been a *joy*, as opposed to a duty.

Steve: Where'd you go to Bible college?

John: In Rhode Island.

Steve: Okay. Very good. So, what have been the parts, after Bible college...what aspects of your life do you really see yourself living out, being a Christian? Like with your boys and with your family, and activity in church over your lifetime, what all kinds of things have you done personally in your personal life to live out that joy and that relationship with Christ?

[John paused for a moment to think]

John: I pastored for a while.

Steve: Oh, you pastored? Oh wow!

John: For a while.

Steve: Where was that at?

John: Just north of Lebanon in a little town. I took over a Presbyterian church for a while. There was some internal conflict that caused the church to fail. So, I don't want to get into that.

Steve: I get it...

John: Just having Christ in family. In your family life you have conflicts, but when you have the Holy Spirit in your life, when you have Christ in your life, there's that peaceful reconciliation, done in the family without getting into fistfights and all that sort of thing. So, Christ's influence in the family has been probably the most prominent thing. Of course, knowing how to live properly makes a difference too.

Steve: Absolutely. Well, I've already learned some great things about you I didn't know before. Now when were you in the Navy?

John: From 1959-1963.

Steve: And did you go to Bible college after the Navy?

John: Yeah.

Steve: Okay, okay. So, you went to the Navy and then, after you got out, you went to Bible College and what did you do after Bible college?

John: You're hurting an 80-year-old man's memory [Laughs]

Steve: [Laughs]...Oh, I know... I guess, how did you get into, because you're an electrical contractor, mostly commercial stuff, right?

John: Industrial.

Steve: How did you get into being an electrician?

John: I took electricity in High School and then I took a job at St. Vincent in maintenance. Then I went to work for a company that built industrial ovens. And I stayed in that for 30-40 years. And then at a certain point they were wanting me to continue to travel too much, so I just decided to open my own business and go from there.

Steve: So, from a timeline standpoint: Navy, Bible College, and then working in commercial/electrical, and working at manufacturing facilities. When you were on the job in the electrical business, which you're still doing to this very day, how have you seen the opportunities to just live out your faith and share the love of Christ? Do you ever get those opportunities in the workspace? In the professional space?

John: Not too much. It's not like you're there as a day to day person. So, your influence is mainly in getting the job done and getting out of their way.

Steve: With a client. You're talking, you go in, fix the problem and then you leave.

John: Right.

Steve: Okay. What about your crews? The people you interact with?

John: Once in a while you get a chance to talk to them. When they're going through something. When an employee is going through a divorce, or especially if they're the injured person… if that's the right way to say it. They're going through a lot of grief and you get a chance to witness then.

Steve: Right. You just have a chance to love on them a little bit and tell them about what the Lord's…

John: And by the way you treat them. The Scripture gives us plenty of advice on how you treat an employee. You don't underpay them. You don't steal their wages. You're generous with them. I learned in the military to praise in public. And to rebuke in private. Which a lot of people don't do. I worked for a guy who was just the opposite. Very little praise. So, I think that shows through as well.

Steve: I know when we were eating breakfast you told me about the pickup truck going through the hills of Southern Tennessee. Why don't you tell that story again? That was funny.

John: Well, we were traveling from one job to another. We didn't have enough vehicles, so I had four of my crew in the back seat...or in the pickup truck under the...

Steve: Camper shell on the back? Right.

John: And they felt I was getting a little too fast going down the curvy roads. One of them opened the back window of the cab and reached his head through and told me, "John, we know you're saved, but we ain't... so slow it down!".

> *One of them opened the back window of the cab and reached his head through and told me, "John, we know you're saved, but we ain't... so slow it down!"*

Steve: I love that! Well, people knew you were a believer. And they knew the concept of being *saved* and... what he was saying is, "it's okay if you died, because you're saved, but some of us back here aren't". That's a pretty profound statement. And I understand, sometimes your crews can be rough and tumble guys sometimes and you had talked about when you were traveling before, maybe a lot of alcohol and the guys partying real hard, did you ever have a chance, with some of your employees over the years, to share the Gospel with them? You said sometimes if they were going through a divorce or something, you could. Any other times that you can recall?

John: Not so much at work, but for a while, I ran a coffee house. I did more there than I did anywhere else, I think.

Steve: At a coffee house? Okay. Really good. Was it just a little breakfast joint or just a…

John: We actually got free rent to the upstairs of a drug store. And the only entrance to it was a fire escape. And there's a lot of miracle stories about that, but we totally revamped that upstairs and we had a coffeehouse up there. We called it *The Fire Escape.* With a double meaning.

Steve: Right. Absolutely.

John: We were able to minister quite well.

Steve: When you say, 'we', was that you and Sandy?

John: Me and a guy named Jim Williams. We spent a lot of hours up there.

Steve: And you used it as a ministry platform, the coffeeshop?

John: Oh yeah. Oh, yeah.

Steve: Tell me about that.

John: Well, we would bring in Christian movies. We had food. We had drink. Not alcohol.

Steve: Coffee or sodas.

John: We had a coke machines and that sort of thing. We had a counseling area. We had a prayer room.

Steve: Oh wow. So, this truly was a ministry.

John: Right. It was a ministry. So local churches helped fund it.

Steve: Wow! Where was this at?

John: In Lebanon, Indiana.

Steve: Okay, in Lebanon. Very good.

John: I think it lasted about four years and then someone broke in and stole everything in the place. And the roof started to leak and we couldn't afford to fix it, but it was a good learning curve for me and I think for Jim as well.

Steve: So, it was an opportunity to help people, feed them, minister to them, share the Gospel with them. Who was your target? Was it for people who were really hurting or was it for homeless people?

John: It was for high school and above.

Steve: High school and above. Okay. Very good.

John: Yeah. One of the founders of Indiana Teen Challenge came and spoke for us. That sort of thing. Betty Violette. You ever heard of her? With the Third Phase in Noblesville?

Steve: Oh yeah. Yeah. Same lady. Okay. That's *Third-Phase*. Familiar with that organization.

John: So, yeah, that was part of our life.

Steve: Very good. Very good. So, how about as a couple with your lovely bride, Sandy? Do you ever do anything together in terms of...other than your core family, of course, but in terms of church or community?

John: Back in the days of song leaders, which seems to have gone out of vogue right now, I led song service for quite a few years. And Sandy would play the piano. And once in a great while, Paul would play the Saxophone. So, we did that for a few years until it kind of went out of vogue.

Steve: Good. I didn't know you were singer. We'll have to have you sing in church sometime!

John: No, you won't! (laughter from both)

Steve: That's great.

John: Those days are gone.

Steve: Okay, okay.

John: My favorite song is *All That Thrills My Soul Is Jesus.* We try to sing in our devotions now and our voices crack.

Steve: If you were telling people about what it means to be a disciple …a follower of Christ, just being a disciple… what advice would you give people? What would you say if you were talking to a group today?

John: The Word is the best teacher.

Steve: Stay in the Bible. Right?

John: Stay in the Bible. If you stay in the Bible, there's no way you're not going to be a good disciple. Unless you don't believe what you're reading. But then, ...that's another question all together. But staying in the Word. The Word has guided Sandy and I all through our lives. Even when we found it impossible to do devotions together, the Word is still the guide. And it doesn't matter what version. There's enough in one Gospel to keep you straight.

Steve: Absolutely. Absolutely. How long have you and Sandy been married?

John: Hmm. (pause, thinking…)

Steve: So, you're 80 now and how old were you when you got married? Do you remember?

John: 21.

Steve: 21. Wow! That's amazing. That's beautiful.

John: So, however many years that is.

Steve: That's 59 years. That's beautiful.

John: No, it's 57, I think.

Steve: 57. Okay. Okay. Very good.

John: Yeah, we were married in 61.

Steve: Married in 61. Okay. Very good. Well, any final thoughts on this topic of being a disciple?

John: To me, one of the best things about being a disciple is knowing what's acceptable and what isn't. I've had opportunities, back in the day, when I would be in people's homes. There was cash left out, not that I would want to steal it, but I made up my mind that I would never even touch anything that belonged to...

Steve: Somebody else.

John: When I went into somebody's house to work on a furnace or to do whatever I was there to do, I would do my job, and that was it. And I felt safe doing that. It gives you that peace factor. You can still be falsely accused, but thankfully that never happened to me. But knowing ahead of time what's acceptable and what isn't, allows you to live your life, free from guilt. That's the best discipleship advice I can come up with.

Steve: In terms of that joy that you spoke of before in knowing Christ, if you were talking to a new believer or somebody that didn't have that joy, what advice would you give to them about finding that?

John: Probably the best advice would be my experience of where I came to that point. It was kind of foolish. I mentioned earlier that we were very strict.

Steve: Legalistic?

John: Very legalistic. Even in the Pentecostal church. Children were not to speak unless they were spoken to. Parents were always right, regardless. So, I guess I had that fear, even going into Bible college. And there was a service during Bible college and everybody was worshiping the Lord. Hands were raised, something I had never done in my life. Here I am in my 20's and I'd never praised the Lord. And I'm looking at this 6, 7, 800 people congregation, 95% of whom had their arms up in the air, and I'm sitting there frozen. And I thought to myself, 'What am I doing here? If I'm not going to be a part of it, why am I even here?' And at this point in my life, I've either got to get up and walk out, or I've got to raise

> And I thought to myself, 'What am I doing here? If I'm not going to be a part of it, why am I even here?' And at this point in my life, I've either got to get up and walk out, or I've got to raise my hands. And that raising my hands was kind of like a surrender... In a real way. And the flood of joy I felt when I broke that chain by raising my hands, has given me joy ever since.
>
> John Gidman

my hands. And that raising my hands was kind of like a surrender.

Steve: Beautiful.

John: In a real way. And the flood of joy I felt when I broke that chain by raising my hands, has given me joy ever since. I'm getting emotional thinking about that time.

Steve: That's awesome.

John: There's been a few times when it's tried to come back because it's an old, old, ingrained habit. I have to remember that experience and...so you'll see me raise my hands in church once in a while.

Steve: Raise your hands - I love that. That was the one big gold nugget. There's lots, but that was the one big gold nugget from our conversation this morning. It almost brought tears to my eyes. Well, thank you sir. This has been great.

2nd Interview with John Gidman - stories:

Steve: Go ahead, John. This is during World War II when you're in England?

John: I was born in '38. The war started in '39. Since I lived in London where the bombing was concentrated, we were bombed out of our home five different times. Five different homes. Each of those times, my family was in church. We would come home from church. There would be no home. Two of those places that I'm aware of, some of the places I don't remember the addresses, there are no homes there today. They've either been made into parks or something. I remember sleeping in the subways because there was nowhere else to sleep.

Steve: Wow!

John: It was quite a life. And the other thing, my dad would take me walking during thunderstorms to get me used to the bombing so I wouldn't be afraid.

Steve: Wow. Wow.

John: There were so many miracles during that time.

Steve: So, if you hadn't been in church, you'd probably be dead. Or you wouldn't have lived because the bombs would have taken you out, right?

John: Right. Correct. There was one story. I told you my dad made it so I was never afraid of bombs. One night there was a thunderstorm going on, of course the war was almost over, and I ran from my parents' bedroom, scared to death of the thunderstorm. Graciously they let me stay in their room until the thunderstorm was over. When I went back, there was a piece of ceiling plaster the size of my body, on my bed.

Steve: It had fallen?

John: Yeah. From the ceiling. It would have killed me. It was the old *hair plaster*. Two inches thick.

Steve: If it hadn't killed you, it would have at least hurt you really bad.

John: Yeah. Yeah. There were stories like that that I could tell. I'm just thankful to be here. God had a purpose for me. And I believe He still does, even though I'm 80!

Steve: Well, you're 80 and you're still running a business and you're still active. And you're still a commercial electrician. Have you slowed down a little bit?

John: Oh yeah. I'm trying to get out of it. I'm going to retire in February.

Steve: Gotcha. Are you selling your business?

John: No, there's not enough left.

Steve: Gotcha. Just winding it down?

John: Yeah. Yeah.

Steve: Well, that's great. Any other stories that you can remember that might be good?

John: I'll think of them after you shut that recorder off. [Laughter]

Steve: If you think of more, you tell me. Thank you, John.

November 2020 Update

In the summer of 2020, John's lovely wife, Sandy Gidman, went home to be with the Lord. A gentle and charming woman who was greatly loved, Sandy was always a joyous presence at church. During the year that she was ill, it was always beautiful to see her at church, smiling brightly with loving eyes and a kind word. She loves the Lord, and we all look forward to seeing her again. Her obituary is following. An exceptionally fond memory from her funeral was towards the end, when John asked everyone to sing *Amazing Grace*, saying "Sandy would like that…"

Sandra Louise Gidman
December 18, 1941 - May 21, 2020

Sandra Louise Gidman, age 78, passed away at her home in Sheridan surrounded by her loving family on Thursday morning, May 21, 2020. She was born December 18, 1941 in Taunton, Massachusetts, to the late Burpee and Mary D. (Wilson) Boehner, and was a 1959 graduate of Taunton High School.

She was a member of Lifepointe Church in Westfield and a member of the Hamilton County Master Gardeners. Sandra was an incredibly special person who quietly helped make the world a better place for everyone who knew her. Her creative nature led her to many different types of outreach during her life. Sandra combined her love of writing and scrapbooking to create her own unique ministry. For some, Sandra wrote daily letters to let them know that she was thinking of them. For others, she compiled scrapbooks filled with inspirational pictures, poems, and words of encouragement to help keep them focused and uplift their spirits during their various struggles. She lovingly sent them to shut-ins, those suffering through cancer and other debilitating diseases, hospice patients, those affected by dementia, nursing home residents, and anyone else that Sandra thought needed a sign that they were not going through this alone. She was also a talented knitter, making hats and scarves for anyone and everyone.

Sandra loved taking care of her Church family as well, using her talents as an organist and pianist for many congregations during her life. And last, but certainly not least, Sandra had a passion for gardening. Her love for plants, the ability to imagine what they could grow to become, and her willingness to help others in their gardening adventures, is why Sandra was a true master gardener. With a true servant's heart, Sandra was a wonderful advocate for those who needed help and an example of God's true love. Her strong faith and love for her fellow neighbor is a legacy that speaks volumes. Sandra was a devoted wife, mother, and grandmother. She loved traveling with her family and going on new adventures.

Observations, Lessons, Application:

- What were your key Observations from John's life and faith journey?

- Are there any parts of John's journey and story that you can relate to personally?

- How do you think God wants you to apply these principles in **your** life moving forward?

Chapter 11

Kyle Condra
Officer, Fire Department
Disciple of Jesus Christ

Kyle Condra is a career Fire Fighter, and Officer, and a servant leader. He is real. He is humble. And he is not afraid to admit his shortcomings. He is a dear friend and brother, and we have served together on numerous teams for men's ministry weekends. Those who know him will say the same – he's a genuine person, authentic. And he loves the Lord, and is not ashamed of the Gospel. He is a son, a husband, and father...and a man that I am proud to call my friend and brother. Here is his story:

Interview with Kyle Condra, May 6th, 2019

Steve: Kyle, please tell me how you came to faith in Christ. How did that happen?

Kyle: I think the biggest thing is... there is a difference, black versus white, day and night; the delineation. There is a difference. I grew up in a very secular home. We didn't even do the Christmas and Easter thing. We never went to church. And so, never growing up with that, it's one of those things, that as a disciple, you're told to go out and preach the word of Jesus. I was the guy who never heard Jesus, and I lived in the United States. So, I was *that guy*, even in the midst of everybody, that had never heard the name of Jesus before. And I got into all kinds of trouble.

My family life was bad. I fought with my dad all the time, got bad grades in school, got threatened to be held back in school, got arrested when I was 15. So, things were bad. And my Aunt and Uncle were the black sheep of the family, if you will. They were the only believers in our family. And they did things so differently.

Steve: Is that Greg?

Kyle: Yeah, Greg and Kathy. And, so the family always looked at them differently. And they're the only ones, for the longest time, that were the black sheep. Everybody talked about them; 'oh, Greg and Kathy...', you know, this kind of thing. But they always stood strong. And in the midst of all the problems that I had been through, had done, and everything, not one single moment of my life that I can remember, did they ever say anything about it. They just loved me completely.

Steve: That's awesome.

Kyle: I never knew that they knew everything. That's how much love and grace they gave me. They didn't treat me any differently. Anything. I got in trouble when I was in high school. I got arrested when I was 15. My dad told me, "If I can't fix you, the church will." So, when I was in high school, my punishment was to go to church to be *fixed* by Jesus.

Steve: Oh, wow.

Kyle: It was kicking and screaming, every Sunday, because they didn't care. They were at their wits-end. They didn't know what else to do about it. So, we started going to church. If you can imagine that scenario. That doesn't solve anything. That just put that much more of a bitter taste in my mouth.

Steve: It was punishment.

Kyle: It was punishment. And they didn't enjoy it either. It's no joke. So, fast forward several years. I get a job and I became a fireman. And that part really started to change my life. It was literally life-and-death decisions. I had to be kind of squared away, and doing my job, and knowing what I was going to do, and be good at my job. And so, there was a little transition in my thinking, in my way of life, just because of that responsibility. I had to grow up, essentially, is what it was. So, I go from high school to becoming a fireman, and having to do that. And so, while I was with the fire department, when I first started off, it was a rough place to be.

Steve: Dangerous job?

Kyle: You're working with a bunch of adult men, and I'm a freshman in college, who became a fireman. Seeing and being a part of men outside of family is very different. So, I fell right into...you know. I don't know if I'm going to be straying off the path or not, but police and fire, the stress that we see, we joke around a lot to deal with that stuff. We drink a lot. And a lot of that is hiding a lot of the pain, but the *brotherhood* of it, everyone is hanging out and doing all that kind of stuff. Make sense?

Steve: High stress job... *gotta-blow-off-steam* kind of thing?

Kyle: So, for several years, just living that life; not necessarily partying, but out drinking a lot. Out with the fire department, joking around, cussing like a sailor. I always say, before I came to Christ, I could embarrass a sailor! I cussed so much. Here's the pinnacle of it: I met this girl and she was a pretty devout Christian. Essentially, I wanted to sleep with her, but she wouldn't have any part of it. I started playing the *Christian-game* to fake her out and work my way into doing what I was going to do. I mean, seriously, that's what it was. So, I started going to church. I started doing these things to impress her and to change her mind. Whatever I could do. So, about six months into our relationship, I proposed and she agreed. So, we were going to get married. We kind of put the marriage on a fast track. And fast forward to the night before the wedding, for many reasons, but one in particular, she decided she was going to call off the wedding the night before. That was the pit. That was the bottom of the bottom. That was everything in my world coming crashing to... Ground Zero.

Steve: Mmmm...

Kyle: Bottom of the pit...this is where Greg and Kathy step back into the story. They're the ones who counseled me through it, scripturally and relationally. Grace-filled, nothing but love. They knew what was going on, but again, they didn't say a word. 'We're here for you. We're praying for you. We love you. What can we do to help you?' This kind of thing. Well, in the midst of all of that, Greg asked me to attend the Great Banquet men's retreat weekend. So, the wedding was cancelled in November and I attended the banquet in March. So, that was November of '03, and I attended the banquet in March of '04. And so, while I was at the banquet, I saw fifteen guys stand up and give their testimony about the things they've been doing and struggling with, and how Christ changed their lives. And recognizing that I wasn't the only one who had the same kind of things that were going on, and hearing about the love and grace, and then being able to see that in Greg and Kathy, and the difference – it was powerful. It was Saturday night that our table went into the back room and had a little quiet time and prayed together, and me and my buddy accepted Christ at the same time together. So, I go back to what I said when I lead this off: it's the difference between black and white, day and night...it's tangible. That change in my life was tangible. So, I went from black to white, day to night. The difference in me was...[pause]

Steve: Dramatic?

Kyle: It was real. It was SO... and to cut out a lot of the middle part of it, my parents saw such a difference in me...fast forward several years; this was not a fast process, but many years. Both my parents accepted Christ because of the change in me. So now, Greg and Kathy are not the black sheep of the family. They're the pinnacle of the family. Everybody strives to be like them. It's just amazing how all the things that happened led to where I'm at now.

Steve: That's awesome. That's beautiful.

Kyle: It's unreal. I'm crying again. Thank you. You're welcome. [Laughter]

Steve: I've only known you since you've been through the banquet. We didn't know each other until after that. So, I know you're active in Great Banquet ministries and you were just telling me about this men's ministry called, *Fight Club*, that was a ten-week Bible study. What other things are in your personal, daily walk with the Lord? What kind of stuff do you guys do? I'm assuming you go to church?

Kyle: Yeah, we do go to church. We go to Harvest Bible Chapel in Carmel. We've been going there for... let's see, Emma's turning nine, so it will be nine years coming up soon. We started as this little portable church, and now we've got our own building. The church has grown. It's been awesome. So, I have to tell you that the biggest struggle that I face with my walk, kind of like the 'doing' side of it, is my schedule. Being intentional with doing things outside of church is very difficult for me. Going to banquet team meetings is very difficult for me. Being a part of any kind of ministry is very difficult for me, because of my schedule.

Steve: the fireman, on-off rotation?

Kyle: So, my work schedule is, I work three days out of five, and then off for four, and it's a rotation. For example, I would work a Monday, Wednesday, Friday, and then be off Saturday, Sunday, Monday, Tuesday. And then work Wednesday, Friday, Sunday; Friday, Sunday, Tuesday. Sunday, Tuesday, Thursday. And that cycle. So, if I'm on duty, I would miss, say, three Mondays in a row, and then be off for six Mondays. And so, for any kind of consistency, I'm going to miss three weeks of something. So, a small group...you miss life. You miss relationship. You miss scheduling. You miss all of those things. So, it's really hard with me, with my schedule, to be plugged in. And that's one of my short falls.

Steve: Challenges.

Kyle: Challenges would be a better word. So, for me to be plugged in, doing ministry, outside of something scheduled, like the Great Banquet or Fight Club, where I know in advance, that I can get trades, or something like that...because it's hard. Because I have to put my vacation days in a year in advance.

Steve: Wow.

Kyle: So, to be able to do all those things, it's not easy.

Steve: It's tough I bet. How would you describe your prayer life? Are you a big prayer? Do you pray throughout the day? How would you describe your prayer life?

Kyle: I will admit, prayer life is probably the biggest weakness in my walk, and has been from day one. So, for me to sit down and just do prayer time, is not something I do enough of. Throughout my day; it might be a quick sentence. It might be, 'Thank you for this' or 'Where am I supposed to go now?' 'What am I supposed to be doing?' or 'What do I need to do with the kids?' or something like that.

Steve: Do you do any kind of devotional reading or Bible reading? What's that look like?

Kyle: So, a lot of my Bible reading is in the car, when I'm driving.

Steve: Listening to scripture?

Kyle: Listening to scripture. The thing that I've really been turned onto here recently is, *The Bible Project*. And it's phenomenal. I don't know if you've heard of it.

Steve: I may have heard of it. So, what is it?

Kyle: It's a YouTube channel, called *The Bible Project*, and it takes you through every book of the Bible. This guy breaks it down both audibly, but then also, visually. And so, the two of them, hand in hand, they draw this picture of the overall theme of the Bible for that book. And they break down the book chapter by chapter, and the meanings, and how it gets all grouped together. I just completed it and I'm getting ready to do it again because it was so fascinating.

Steve: It does the whole Bible?

Kyle: It does the whole Bible. Yeah. Each book has at least one video, sometimes two or three, depending on the length, like Isaiah; it was at least two or three videos because it was so long.

Steve: I'll have to look that up.

Kyle: It's really neat. And then there's another app that I use. It's really good, too. It's called, *Through the Word*.

Steve: *Through the Word* is a phone app?

Kyle: Yeah. And it's similar to *The Bible Project* except it's just an audio and it digs a little deeper. *The Bible Project* gives more than a general overview, but it's preparing you to read the text. *Through the Word* really breaks it down and puts it in cultural history and language. So, if you put those two together, and then reading on top of that, it really helps to understand the Bible. It makes it...like I've never understood the Bible before. For me to just sit down and read the Bible, I miss a ton of stuff, because you have to put it in context. If you don't read it in context, it's not necessarily wrong, but it's not necessarily right either.

Steve: It's hard to maybe comprehend some of it. I understand. So, we talked about police and fire can be a bit of a rough environment sometime and it's a bunch of testosterone-festival kind of environment, a para-military kind of groove to it, but do you ever find opportunities to live out your faith, in your profession? Whether it be praying with another firefighter, or praying with a family that just had a tragedy? Do you ever find opportunities to live out your faith in the professional world?

Kyle: Short answer; yes. Long answer; it's hard. There are not a lot of believers in the fire service. And so, I go back to the transition in my life; the change in my life, when I accepted Christ. The Thursday before I left for the Great Banquet, I was 'just one of the guys'. After I came back that next Monday, when I went back to work, I was no longer one of *those guys*.

Steve: Oh really? You could feel it.

Kyle: Oh, it was instantaneous.

Steve: So, is it you feeling it, or was it them feeling it?

Kyle: Both. It went both ways, that fast. And it was because of the fraternity lifestyle; the coarse joking, the swearing, the googling it…whatever, you know what I'm saying? I got back to the firehouse the next day, and that stuff wasn't funny anymore…at all. It was everything I had been a part of, and the next day, I had changed so much, that I didn't know how to live life. Being born again, to me, was so literal, because I was lost for so long, when I was an infant trying to figure out how to be a Christian in this non-Christian lifestyle that I had been living for so long. I mean, to be brutally honest, I lost every single one of my friends after I became a Christian. And it wasn't that I had treated them necessarily different, but I treated me differently. I was acting differently, and they saw that enormous change and didn't want to be a part of it. And so, I had to literally find all new friends. And it was extremely challenging.

Steve: I bet. So, who discipled you, in terms of coming along side you and teaching you and coaching you, sharing and guiding you? Was it Greg?

Kyle: It was the banquet...

Steve: The banquet community?

Kyle: For many years.

Steve: Any one in particular? Or just some friends you knew there?

Kyle: I didn't have that, so when I became a Christian, and it was in 2004, and I struggled for two years, because I didn't know what I was supposed to do. I didn't know what life was supposed to be like. I didn't have a mentor and that would be the biggest thing for me to tell somebody is: 'When you become a Christian, you have to have somebody that you trust. Somebody that you can count on. Somebody that can lead you through everything'. I didn't have that and that's one thing I wish I had, because I think my walk would have changed if I would have had somebody like that. If I would have known to go to Greg, he would have bent over backwards for it, but I didn't. So, I was blessed that I was able to serve on banquet teams. I learned just an absolute ton, just by being able to serve on teams and writing many talks, and serving in different

> '*When you become a Christian, you have to have a mentor. You have to have somebody that you trust. Somebody that you can count on. Somebody that can lead you through everything*'
>
> - *Kyle Condra*

DISCIPLE-ing

capacities and learning how people lived, by seeing it, through the banquet community. That's where I got mentored.

Steve: It's community. That's what all of us believers need is, community. Can you be a Christian on a desert island? Sure. Is it harder? Yes. Being in community. You found your mentorship in a group of people. I love your "You need a mentor. You need somebody to help you, guide you to be a disciple" and help you with that journey. Have you ever had opportunities where you could pray with somebody or encourage them in some way, or live out your faith in some way while you're in uniform?

Kyle: Yeah. But it's very, very hard. But it goes back to what I was saying about after I accepted Christ, coming back to the firehouse…I was a totally different person. It became very palpable at the fire department, because, "Hey, Kyle, what in the world is going on with him?" For several years, it was a challenge. Knowing that people were watching me, microscopically, after that point in time…

Steve: You were different…

Kyle: Right. So, for those first couple years, I really struggled. Like I had said before, I didn't know. I didn't have a mentor. I didn't have any leadership. I didn't have any guidance. I was figuring this all out on my own. So, 2006, I literally had a miracle worked in my life; cannot move me off of that in any way, shape, or form. February 12th, 2006, the Holy Spirit worked a miracle in my life.

Steve: What was that?

Kyle: I had an addiction. I had an addiction since I was in second or third grade. I was at a banquet. We were at closing. The lay director had asked me to preview the closing. We get up there, and we preview the closing, and I'm standing in front of seventy something guys, and it was a wave of the Holy Spirit. I will never forget it. I said, I gave my life to Christ two years ago, but now I'm dedicating my life to the Lord. And this wave of the Holy Spirit just moved right through me and right then and there; that moment in my life, that addiction was cancelled. 2000 some odd days later, here I am, still without that. Okay, back on track.

Steve: No, that was on track.

Kyle: So, you were asking about living my life out.

Steve: Yeah, sharing your faith on the job.

Kyle: People are seeing me microscopically now. So, understanding that and knowing that I have to live the Christian life to the best of my ability, and nobody's perfect; I get that. I make mistakes just like anybody else, but having somebody see a difference in me enough to notice it, and be like, 'something's different about him'. In my walk at the firehouse now, it's changed a little bit, because I was promoted five years ago.

Steve: You're an officer now, right?

Kyle: I'm an officer now, so now I have different responsibilities, but I also have people working for me. So, now I get to exemplify servant leadership at the firehouse. When I decided I was going to become an officer, that's where I was putting my stake in the ground. I was like, if I do this, this is what my principles are. I'm going to be a servant leader. And I'm going to serve my guys.

Steve: I love servant leadership. But describe it for me. How would you describe this calling that you feel, living out servant leadership?

Kyle: It's bigger than what the words are. It's challenging. It's becoming less than the people who work for you. I'm not special. I'm no better than them. And that's the way I look at it. I took a test, and I'm in charge. I have that responsibility. But just because I have that, doesn't make me better. It doesn't make me special. It doesn't give me power. It gives me more responsibility to do what's right. And it gives me an opportunity to show Christ's love; that He came and suffered and died. And so, when I lead my guys, it's completely out of humility. I cannot count how many times I say, 'thank you' throughout the day. I cannot tell you how many times I'm the first one jumping in and doing something and then the guys follow me.

Steve: Lead by example...

Kyle: Not me asking or telling them, 'Hey, you've got to do this', but it's me starting something and those guys knowing and feeling that it's the right thing to do, that they'll come in and follow me, because I'm not forcing them. I'm humble in the fact that I know I make mistakes, but those guys know that. And I'm open with that, that if I do mess up, it's an open forum. We get to talk about it. We get to, 'Hey, why'd you do this?' or 'Where could we have done something differently here?'. I don't think I know it all. I don't act like I know it all. That old saying, *'Treat people like the way you want to be treated'*... somebody I heard once said, 'Treat people better than you how you want to be treated'. Not as equal, but treat them better than you would want to be treated. It's free to be nice.

Steve: It's free to be nice.

Kyle: It's free to be nice. It doesn't cost you anything to be nice.

Steve: It's true.

Kyle: I totally believe that. I absolutely, heart and soul, believe that...I've seen it in my firehouse, where being humble, treating your guys better than the way you want to be treated, and being in a firehouse before Christ, and being a part of that group, where it's just free for all, versus someone who's leading humbly. There is an absolute palpable difference.

Steve: Have you noticed a difference, when you're the officer in charge of the shift, or whatever, are you influencing those men by example, you think?

Kyle: That's a hard question. I would like to think so. I don't know how to answer that. The one thing that I do know is that, I've had several people tell me that working in my firehouse is different than any other station or crew they've ever worked with before. Guys have told me that it's so refreshing, that it's not negative. People aren't running around cursing. We aren't watching movies on TV that are bad. In my station, the TV is hardly ever on anymore. Guys are sitting around talking or doing stuff around the firehouse, making it better, where we have been in firehouses before, where movies that shouldn't be on, are being watched and guys are cutting up, or whatever. And I'm not judging. I'm not saying that at all. Because I was there. And it's Christ that made the difference. It's not the officer. It's not the firefighters. I mean, that's the change. If we can get Jesus in, anywhere, it doesn't matter where, that's the change. And that's the palpable difference. When you start doing that kind of stuff. Since I've been an officer out at my station, I don't know, but I've had more Christian guys come in and work with me, work for me, decide to come work with me, because they know the difference. They see the difference. They want to be a part of that. So, we, instead of watching movies, we'll watch church. At the firehouse. On TV. We'll stream a sermon. We've had Bible Studies. I mean, it's insane. It's insane. It's crazy.

Steve: That right there is a perfect example of living out your purpose of being a disciple and making disciples. Not only in your personal life, but in the workplace. You've allowed God to work through you in that capacity. That's cool. It's not like you forced it on anybody.

Kyle: No. Heck no.

Steve: It just happens.

Kyle: Right now, just currently, I've got a guy who's probably a stronger Christian than I am, who pushes me. So, just become the leader. Just because I'm the officer, or whatever, he really comes in and flips things around for the good. He is bold. He's not afraid. I'm timid, because I'm an officer. I don't want to cross that line of work versus faith. But he doesn't have that leadership position, and he gets out and preaches. And he's not afraid at all. And, so it is awesome.

Steve: He is bold.

Kyle: He is very bold. Not shy at all to speak the name of Jesus. It's cool. It's very cool.

Steve: Very good! So…the fruits of the spirit are: love, joy, peace, patience, kindness, gentleness, and self-control. From Galatians. How would you say you, and obviously, you have a very life transforming change in a very short period of time, after becoming a Christian, especially after having, not only becoming a believer, but then dedicating your life to Christ… but how would you say you see those kind of things playing out in your personal or your professional life? How would you say you see those things play out?

Kyle: I feel like I have a calling on my life to be a fireman. I cannot imagine…mentally, emotionally, physically, cannot imagine doing anything else. I've been a fireman since I was 19 years old. I'm 42 and there hasn't been…I take that back. There was a period of time, right when I became a Christian, that I didn't know if I wanted to do it anymore. Because of the living environment that I was in. That period of time and change, that two years, was pretty rough. Outside of those two years, I dread the day where I'm not a fireman anymore. Me going to work is just joy. I LOVE going to work. I don't dread going to work. The joy I get out of it is amazing. That part of it is the career side of it. I love working with my guys. The comradery that we have. Building those relationships. Being a part of each other's families and getting to know their families. We were talking literally yesterday about having a family dinner at the firehouse and inviting the families and kids and all that kind of stuff.

Steve: Hopefully you don't get a big run right in the middle of it. [laughter]

Kyle: It always happens. And that kind of thing. We were talking about going to an Indians game this summer and being more than a crew at the firehouse; but investing in each other personally and professionally. And part of investing in personally and professionally is, I've tried to spur on younger guys that are coming up and getting ready to be promoted and really working with them and mentoring them, unofficially, and helping them in the transition...

Steve: In their firefighter career?

Kyle: In their transition from going from firefighter to officer. I see such a huge lack of that. And I think that totally goes back to service; to serving. I serve these guys. I'm taking myself out of the position that I love to do, which is being an officer, and giving them that opportunity to practice and learn, with me being in the back helping them if they have any questions. So, taking everything a step further and letting me get out of my way and out of my wants; putting my wants and desires second, and putting somebody else, who needs it more than me, get up there and do something and learn something to be better at what they do. I don't need to prove myself. I am who I am. I do what I do. I make my mistakes. I make my good calls and judgements.

Steve: That's cool.

Kyle: I don't know. How it manifests in your work? Self-control....

Steve: For example, do you feel you're more patient and more kind and more self-controlled, obviously, since becoming a believer? You've probably seen that change, right?

Kyle: Oh, for sure. Look, I struggle. There are a couple guys in the firehouse that I would just...

Steve: They push your buttons? [laughter]

Kyle: More than you know. And look, so, I'm real. I have my struggles. I sin. I'm angry. Things that upset me, probably are different because I see people treating people poorly. That really bothers me. Self-control; I don't cuss at the firehouse. I had one guy come up to me; I cussed once and I was making a quote from somebody else. And the guy came up to me afterward and goes, "Kyle, I've been here and in the five years I've been here, I've never heard you cuss once." And so, that was eye opening, in the fact that, I'm being watched that much more. And for somebody to be able to give a date and time of not seeing me cuss before, that was eye opening. That was crazy. That five years, whether he knew it or not, or consciously or subconsciously. So, the self-control is not talking bad about people.

Steve: Your kids watch you too.

Kyle: Oh, my goodness... [Laughter]

Steve: You and Tracey have two kids, right?

Kyle: Yeah, Tracey and I will be married 12 years in September. We have two kids. They're seven and nine; Molly and Emma. I have never once spoken poorly about my wife. Period.

Steve: That's great.

Kyle: Divorce is rampant through the fire department and through the police department.

Steve: Is it?

Kyle: Rampant. So, hearing the number of guys, who will belittle their wives, in front of a group of people, is excruciatingly painful. Even that side of it, bringing my personal life into the firehouse; guys seeing me that I'm not complaining about my wife. I don't bad mouth her. So, guys sit around at the firehouse, at the dinner table, and everybody complains. There are things that people don't like. Right? But the number of people who have told me that they just sit, and 'I just watch. And don't partake. And keep my mouth shut.' And everybody's doing whatever. That I don't... so, my self-control. That's what I'm getting back to. My self-control is not being a part of the group of complainers. I'm sitting there, and I'm still a part of the crew. I don't want to ostracize myself and put a divide in or anything like that. I'm still there. But I'm not a part of the conversation. I sit and listen and keep my mouth shut. People know it and they see it. So, all of those micro things that I do throughout the day add up. My self-control; I don't cuss. I don't take part in course conversation; in course talk, that kind of thing. Putting others before for me. Being an example. Sacrificing my hopes and desires, for somebody else, so that they can get better. I say this stuff out loud and I feel like I'm boasting, but to me it's that whole servant leadership thing. Getting out of the way to help other people become better. So, finding the strengths of your guys and using that instead of focusing on of the negatives...

Steve: Helping them grow...

Kyle: Everybody has weaknesses. You have weaknesses. I have weaknesses. If I focus, and microscopically look at your weaknesses, they become much bigger than they actually are. So, if I can just focus on your positives and your strengths, and magnify those, they become even bigger and better strengths, right? So, I look for those powerful things the guys are good at. And really, talk about it. Build it up. Complimenting people in big crowds and keeping bad things private, between just the two of us. Any opportunity I have to say, 'Thank you', in front of people is just huge. It makes you feel like a million bucks. It makes you want to do it again. I don't have to tell people to do something, because they already want to do it. It's just my...

<u>Steve</u>: That's good leadership.

<u>Kyle</u>: It's just my thoughts on the whole thing.

<u>Steve</u>: It's great. I love it. Very good. Any final comments before we wrap?

<u>Kyle</u>: Being a Christian is extremely hard. It's extremely hard in the fact that, you are a built-in hypocrite and that's what the world sees. You and I are not perfect. We cannot be perfect. And so even though the world sees Christians as being held to a higher standard, they magnify the weaknesses of, 'Well, you messed up. You cussed. You watched a movie that you shouldn't. You are angry. You are this...' instead of the grace that Christians extend to one another about understanding sin, and that it's a poison and that we can't get away from it. Even though we're Christians and we love Jesus, being a built-in hypocrite is hard. I try my best. But boy do I ever fail. So, living out my Christian walk - I do it to the best of my ability, and when I mess up, I'll be the first one to apologize. Living and treating others better than the way you want to be treated. Serving others, putting others before yourself...leading by example... leading from the front. Being okay with being different. Being okay standing up for what you believe in. And just loving other people. That's it. It's easy to say. But in real life, it's hard. Being a Christian is extremely

difficult. Now, with that being said, it is absolutely life changing. It is black and white. Day and night.

Steve: I love that saying: Black and white. Day and night.

Kyle: It is the difference in my life…it's opposite. Everything that I lived for was for the world before Christ. After Christ, everything is to the best of my ability…is Christ centered. It's just different. And unless you've experienced that difference, it's hard to understand what that really means. But if you're reading this and you're a Christian, you know exactly what I'm saying. Right?

Steve: Absolutely. Thank you.

Observations, Lessons, Application:

- What were your key Observations from Kyles's life and faith journey?

- Are there any parts of Kyles's journey and story that you can relate to personally?

- How do you think God wants you to apply these principles in **your** life moving forward?

Chapter 12

Scott Beck
President, Beck's Hybrids
Disciple of Jesus Christ

Scott and I have known each other since 1984, having met at Purdue University and having been fraternity brothers at FarmHouse Fraternity, and roommates for one of those years at Purdue. Scott is a successful businessman, heading-up the large, multi-generational family business, *Beck's Hybrids*, which is a leader in the agricultural seed technology industry. Scott is also an extremely devoted family man, and he and his wife are very active in the lives of their children and in their community, in the agricultural industry, Purdue University's School of Agriculture, and with the FarmHouse Fraternity Foundation. And, Scott is a true gentleman. A polite, kind, thoughtful, and reflective person who carefully thinks through challenges and problems, and has shown incredible leadership throughout his life and career. Most importantly, Scott is a devoted disciple of Jesus Christ, aspiring to give honor to God in and through his life, both personally and publicly. Following is the interview discussion with Scott:

Interview with Scott Beck, May 11th, 2019

<u>Steve</u>: So, Scott... How did you come to personal faith? Did you grow up in the church or was it later in life? Just, how did you come to faith in Christ?

Scott: I did grow up in the church. It was a Lutheran Church. We attended regularly. Part of the youth group. But what I didn't get there was what God desired in terms of *relationship*, with Him personally. With Jesus Christ as Lord. At church there was liturgy - it's all sound doctrine, for the most part, I believe. But it wasn't until I was at Purdue and a member of Farmhouse Fraternity…there were guys in the house that were truly *believers*.

Steve: Dave, Neil, Sheldon, Kent, and all those guys, right?

Scott: Yeah. They organized a spiritual retreat. I remember going on that my freshman year. And the guy leading it called me out about some things. It was one of those things that got me started in the right direction. I went home that summer and was really seeking God more. And then I also heard this voice that said, 'You're going to get home this summer and kind of get back with your old friends and start doing the old stuff'. So, that's the voice I eventually listened to. And, so, the rest of my college days were really not all that glorifying to God. But toward the end of college, it really became apparent that I was really searching for the truth. And I went to a series of films that Campus Crusade had put on, on the Billy Graham series: *Distant Thunder*...end-time type things. And I went to those… and it got my attention that God was really talking to me about needing to surrender my life. I came to a point where I realized that He was speaking to me and I needed to make Him Lord of my life, but I needed to do some things to show that repentance. I remember one night… I took my hard rock albums out and I broke them, and I put them in a dumpster.

Steve: I've heard this story. So, you went through… where you transitioned from going through the liturgy of being in *religion* to an actual deep, personal, relationship with Christ. In your personal life today, and I know you're married and you've got kids, and you've got a business and you've got a farm, so how do you live out your faith in your personal life?

Scott: I appreciate you sending me these questions ahead of time.

Steve: Sure!

Scott: What came to mind, in that regard, is just the simple things of meditating on God's Word at the beginning of the day. Starting out with thinking about and speaking His Word and offering up thanksgiving and praise in the morning and then just throughout the day believing and receiving what He says is mine; who I am in Christ and who He is in me. Working to orient my thoughts and beliefs according to His Word. And then doing the important things rather than just thinking about them or talking about them. To me, that's the key - taking action. I think that's probably where I don't do enough. It's easy to talk about and we need to have good conversations, but to continue to trust Him more, just in daily conversations, or when making work decisions. Family.

Steve: You're a dad. Are you a grandpa yet?

Scott: No. No, not yet. I've got two boys that are engaged. They're getting married this fall.

Steve: Very good. You start the morning with the Word and prayer time, and stuff like that. Many days. Maybe not every day, but many days?

Scott: Yes. One of the good things of the technology is I get a *Verse of the Day*. That's kind of the minimum, but...

Steve: It shows up in your inbox or in your text… and stuff like that?

Scott: Yes.

Steve: Absolutely.

Scott: So, I try to make a habit, even mentally, if I pick up my phone in the morning…and I don't always do this, but I think, 'Read the verse first'. Orient my thoughts around that as opposed to checking other things. I don't always do that, though.

Steve: Well, you're farming and it's planting season. Just all year long. And then you've got your crews and your people. And your team and all of that.

Scott: As far as the farming part, I'm not as involved in the day to day stuff on that, at this point. But just spending some time, either at my home office, or at work in the office, going in early enough, where I've got five to twenty minutes to read. It might be a couple chapters. So, that's how I orient my thoughts and my day and try to bring things into perspective and focus on how to…what's the priority that day?

Steve: Excellent. How often do you go to church? Do you do family devotional time or pray over meals? Within your family context, how do you try to live out your discipleship and your role as spiritual leader in the home, with your family? How do you normally try to live that out?

Scott: Certainly, prayers at meal time. We've, historically, been in more of a routine and habit, once a week, having a devotion time. We've been very lax on that. I've got five children. The three boys are the older of the children and they're out of the house now; college or graduated from college. And my two daughters are still at home. We just have not kept up that practice on a regular basis. We still do it intermittently. I guess it tends to come up in general conversations. With my older daughter, whose 17, asking her about her relationship with her boyfriend. 'Are they praying together? Are they studying the word? What are you reading in the Bible now?' My younger daughter, similar. I try to have a conversation around 'what did they talk about at youth group?' So, just incorporating conversation with the kids. And certainly, when it's time for disciplinary actions, there's the opportunity to talk about, 'What's God see this as? What's He think about this? What's He think about you? And how do you deal with this in light of Him and His Word?'

Steve: Understand. So, in your professional life… how about, like as the leader of a company and working with your other managers, your agronomy managers, and your business managers, how does God provide that as a platform where you can be a disciple and maybe share your love of Christ in the professional space? What's that look like?

Scott: Culture is really important. We work diligently to foster the right type of culture. In our workplace, it is okay to live and be a Christian, to express your faith. But I would say, how is that lived out? The things that came to mind, was really focusing on listening to others, caring for them, and what they're dealing with. And in situations where they haven't made the right choices or the best choices, see if...what is their frame of mind in this? Is this something where they can learn from it? Are they taking a path of recognizing their wrong, where we can give them grace and mercy and a second chance?

Or is it something where the person just really needs to experience the discipline of losing a job or getting moved to a different position. You know, something to really help them understand that they do need to change, that they cannot continue on this path as an employee here with those similar types of behaviors. As leaders, we balance two things. As followers of Christ and leaders in a business, we balance two things. There's the servanthood aspect, where we want to be forgiving, caring, and give people second chances; just like God extends His grace to us. On the other side of that, there's the stewardship part, where we're stewarding the larger organization. What's the impact of that individual's behaviors on all the

> *As leaders, we balance two things. As followers of Christ and leaders in a business, we balance two things. There's the servanthood aspect, where we want to be forgiving, caring, and give people second chances; just like God extends His grace to us. On the other side of that, there's the stewardship part, where we're stewarding the larger organization.*
>
> *-   Scott Beck*

other employees? Or on all the customers? And are they at a place where a second chance will bring hope to others? We will recognize God's grace and mercy and others can see that? Or is the stewardship aspect more important at that point, because of the severity of the infraction, or the place where that person is, in terms of their journey. They're not seeing it the way they need to see it, so they need to experience some severe consequences to help them, hopefully, to get them to a better point.

Steve: I like that. Servanthood and stewardship. I like that. That's good. Do you...and obviously as an industry leader you have to, you can't force your faith on people, but you can provide a culture...that it's okay if you exhibit that culture. Is that what you're saying?

Scott: Exactly.

Steve: Is there an optional Bible study within your group, so if they want to, they can participate?

Scott: We recently started a series of classes we call, *Aiming High.*

Steve: *Aiming High.* Okay. Very good.

Scott: *Aiming High.* And one of the members of our education team, who has spent years in youth ministry, presents a topic. I think the first one was, 'What is faith?' and then he did one on 'the Love of God'. Recently did one on the Resurrection. These are optional classes. He travels around to our different locations. It's about a 50-minute time slot. We offer it and those that want to attend, can. We treat it like any other educational opportunity we offer. People can attend classes on how to manage your time better. Or how to deal with conflict. Or how to improve your public speaking.

Steve: It's just an optional thing. If you want to participate, you can. Okay. I love that. Very good.

Scott: We make a lot of decisions in relation to people. And yes, we have to have policies to help set the guardrails, but sometimes those don't always speak to every situation. In fact, they can't. There's no perfect contract. There's no perfect policy. So, we do make an effort to actually consider the individual when there are things involved, involving whether we need to practice stewardship or the servanthood aspect. And treat that person as an individual, not as someone we apply a policy to.

Steve: Okay. I've heard lots of amazing stories about this from lots of different people, but has there ever been an opportunity for you with somebody who asked or said, "Scott, there's something different about you, what is it?" Or, have people ever asked you about your faith? Or have you ever had the opportunity to present that? To share the Gospel with other people?

Scott: I do. Usually in a public setting, like when I meet with our new employees coming on board, I meet with them their first day. I don't always talk about it, but I'll often times make reference to the fact that one of our stated business goals is to honor God. You don't have to be a Christian to work here, but we don't suppress it either. I personally believe that God has created each one of us with a purpose and that we are better off when we are linked up with Him, and understanding that purpose and living it out.

Steve: Absolutely.

Scott: But you don't have to be a believer to work at our company.

Steve: Sure. I get that.

Scott: And then, one-on-one, there's definitely times…in fact, I'm in the midst of, not a process, it's an investment of time, over probably the next 12-18 months. I'm meeting with every employee in the company. We've got 660 some now.

Steve: Wow!

Scott: So, I'm taking 27 minutes, and there's a story behind that, why 27 minutes, but it's a time to really help me understand and learn more about them, what they do, what they enjoy about their job and about the company, what they would like to change. And then, I often talk about how they connect what they do with our purpose of helping farmers. We say our purpose is helping farmers succeed. And so, whether they're the person that's helping take care of the grounds and the facilities or whether they're programming in our IT department, or whether they're on the front line of customer service or sales, how they contribute to helping farmers. And what we call the *'Exceptional Brand Experience'*. So, ask them how they connect what they do. When they show up at work every day, 'What do you do that's different? What do you do that you know you're making a difference?'

Steve: Excellent.

Scott: So yeah, I'm in the midst of doing that. And then I ask them for advice. I ask them if they have any advice for me.

Steve: Okay. Some employee feedback to the boss. I love that. 27 minutes? Is that something you can talk about or is that a whole different story?

Scott: I'll give you the very short version of that. We had an initiative a couple years ago... we asked employees to think about how they could save the company 27 dollars a day. There's a story behind that as well. I built off of that theme of 27 dollars a day and I'm calling this the '27 Minute Investment'.

Steve: Okay. Very good.

Scott: I've really enjoyed it. It's been energizing to me.

Steve: I bet your employees love it too. They get one-on-one time with you for 27 minutes.

Scott: Going into this, that's something that I've learned, that I didn't realize...how impactful and how meaningful it is to them. I'm thinking this is a chance for me to meet with them - they're thinking about how there aren't too many places that they've worked before that they would get to meet with the president. But it's been fun and it's been rewarding when they've been willing to share ideas of things that they would do different. We've implemented some of those immediately, or sometimes just little tweaks; things that we can do.

Steve: From a leadership perspective, that is excellent. Then they feel like they've gotten to know you personally, whereas, maybe before, they've just been in meetings with you...but they never got one-on-one time with you. I love that.

Scott: And there are employees that we've hired that I've never met. Or at least, I might have met them for 20 minutes during our onboarding conversation. But it's a group of people, so it's not really one-on-one time.

Steve: That's excellent. How have you felt the Lord's leading in your leadership or in your professional role? Do you ever feel like the Lord is guiding you in a particular direction?

Scott: There have been times when...and this one example goes back years ago, back when my mom was working in the company. We were working on our Plot Book Project. We were having lunch and I felt impressed to ask her a question about something. And so I did, and what it did is it uncovered an issue that we needed to deal with. I forget exactly what it was, but it was the way we were doing the test plot or the data or something…but it was just that prompting that I felt to ask her this question. I guess the 27-minute thing came out of a prayer and reflection time that I had early in the year. It was on a Saturday morning and I was just at home, really praying about, 'Okay, God, what do you want for this year? What do you want me to do? How do I use my time?' And so, I had just seen the list of our employees that our HR person sends out once a month or so. And on January 1st, we had 638 full time employees. That number stuck out in my mind. Just thinking, meditating, and praying about that, thinking, 'What if I meet with each employee?' And then I started doing the analytical part of it. 'How much time would that take?'

Steve: That's a lot of hours!

Scott: At that point I'm still thinking 'Is that 15 minutes? Is it 30?' You know, how much time it is. So, it just got me thinking about that. And I shared it with a few people. And I began to realize that this is something that I'm supposed to do…and *want* to do.

Steve: Very good! So, what would you say are the main Biblical leadership principles that God's Word has presented to you?

Scott: That breaks down into three main categories: Humility, Servant Leadership, and Direction:

- **Humility** – God is opposed to the proud, but gives grace to the humble. Hebrews says: "Let us come boldly to the throne of grace that we may obtain mercy and find grace to help in the time of need."

- **Servant Leadership** – Leaders don't lord over their people. They work along with them and support them with the tools, training, and encouragement to do their work.
- **Direction** – Clarity of communication. "Without vision, the people perish" (Proverbs 29:18) People need direction and purpose and to know that their work is meaningful and that their values align with mine.

<u>Steve</u>: Excellent summary. I love the Proverbs 29 quote. So, how about how the Fruits of the Spirit manifest in professional life for you? Any insights?

<u>Scott</u>: I would say: Caring for, giving to, and believing in our people produces good results. The fruits of the Spirit are present in each of these three things!

> *"Caring for, giving to, and believing in our people produces good results. The fruits of the Spirit are present in each of these three things!"*
>
> Scott Beck

<u>Steve</u>: Excellent. Totally agree. Thank you, Scott.

<u>Scott</u>: Thank you.

Observations, Lessons, Application:

- What were your key Observations from Scott's life and faith journey?

- Are there any parts of Scott's journey and story that you can relate to personally?

- How do you think God wants you to apply these principles in **your** life moving forward?

Section Two:
Principles Illustrated

Principles Illustrated in the Interviews

As previously stated, it was the goal that you, the reader, make your own observations from each of the twelve disciple interviews. I wanted you to allow the Holy Spirit to speak to you from each story – to illuminate key principles of what each person said. That is the most important thing that can happen. Holy Spirit illumination, instruction, and guidance.

As the narrator, or guide, on this case-study-series of discipleship stories, I also felt led to give you a summary of my thoughts, my observations – the things that I felt the Holy Spirit illuminated to me. Prayerfully, and humbly, following are the key observed *principles* that I received from each interview after reading and studying them numerous times. As well, at the end of this chapter, there is a combined list of points compiled from all of the interviews – and scriptural references that seem to support the conclusions drawn. The process for evaluating these illustrated principles points was as follows:

1. Pray to the Lord Jesus, asking for the Holy Spirit to guide me and give discernment and inspiration.
2. Identify key comments by the disciple(s) being interviewed that seemed to jump out as *Key Illustrated Principles*;
3. Test those points to assure that they are in alignment with and are in no way contradictory to God's Word, the Holy Bible;
4. Identify scriptures that are in harmony with the key principles/teachings.
5. Compile the points into a succinct, helpful list for our walk as disciples, and for making disciples.

It is my hope and prayer that you have found the interviews to be insightful, thought-provoking, inspirational, and encouraging – and most of all, point you to a closer walk as a disciple of the Lord Jesus Christ, and a humble kingdom builder in the Lord's service. As well, I hope that my observations will aid you in processing the stories and information that has been presented. For the Glory of God, and in praise of the Lord Jesus Christ!

Chapter 13

Key Illustrated Principles from the Interview
ADAM M. - from Chapter 1
Career Police Officer
Disciple of Jesus Christ

Adam's interview had many layers: what he was like before-Christ, and after he became a disciple; how he is able to grow into deeper relationship with the Lord through study of the Word; and how he is able to express his faith in Christ in his personal life, and in his very public role as a police officer. Key illustrated points that I observed from his interview would fall into the following categories:

Loving Others

> "it's funny...strangers when they see a police officer walk into a store and I make eye contact with somebody and say, "hi, how are you doing?" and they're shocked by a police officer being approachable because we're typically like robots."

Being Christ-like

> "My prayer every day is to be a little more Christ-like..."

God's Word – Bible Study

> "However, I'm <u>really involved in the Bible Study Fellowship</u>... I've been doing that about nine years

or so… It's really a blessing… <u>And I love it because it makes me stay intentional</u>."

Not Condemning, Forgiving, Encouraging

"Adam: So, I try to see the *person*. The biggest thing I try to keep in mind is: I've obviously sinned; they've sinned. <u>I'm not here to condemn them</u>, just like I don't want to be condemned either. So, I try to keep that in mind. <u>I have to do my job, but I can still be compassionate toward them…</u>

"don't give up. Have faith".

Sacrificing for Others, Protecting

<u>"If I gave up my life for somebody on duty, I would hope they would spend the rest of their life trying to make it up…"</u>

"I want to make somebody else's life better. I've got that opportunity to make somebody's life…or the police department…better".

Leading by Example, Shining Our Light

<u>"I just try to lead a good example. The guys who work for me, I try to be a good example for them.</u> And the bad part is, and it's not just us in the police world, but anybody, you may never know who you touched. And that's why we always have to go out there, every single day, trying to make a difference, and not get frustrated by not seeing the fruits of our labor"

Confidence and Faith in God's Promises

"Before, I was afraid to die, because of selfish reasons. Once I was saved, I don't want to die, but I'm not afraid to die, because I know where I'm going, and I know I'm not going to die until God's ready to take me home. So, I have a confidence, not to be reckless, but not to be in fear either"

One Person – Personal or Professional

"You know, this endeavor, the whole 'showing faith at home versus showing faith at work,' the closer I get to Christ, I don't see a difference between the two. It's an internal change. It's a heart change. It's a mind change. I think the more Christ-like we get, we're going to be that way no matter what we do."

Principles Illustrated – Adam M.

- Loving Others
- Being Christ-Like
- God's Word – Bible Study
- Not Condemning, Forgiving, Encouraging
- Sacrificing for Others, Protecting
- Leading by Example, Shining Our Light
- Confidence and Faith in God's promises
- One Person – Personal & Professional

Chapter 14

Key Illustrated Principles from the Interview

Andrew – from Chapter 2
Senior Director, Consultant
Disciple of Jesus Christ

Coming to faith is a process

"But really it was really someone in the workplace who approached me and was new to the team. I was kind of getting them introduced to what we were doing. *They said "that's interesting and all, but have you accepted Christ?"*

Bold, confident disciple led me

"And, so I went down that path. But anyhow, it started with being in the Word. It was a challenge to go off and read the Gospel of John. I did that. It raised a ton of questions. And just dove in. He very confidently said, "Look, I don't care what questions or doubt you have about the Bible. It's truth. It will hold up to whatever you've got, so, why don't you just outline for me what your questions are; your doubt is, and let's just walk through the word and I'm going to show you how all your doubts are going to get addressed. He was so confident and so bold. I was, if nothing else, intellectually curious enough. And they say, 'Faith comes through hearing', but it was a process over time of just being in the Word."

Responsibility to be the spiritual leader in the home

"It's my responsibility to teach my family. So, it's one thing for me to go off and take on a Bible study, but if I'm not helping that to grow my family and help them in their knowledge and understanding of the Word of Christ, then that's on me. I take that responsibility very seriously."

Prayer without ceasing

"When you wake up and go to sleep, your commute time, and lunch, you're guaranteed five times, so you want to be continuously in prayer. I don't try to pray selfishly. I truly try to pray for Kingdom work being exposed and being wise enough to see opportunities to do things."

Kingdom Focus

"Again, praying that you handle things in a way that's going to show that you are a *Christian*. And not let other things motivate you. But overall, to me it's the Lord's prayer, over and over a lot. And thinking about that and being very intentional, about every word in there, but really focusing on His will and His kingdom."

Bible Study and Application

"This is tying, backward and forward, into other scriptures, exploring larger themes, getting into application. It's really meant to be a nice expository discussion, followed up by application. And then we bookend it with prayer. We're going to open up in prayer and we're going to close in prayer, and that prayer is going to be tied to, 'What did we learn?' We can apply this. We can share this."

Being *Salt and Light*

"I think it's a couple of things. Again, going back to scripture, we're called to be *salt and light*. I know that sounds cliché' to answer, but it's true. People should be wanting some of whatever you have, so I think there's a joy aspect. So, when people see you going through trials and yet, you have a smile on your face…"

Chess Board Position – Prioritization

"…I also think this answer is about being at the right spot on the *chess board*. In a fairly conservative Christian community, in the middle of Indiana, those opportunities aren't going to be… they're there, but consider if you plop yourself in the middle of a prison ministry or a rehab ministry, those kinds of things, where you've just got, if you chose to, you'd have a lot more opportunities. It's about how you prioritize and where do you spend your time on the chess board."

Seek Opportunities to discuss Faith

"So, I think just the more activities you're involved in; the more ministries you're involved in, the more you can talk about them. I think the more you're inundated with Kingdom work; if that's what you do and that's what you focus on… just because you're just dripping in it."

Active Yeast spreading the Gospel

"The sermon this Sunday was talking about this idea of yeast and the fact that you have starter loaves. And basically, those characteristics are carried through the loaves that are descended from that starter. But yeast has to be active; it has to be living to have an affect."

Principles Illustrated – Andrew

- Coming to faith was a process, beginning with a question by a bold disciple co-worker
- Bold, confident disciple led me
- Responsibility - spiritual leader in the home
- Prayer without ceasing
- Kingdom Focus
- Bible Study and Application
- Being *Salt and Light*
- *Chess Board Position* – Prioritization to Share the Gospel
- Seek Opportunities to discuss Faith and Faith-Activities
- Yeast must be Active to spread - engaging others, SPREADING the Good News of Jesus

---

Chapter 15

Key Illustrated Principles from the Interview

Dr. Barb Haehner - from Chapter 3
Medical Doctor, Medical Director
Disciple of Jesus Christ

Kingdom Focus, Christ-Centered

"...(that difficult trial in my life) really gave me a lot more empathy and compassion for people that were going through lots of personal pain. And so, I think God has really used that nine years of my life to put me on the Kingdom path, and to know that's really the only path that ever leads anywhere. And that purpose, that you're serving the Kingdom, in everything you do, and the way you live...everything has to be Christ-centered!"

Follow the Leading of the Holy Spirit

"Because He had His plan for me, that if I had not been sitting there, that day, in the congregation, listening to (Her)...the Holy Spirit couldn't have *[spoken to me that day]*..."

Trusting God's Leading

"When I just think about how He promised me, that if I took this on, and did my part, that I wouldn't have to worry about it growing and doing what it's doing now. And before my very eyes."

Excellence for the right reasons

"You <u>do it with excellence, as if you were doing it for Christ</u>…

…It's <u>*personal excellence for the right reasons.*</u>"

Learning to Hear God's voice – Quiet Time with God

"But sometimes it's being in a very quiet place and opening my heart and my mind and saying, <u>'What do you have for me today? What is your Word for me today?' And learning how to hear from the Holy Spirit and let His word and His influence be the number one driver of your actions, as opposed to your flesh.</u>"

One Life – Not Compartmentalized

"But taking the time you need to, in a crazy life, to make sure that you can hear the still small voice and pick as much as you can, that direction, and not your flesh. That is the key to living a Kingdom centered life. <u>It's not about dividing my professional life, my family life, my friend life, my whatever life. It's one life. It's Christ centered.</u> And everything you do and every action you make is being directed by the Holy Spirit."

Praying & Speaking into Someone's Life, led by the Spirit

"…<u>if you feel like God is urging you to pray for someone,</u> and even though you might not have any idea what that person is doing at this moment, that you're supposed to share that with that person…"

Principles Illustrated – Dr. Barb

- Kingdom Focus, Christ-Centered
- Follow the Leading of the Holy Spirit
- Trusting God's Leading
- Excellence for the Right Reasons
- Learning to Hear God's voice – Quiet Time with God
- One Life – Not Compartmentalized
- Praying & Speaking into Someone's Life, led by the Spirit

Chapter 16

Key Illustrated Principles from the Interview

David Harbaugh – from chapter 4
U.S. Government Employee
Disciple of Jesus Christ

Seek Lord's Guidance on what to say

"I try to <u>let the Holy Spirit guide me on what to say or what to do</u>; how to approach certain situations and certain people. It's not always the same. I try to seek the Lord's guidance."

Using Common Sense as to appropriateness of when to share with people

"we all have to <u>use some common sense</u>, but I've found that, as long as the purpose is to share the happiness of my own faith, and not to tear down anybody else's...as long as I don't tear down anybody else's, I feel very free."

Good work ethic = Good witness

"I have <u>the work ethic that is supposed to be associated with Christians</u>, that I'm not lazy. So, a big part of that is sharing my faith, but it's also doing my actual job to a very high standard."

Offering to Pray for them

"Is there anything I can pray for you about?"

"Yes, I ask that as a question sometimes, and what happens more often is, they'll tell me what's going on in life, and I'll say I'll pray for you."

Allowing God to be glorified in your unique circumstances

"I think until, or unless, God heals me completely of Cerebral Palsy, then I need to use my unique situation to be a witness for the Lord and to our world."

"...And I think as long as I'm the only person that a lot of people see who walks kind of crooked, walks on a walker or a cane, as long as I'm not able to just blend in, then I need to use that to God's glory as much as I'm able and as much as the Lord will use me."

Co-worker time – don't waste it!

"Look for opportunities, because in a ten-hour work-day, like mine, or an eight-hour work day, the time you spend with those people are going to add up. There might be more waking hours than you spend with your family at home.... but the sheer number of hours that we spend with people we work with... don't let them go to waste!"

(summary next page)

Principles Illustrated – David Harbaugh

- Seek the Lord's guidance on what to say
- Using Common Sense as to appropriateness of when to share with people
- Good work ethic = Good witness
- Asking: "Is there anything I can pray for you about?"
- Allowing God to be glorified in your unique circumstances
- Co-worker time – don't waste it!

Chapter 17

Key Illustrated Principles from the Interview

Devon McDonald – from chapter 5
Businessman, Leader, Linebacker, Missionary
Disciple of Jesus Christ

Only relationship with God will satisfy the soul's desire - Fame and Money will not

> "Then I felt HOPE for the first time in my life! I felt like *tomorrow going to be better than today!* Never felt like that before. Then I felt joy. I felt happy. I've won Championships. I've got money. But I've never felt like I feel right now."

Being Pure in our *secret life*

> "There are three lives that we live: We live a public life. We live a private life. And we live a secret life. The devil will fight you in your secret life, because if he can corrupt your secret life, the other life is fake; it's a fraud. And we see it every day. We see all these people that we thought in public were sort of dynamic. We find out in secret, they're hellish. So, what I do, I pay particular attention to my secret life."

People are watching – be an example

> "So, for me, I seek to be an example, because people are watching. They watch your actions. They watch what you do in situations"

Three Levels: Be Discipled, Peer Discipling, Disciple others (Paul – Timothy Model)

> "So, we should be hearing from God, have someone that's discipling us, have people on the same level, iron sharpens iron, and we should always have people that we're pouring into. And if you don't have that order, then you don't have the flow of God moving in your life. I'm conscious of that and I believe in that."

God will move you to a *Bigger Tank* so you can GROW!

> "I want the fish to grow bigger"... "Yeah, they grow to the size of the tank proportionately"

Principles Illustrated – Devon McDonald

- Fame and Money does not satisfy the soul's desire...only God
- Being Pure in our *secret life*
- People are watching – be an example
- Three Levels: Be Discipled, Peer Discipling, Disciple others (Paul – Timothy Model)
- God will move you to a *Bigger Tank* so you can grow!

Chapter 18

Key Illustrated Principles from the Interview

Don & Karol – from chapter 6
Career Military Officer (Retired) & School Teachers
Disciples of Jesus Christ

Discipled through relationships

> "I was in Okinawa and my dad was stationed there. There was a group of missionaries who ministered to the local community there. But they also had local churches and their kids were magnificent kids. And we bound together. We just had a terrific relationship. And through that environment, <u>through that relationship, I began to realize what life in Christ was all about."</u>

Jesus calls people to a personal relationship

> "And I was taking a class at Northside called *Master-Life*. I completed the second section and as we were sitting there, <u>and I felt God say, "You don't have a personal relationship with me."</u>...And so, I was rebaptized at the age of 40, on Mother's Day."

Giving every day to God – asking for His lead

> "<u>I give every day to God and I let Him open doors.</u> And He often will give me a thought. And I'll make

a call to a friend. Opening doors is the best way, I think, in my own personal life, that I start everyday asking God where He wants to take me - What He would like me to do that day…"

"I start with, *This day is yours. Every thought. Every word. Every action. Every reaction. Let it all be yours. And lead me to where You want me to be and who you want me to talk to.* " And I've done that for many, many years, every day."

God will burden our hearts

"God burdens my heart with certain students and I don't know why I feel burdened more with certain students than I do with others. Maybe it's because the need there is greater and there needs to be more of a personal contact and a personal relationship with a Christian."

Being Prepared to Pray

"our *opportunity* is, that if a student comes to us with spiritual questions, and I say this as 'us' because my entire three person staff is Christian, but if they come to us with a specific question or a specific desire for prayer, we can and we do."

Asking to Pray with Co-workers

"And then, as I got to know people and I saw that they were hurting, I would say, "Would you like me to pray with you? Is there anything I can pray about?" With Rabbis, with Israelis. And people, most often, said yes. …It built relationships"

Caring. Kindness. Love.

"However, as I started to pray over my classroom, to anoint the classroom, and to ask for opportunities in ministry, God was very, very steady in that. And that was about the last five years at the Hebrew Academy. But He built me up to building relationships and trust with families and respect. And caring and kindness."

Prayer with Focus

"my advice would be: don't discount the power of prayer. And consistent prayer. Prayer with focus. And then to be receptive to the fact that doors will open and opportunities will present."

Principles Illustrated – Don & Karol

- Discipled through relationships
- Jesus calls people to a personal relationship
- Giving every day to God – asking for His lead
- God will burden our hearts
- Being prepared to pray
- Asking to Pray with Co-workers
- Caring. Kindness. Love.
- Prayer with focus

Chapter 19

Key Illustrated Principles from the Interview

Jeff Carson – from chapter 7
Barbeque Master, Entrepreneur
Disciple of Jesus Christ

Gratitude to God for salvation leads to sharing the Gospel

> "God was working on me. Inside our church, grounding and rooting me as a solid foundation and having a personal relationship with Him. So, I was really on fire for the Lord, because I had seen what He did in my life. And a lot of people don't understand, <u>when God releases you of your past sins, no matter what you've done, and gives you a new lease on life, you want to go share the Gospel."</u>

Need to have a Mentor

> "He had a passion for us to know the Bible and give us all kinds of study work. You name it, we'd be ten or twelve of us; my sister and some other families, Wednesday night, we'd be in the pews. <u>We'd have six to twelve books out, just studying. From that point on, the hunger kept on going."</u>

God opens doors

"…I can see Him at work. God is at work, even when we don't see it. He was opening up doors and doing some wonderful things. So, from that point on, I just started serving Him. Started doing ministry."

Disciples are to be *making* disciples

"We are to be making disciples continuously, Steve, like I said. And that's Matthew 28, the *Great Commission* to go make disciples. And it's a humbling experience, whenever you get a chance to share the Gospel of Jesus Christ with someone, and get a chance to share your testimony about what Christ has done in the midst of your life and how He's working…"

The more we learn, the more we have to tell others

"The more we learn, the more we have to go out and tell somebody. Tell them that Christ loves them and share the Gospel in a capacity and in a way that's plain and simple, that they would want to go out and do the same thing."

We can't save anybody – we can only share the Gospel of Jesus Christ out of Love

"We can't save anybody. It's by God's grace that we've been saved, through faith. Not of works. So, there's nothing we can do to add to it or take away, but we can be obedient, in a sense, in sharing the Gospel with those who do not know. And if we love them, we're going to tell them the truth out of love.

Then we're going to share the Gospel. And hopefully, the Holy Spirit tugs at their heart..."

We have to listen to people

"you have to have that discipleship heart. You have to have the discernment for individuals to see where they're at. <u>You have to listen. You have to listen to people.</u> You've got to see where people are at."

Earn the right to share the Gospel

"But the long story short, as I'm sharing the Gospel with people, they see Christ in me. I see if they're crying or if they're hurting, or whatever, and then I get to know them. And at that time, you can work your way in. "Look, you don't mind if I pray with you, do you?" <u>They see something different about you, but yet again, you have to earn that right to share the Gospel with them.</u>"

People watch us as Christian disciples

"I have one brother that goes to my church and he gave his testimony. He came in maybe two months ago and he said, <u>"I was watching you, Jeff. Everybody that came in, you shared the Gospel with them. Or you prayed with them. Or you got to know them. Whatever it took.</u> You took the time to talk to them and see how the family was. To see how church was if they were church-going. You found that niche with those individuals." And I think that's what Jesus Christ does. He comes alongside people. He picks ordinary people to do extraordinary things."

God uses ordinary people to do extraordinary things

> "And I think that's what Jesus Christ does. He comes alongside people. He picks ordinary people to do extraordinary things."

Your business _is_ your ministry

> "People say, 'Well, your business is your ministry!' And that's so true. But people I talk to say, 'Jeff, your ministry, your business. You talk to people. You do this.' I feel like there's something else."

The more you learn and do, the more God provides opportunities

> "If you're grounded and rooted in the Gospel, the more that you learn about Him, the more you read the Bible, the more that you share the Gospel, the more that you pray, the more things that you do for Christ, the more He opens up opportunities for you and a chance to be a disciple - but also to disciple one another. We are to disciple. We are to teach those who do not know"

Humbleness is seen

> "And then as you humble yourself, people will see it in you. And then you'll have that passion. You'll have that desire to go out and share the Gospel with others"

Principles Illustrated – Jeff Carson

- Gratitude to God for salvation leads to sharing the Gospel
- Mentor encouraged us to study God's Word
- God opens doors
- Disciples are to be *making* disciples
- The more we learn, the more we have to tell others
- We can't save anybody – we can only share the Gospel of Jesus Christ out of Love
- We have to listen to people
- Earn the right to share the Gospel
- People watch us as Christian disciples
- God uses ordinary people to do extraordinary things
- Your business *is* your ministry
- The more you learn and do, the more God provides opportunities
- Humbleness is seen

Chapter 20

Key Illustrated Principles from the Interview

Jim Laidlaw – from chapter 8
Carpenter, Contractor, "Sawdust"
Disciple of Jesus Christ

Not Judging others, meeting them where they are

> "And when we go in there, we don't care what these
> guys have done. <u>All we care about is what's in their
> heart</u>. A lot of these guys come into a weekend
> with a lot of hate...lot of hatred, a lot of
> bigotry...racism in their hearts. All that stuff is
> *taught* to them...it's a learned behavior. And by the
> time the weekend is over...again, *Christ shows up,
> He shows out*... these guys are Aryan Brotherhood,
> and Muslims... are hugging it out!"

Many accept Christ at great risk to themselves

> "...these guys are in an enclosed environment, and
> they cannot escape it. They cannot get away. So, if
> these guys change their ways...they are changing
> their ways knowing that the <u>repercussions of this
> could be serious</u>! <u>And they do it anyway</u>. That is
> powerful to me."

God's Love in Jesus transforms men's hearts

> "Crying or hugging is seen as a sign of weakness.
> I'm telling you these guys are balling their eyes out!
> And hugging on each other. It's quite the
> transformation, and you're correct in that..."

Not forcing, Just Being Present

"I don't force anything. I let the situation present itself. And it does present itself. Whatever that opportunity is… I go with it. Just through conversation and talking with people. I don't want to know what's in their head, I want to know what's in their heart."

"God's timing…it appears. Right? There's my opportunity. Just like we were talking about in discipleship: There's my opportunity! I don't try to force anything. I'm there."

As business leaders, we have an effect on our team

"The guys that worked for me clearly understood who I was and what I do and it did have an effect on them… because they told me I did."

We are to *Believe* and *Take Action*

"in John 3:16, we are to believe….Matthew 25:36 is ACTION by somebody. So, that's how I do what I do. I go visit people, I roll up next to them, I'll feed them, I'll give money, even if I don't have it… I'll still do that. And I'll listen and be compassionate."

Get with it! – Get on it! (Don't Wait)

"Get with it! [laughs] Get on it! Because this is your one and only opportunity. This is not a *dry run*. At one point I thought I was invincible. No, this is the *real deal*."

Get out of your head, and get into your heart

"Get out of your head, and get into your heart. Let your heart do the driving versus your head. I understand we have to be logical and do certain things, but once you allow your heart to get after it, then you're starting to figure out and understand what Jesus has been talking about all along."

Principles Illustrated – Jim Laidlaw

- **Not Judging others, meeting them where they are**
- **Many accept Christ at great risk to themselves**
- **God's Love in Jesus transforms men's hearts**
- **Not forcing, Just Being Present**
- **As business leaders, we have an effect on our team**
- **We are to *Believe* and *Take Action***
- **Urgency - Get with it! – Get on it!**
- **Get out of your head, and get into your heart**

Chapter 21

Key Illustrated Principles from the Interview

Jim & Anita VarnHagen – from chapter 9
Rescue Mission Leaders, Engineer
Disciples of Jesus Christ

Children Seek God

"So, I went out there by the barn, and I sat down and I looked up in the sky and I said, "I wish I knew more about God." So, I'm talking to God. So, I think that was my first prayer." (Age 5)

Growing in faith through the Word and church

"While we were in Greenville, we attended Southside Baptist Church. It was there that I really grew in faith."

"…I think just the activities of the church and attending the meetings. And realizing, by reading the Bible".

Discipled and Mentored by a friend

"And I had a friend. He was very interested in witnessing to anybody that came along. And so, he would take me with him. One of the places we went was down to near the railroad station where the

Rescue Mission was. So, <u>I got involved in working with down and out people.</u>"

Encouraged friend to read Gospel – he came to Christ

"So, I went to a couple meetings with him. <u>I gave him a New Testament and told him that he needs to read this and really receive Christ into his life.</u> It didn't happen right away."

Anita: "But it was building a relationship with him"

Jim: "Building a relationship with him. Sure enough, over time, I saw that there was a change. And I said, "You know, I see a change in you." He says, "Yeah." He says, <u>"Jim. I received Christ into my life."</u>

Praying for God's guidance

"And so, <u>we prayed together and asked the Lord to lead in what our next steps should be.</u> About 11 o'clock that evening, we got a knock on the door. It was the director of the Rescue Mission in Detroit. He says, "Jim, the board has decided to offer you a position." That was the answer to prayer. We've been on that track ever since. <u>And I can tell you, that through prayer, at the last minute, we've seen God give us a definite answer.</u>"

Baptism was witness for the Lord

Anita: "Well, it's a curious thing. He hasn't brought out a number of things, but <u>even when he was saved in Morocco, he was ultimately a witness for the Lord,</u> because they had a whole convoy of cars that went up into the Atlas Mountains and watched him be baptized along with some Muslims."

Trusting in the Lord's plan

Jim: "Well, I was with the Light Bearers for four or five years, I guess. We had reorganized the Light Bearers, to the point where each Light Bearer Chapter was independent. When that occurred, they didn't need somebody to head the organization up. I kind of worked myself out of a job. So, then there was another organization that wanted me to join their staff in Chicago, but I wasn't confident that that was where the Lord wanted us. Again, we prayed, "Lord, help us." I gave them the same thing. I said, "I'll let you know Friday morning.""

Jim: "Lo and behold, without my knowledge, the Executive Director of the Mission in New York, whom I had met and had known and knew his family and so on, through church acquaintances in the past. He gave me a call. He says, "Jim." He says, "I'm planning on retiring." He says, "We have a board meeting coming up." He says, "I'd like you to come here and interview.""

"…I went and visited with the board. They offered me a position. We had about six months to prepare to get there. And it all worked out. We went to New York, and we spent 23 years at that Mission. That's the longest I've spent at any position."

Let others see us trusting in Christ

Question: What's most important to BE a disciple?

"I'd say, to be a witness, but we're all witnesses in a sense. How good are we as a witness? We just let our lives show that we're trusting Christ. And others can see that in us. We're a witness regardless. How effective are we at being a witness? I think being a disciple means that you need to be a witness for the Lord. I think others see Christ in us without the fact that we'll even verbally tell them."

Asking a question can lead people to seek Jesus Christ

"I just happened to say to this guy, "Do you know Jesus Christ as your personal Savior?" And he sort of sat back in his chair. And he said, "Yes." And so, we just kept eating our soup and I wished him well… But two years later, I saw him up at the Harvard Club where there was this Bible study… I was getting my coffee and everything to go sit down and he says, "Why don't you sit down with me." So, I sat down there. He says, "Jim, do you remember asking me, 'Do you know Jesus Christ as your personal Savior?'" And I said, "I think I do. In that Chinese restaurant." And he says, "You know, I never knew the Lord, but that just registered in my mind." And he says, "I started reading the Bible and I received Christ in my life. And I'm going to this church" and so on. You know, you don't have to say a whole lot sometimes, to a person. But that triggered him to want to… Learn more. And he received Christ!"

Conscious effort to talk about the Lord, and live so they see Christ in you.

> *Question: What would you say are the most important things in terms of making disciples?*

> Jim: "I think you just have to make a conscious effort to talk to people about the Lord. And live your life in a way in which they can see Christ in you. I think you have to do both things. If you're honest and faithful to the Lord, I think that people can see that. We're all sinners. I haven't ceased to be a sinner, but yet I know I'm saved. And I want others to know that too. You can't continue to live like you were a sinner at one time. So, you have to continue to develop and grow in your faith. There's no end to that. So, I think as we continue to develop and grow, other people can see that in us."

Be *real*, become friends with people

> Anita: "You have to be *real*. And become friends with people. Be open with your life. And then they're open with you and that encourages the Lord to work within the hearts of other people."

"Listen to the Lord's call on your life" - Jim

"Never stop learning" - Anita

Principles Illustrated – Jim & Anita

- Children Seek God
- Growing in faith through the Word and church
- Discipled and Mentored by a friend
- Encouraged friend to read Gospel – he came to Christ
- Praying for God's guidance
- Baptism was witness for the Lord
- Trusting in the Lord's plan
- Let others see us trusting in Christ
- Asking a question can lead people to seek Jesus Christ
- Conscious effort to talk about the Lord, and live so they see Christ in you.
- Be *real*, become friends with people
- Listen to the Lord's call on your life
- Never stop learning

Chapter 22

Key Illustrated Principles from the Interview

John Gidman – from chapter 10
Career Electrician
Disciple of Jesus Christ

Relationship with Christ is a *Joy*, not a *Duty*

"Even though my background was Pentecostalism, it was not what you would see over in the States. It was a very stayed, rigid, type of life…. And so, I never felt the joy of salvation. It was just a duty. And not until, I almost can say, that not until I went to Bible college, did I really become a disciple of Christ. There's a difference between, in a sense, a *follower*, because you know that's the right thing to do - and having a *relationship with Christ*. I grew up in the era when you were a *Soldier*, and to have a relationship with something, not talk even. So, when I got to Bible college, my whole view of God, of Christ, of the Holy Spirit, all of that changed. And from there on, being a disciple has been a *joy*, as opposed to a duty."

Peaceful reconciliation in Christ

"Just having Christ in family. In your family life you have conflicts, but when you have the Holy Spirit in your life, when you have Christ in your life, there's that peaceful reconciliation, done in the family without getting into fistfights and all that sort of thing. So, Christ's influence in the family has been probably the most prominent thing. Of course, knowing how to live properly makes a difference, too…"

Engage the community creatively for ministry

"We actually got free rent to the upstairs of a drug store. And the only entrance to it was a fire escape. And there's a lot of miracle stories about that, but we totally revamped that upstairs and we had a coffeehouse up there. We called it *The Fire Escape.* With a double meaning."

"…We were able to minister quite well."

"…we would bring in Christian movies. We had food. We had drink. Not alcohol."

"…We had a coke machines and that sort of thing. We had a counseling area. We had a prayer room"

"…It was a ministry. So local churches helped fund it."

Bible reading - the Word is the best teacher

"The Word is the best teacher…. Stay in the Bible. If you stay in the Bible, there's no way you're not going to be a good disciple. Unless you don't believe what you're reading. But then, …that's another question all together. But staying in the Word. The Word has guided Sandy and I all through our lives. Even when we found it impossible to do devotions together, the Word is still the guide. And it doesn't matter what version. There's enough in one Gospel to keep you straight."

Surrender to Christ brings Joy

"So, I guess I had that fear, even going into Bible college. And there was a service during Bible college and everybody was worshiping the Lord. Hands were raised, something I had never done in my life. Here I am in my 20's and I'd never praised the Lord. And I'm looking at this 6, 7, 800 people congregation, 95% of whom had their arms up in the air, and I'm sitting there frozen... And that raising my hands was kind of like a surrender."

"... And the **flood of joy I felt** when I broke that chain by raising my hands, has given me joy ever since. I'm getting emotional thinking about that time."

Principles Illustrated – John Gidman

- **Relationship with Christ is a *Joy*, not a *Duty***
- **Peaceful reconciliation in Christ**
- **Engage the community creatively for ministry**
- **Bible reading - the Word is the best teacher**
- **Surrender to Christ brings Joy**

Chapter 23

Key Illustrated Principles from the Interview

Kyle Condra – from chapter 11
Officer, Fire Department
Disciple of Jesus Christ

Some have never heard the Gospel

"I grew up in a very secular home. We didn't even do the Christmas and Easter thing. We never went to church. And so, never growing up with that, it's one of those things, that as a disciple, you're told to go out and preach the word of Jesus. <u>I was the guy who never heard Jesus, and I lived in the United States.</u> So, I was *that guy*, even in the midst of everybody, that had never heard the name of Jesus before."

Christians Just Loved Me Completely

"And, so the family always looked at them differently. And they're the only ones, for the longest time, that were the black sheep. Everybody talked about them; 'oh, Greg and Kathy…', you know, this kind of thing. But they always stood strong. <u>And in the midst of all the problems that I had been through, had done, and everything, not one single moment of my life that I can remember, did they ever say anything about it. They just loved me completely.</u>"

Scripturally, relationally, grace-filled, nothing but love

"Bottom of the pit...this is where Greg and Kathy step back into the story. They're the ones who counseled me through it, <u>scripturally and relationally. Grace-filled, nothing but love.</u> They knew what was going on, but again, they didn't say a word. <u>'We're here for you. We're praying for you. We love you. What can we do to help you?'"</u>

Honest testimonies are powerful

"<u>I saw fifteen guys stand up and give their testimony about the things they've been doing and struggling with, and how Christ changed their lives. And recognizing that I wasn't the only one who had the same kind of things that were going on, and hearing about the love and grace, and then being able to see that in Greg and Kathy, and the difference – it was powerful.</u> It was Saturday night that our table went into the back room and had a little quiet time and prayed together, and me and my buddy accepted Christ at the same time together."

Transformational Change After Encountering Christ

"So, I go back to what I said when I lead this off: <u>it's the difference between black and white, day and night...it's tangible. That change in my life was tangible. So, I went from black to white, day to night.</u> The difference in me was...[pause]... It was real. It was SO.... and to cut out a lot of the middle part of it, my parents saw such a difference in me...fast forward several years; this was not a fast process, but many years. <u>Both my parents accepted Christ because of the change in me.</u> So now, Greg and Kathy are not the black sheep of the family. They're the pinnacle of the family. Everybody strives to be like them. It's just amazing how all the things that happened led to where I'm at now."

Bible study - Listening When Driving

"So, a lot of my bible reading is in the car, when I'm driving…. Listening to scripture. The thing that I've really been turned onto here recently is, *The Bible Project*. And it's phenomenal. I don't know if you've heard of it…. It's a YouTube channel, called *The Bible Project*, and it takes you through every book of the Bible. This guy breaks it down both audibly, but then also, visually. And so, the two of them, hand in hand, they draw this picture of the overall theme of the Bible for that book. And they break down the book chapter by chapter, and the meanings, and how it gets all grouped together. I just completed it and I'm getting ready to do it again because it was so fascinating."

"…. And then there's another phone app that I use. It's really good, too. It's called, *Through the Word*."

Born-Again was so literal – struggled, lost friends

"…when I went back to work, I was no longer one of 'those guys'."

"…I had changed so much, that I didn't know how to live life. Being born again, to me, was so literal, because I was lost for so long, when I was an infant trying to figure out how to be a Christian in this non-Christian lifestyle that I had been living for so long. I mean, to be brutally honest, I lost every single one of my friends after I became a Christian."

New Disciples Need a Mentor

"I didn't have that, so when I became a Christian, and it was in 2004, and I struggled for two years, because I didn't know what I was supposed to do. I didn't know what life was supposed to be like. I didn't have a mentor and that would be the biggest thing for me to tell somebody is: 'When you become a Christian, you have to have a mentor. You have to have somebody that you trust. Somebody that you can count on. Somebody that can lead you through everything'. I didn't have that and that's one thing I wish I had, because I think my walk would have changed if I would have had somebody like that. If I would have known to go to Greg, he would have bent over backwards for it, but I didn't. So, I was blessed that I was able to serve on banquet teams. I learned just an absolute ton, just by being able to serve on teams and writing many talks, and serving in different capacities and learning how people lived, by seeing it, through the banquet community. That's where I got mentored."

Servant Leadership Following Christ

"I'm an officer now, so now I have different responsibilities, but I also have people working for me. So, now I get to exemplify servant leadership at the firehouse. When I decided I was going to become an officer, that's where I was putting my stake in the ground. I was like, if I do this, this is what my principles are. I'm going to be a servant leader. <u>And I'm going to serve my guys</u>…. It's bigger than what the words are. It's challenging. It's becoming less than the people who work for you. I'm not special. I'm no better than them. And that's the way I look at it. I took a test, and I'm in charge. I have that responsibility. But just because I have that, doesn't make me better. It doesn't make me special. It doesn't give me power. <u>It gives me more responsibility to do what's right. And it gives me an opportunity to show Christ's love; that He came and suffered and died. And so, when I lead my guys, it's completely out of humility.</u> I cannot count how many times I say, 'thank you' throughout the day. I cannot tell you how many times I'm the first one jumping in and doing something and then the guys follow me."

Different, positive

"I've had several <u>people tell me that working in my firehouse is different</u> than any other station or crew they've ever worked with before. Guys <u>have told me that it's so refreshing, that it's not negative.</u> People aren't running around cursing."

Before Christ, After Christ

"Being a Christian is extremely difficult. Now, with that being said, it is absolutely life changing. It is black and white. Day and night."

"… It is the difference in my life…it's opposite. Everything that I lived for was for the *world* before Christ. After Christ, everything is to the best of my ability…is Christ centered. It's just different. And unless you've experienced that difference, it's hard to understand what that really means."

Principles Illustrated – Kyle Condra

- Some have never heard the Gospel
- Christians just loved me completely
- Scripturally, relationally, grace-filled, nothing but love
- Honest testimonies are powerful
- Transformational change after encountering Christ
- Bible study - Listening when driving
- Born-Again was so literal – struggled, lost friends
- New Disciples Need a Mentor
- Servant Leadership following Christ
- Different, positive
- Before Christ, After Christ

Chapter 24

Key Illustrated Principles from the Interview

Scott Beck
President, Beck's Hybrids
Disciple of Jesus Christ

Relationship vs. Religion

"I did grow up in the church. It was a Lutheran Church. We attended regularly. Part of the youth group. But what I didn't get there was what God desired in terms of *relationship*, with Him personally. With Jesus Christ as Lord. At church there was liturgy - it's all sound doctrine, for the most part, I believe. But it wasn't until I was at Purdue and a member of Farmhouse Fraternity...there were guys in the house that were truly *believers*."

God calls us to humble ourselves, repent, and *Surrender*

"But toward the end of college, it really became apparent that I was really searching for the truth. And I went to a series of films that Campus Crusade had put on, on the Billy Graham series: *Distant Thunder*...end-time type things. And I went to those and it got my attention that God was really talking to me about needing to surrender my life. I came to a point where I realized that He was speaking to me and I needed to make Him Lord of my life, but I needed to do some things to showed forth that repentance. I remember one night; I took my hard rock albums out and I broke them and I put them in a dumpster."

Starting the day in God's Word, thanksgiving, and Praise

[regarding living out faith in our personal life]

"What came to mind, in that regard, is just the simple things of meditating on God's Word at the beginning of the day. Starting out with thinking about and speaking His Word and offering up thanksgiving and praise in the morning and then just throughout the day believing and receiving what He says is mine; who I am in Christ and who He is in me. Work to orient my thoughts and beliefs according to His Word. And then doing the important things rather than just thinking about them or talking about them. To me, that's the key; is taking action."

Engaging children in conversation about God

"With my older daughter, whose 17, asking her about her relationship with her boyfriend. 'Are they praying together? Are they studying the word? What are you reading in the Bible now?' My younger daughter, similar; I try to have a conversation around 'what did they talk about at youth group?' So, just incorporating conversation with the kids. And certainly, when it's time for disciplinary actions, there's the opportunity to talk about 'What's God see this as? What's He think about this? What's He think about you? And how do you deal with this in light of Him and His Word?'"

Leadership: Servanthood & Stewardship balance

[regarding living out faith in professional life]

"Culture is really important. We work diligently to foster the right type of culture. In our workplace, it is okay to live and be a Christian, to express your faith. But I would say, how is that lived out? The things that came to mind, was really focusing on listening to others, caring for them, and what they're dealing with. And in situations where they haven't made the right choices or the best choices, see if...what is their frame of mind in this? Is this something where they can learn from it? Are they taking a path of recognizing their wrong, where we can give them grace and mercy and a second chance? Or is it something where the person just really needs to experience the discipline of losing a job or getting moved to a different position. You know, something to really help them understand that they do need to change, that they cannot continue in this path as an employee here with those similar types of behaviors. As leaders, we balance two things. As followers of Christ and leaders in a business, we balance two things. There's the servanthood aspect, where we want to be forgiving, caring, and give people second chances; just like God extends His grace to us. On the other side of that, there's the stewardship part, where we're stewarding the larger organization; what's the impact of that individual's behaviors on all the other employees? Or on all the customers? And are they at a place where a second chance will bring hope to others? We will recognize God's grace and mercy and others can see that? Or is the stewardship aspect more important at that point, because of the severity of the infraction, or the place where that person is, in terms of their journey. They're not seeing it the way they need to see it, so they need to experience some severe consequences to help them, hopefully, to get them to a better point."

Providing Optional Educational Opportunities

"We recently started a series of classes we call, *Aiming High*."

"*(Aiming High)*. And one of the members of our education team, who has spent years in youth ministry, presents a topic. I think the first one was, 'What is faith?' and then he did one on "the Love of God". Recently did one on the Resurrection. These are optional classes. He travels around to our different locations. It's about a 50-minute time slot. We offer it and those that want to attend, can. We treat it like any other educational opportunity we offer. People can attend classes on how to manage your time better. Or how to deal with conflict. Or how to improve your public speaking."

Honoring God with our business

"Usually in a public setting, like when I meet with our new employees coming on board, I meet with them their first day. I don't always talk about it, but I'll often times make reference to the fact that one of our stated business goals is to honor God. You don't have to be a Christian to work here, but we don't suppress it either. I personally believe that God has created each one of us with a purpose and that we are better off when we are linked up with Him, and understanding that purpose and living it out."

Personally connecting with people

"…I'm meeting with every employee in the company. We've got 660 some now…"

"So, I'm taking 27 minutes… it's a time to really help me understand and learn more about them, what they do, what they enjoy about their job and about the company, what they would like to change"

Biblical Leadership: Humility, Servant Leadership, and Direction

[what are the main Biblical leadership principles that God's Word has presented to you?]

"That breaks down into three main categories: *Humility, Servant Leadership*, and *Direction*.

Humility – God is opposed to the proud, but gives grace to the humble. Hebrews says: "Let us come boldly to the throne of grace that we may obtain mercy and find grace to help in the time of need."

Servant Leadership – Leaders don't lord over their people. They work along with them and support them with the tools, training, and encouragement to do their work.

Direction – Clarity of communication. "Without vision, the people perish" (Proverbs 29:18). People need direction and purpose and to know that their work is meaningful and that their values align with mine."

Principles Illustrated – Scott Beck

- *Relationship vs. Religion*
- God calls us to humble ourselves, repent, and *Surrender*
- Starting the day in God's Word, thanksgiving, and Praise
- Engaging children in conversation about God
- Leadership: Servanthood & Stewardship balance
- Providing Optional Educational Opportunities
- Honoring God with our business
- Personally connecting with people
- Biblical Leadership: Humility, Servant Leadership, and Direction

Section 3:

Principles Categorized
Scriptural Correlation
DISCIPLE-*ing* Matrix

Chapter 25

The Why? What? How? & Bringing It All Together

Not Thesis-Proving, but a Quest for Understanding

Unlike many writing or research projects, this book did *not* start out with a thesis - and then the author sets out to prove the thesis. For example, I did not set out to tell the world how to be a disciple or make disciples based on my knowledge or experience or what I saw the Bible telling us; nor did I set out to prove or disprove any existing models for being a disciple or disciple-making, modern or ancient.

Rather, this was an exploration project – a *Quest!* Seeking to examine the Scriptures, following the Holy Spirit's guidance, and to glean understanding of the Biblical model for *BE-ing* a disciple of Jesus, *MAKE-ing* disciples of Jesus, and living out our faith in our lives, personal and professional. And to better understand how God's Word instructs us to believe in, trust in, and rejoice in Him as we do the work for His Kingdom that He has called us to.

As mentioned in the introduction, this process was started because I felt the Lord call me to (1) grab my Bible (2) talk to fellow Christ-followers that He put on my heart (3) glean from the Bible and from their stories in the interviews (4) examine the information gleaned (5) test it against Scripture (6) see what God brought forth from the effort.

Was this just for our understanding, those involved in this project? Or, does God have larger plans for it? I give that to the Lord – may He be glorified – I will follow His lead.

These three chapters of Section 3 show the results from the interviews, the categorizing, the Biblical validation, and the model that originated from the interviews.

I feel it very important to state that these topics (the Biblical model for being a disciple of Jesus, making disciples of Jesus, and living out our purpose in our lives, both personally and professionally) is clearly written about in Scripture, and has been taught, studied, written about, and practiced for nearly 2000 years. There are hundreds or thousands of extra-Biblical books on these topics – and I don't know if anything presented here would be considered truly *New* or original... probably not. But true, on-fire-discipleship for the Lord Jesus in North and South America and Europe is declining – and in prayer and devotional times over the last few years, I have asked the Lord "Why is the church struggling with luke-warm, scripturally illiterate, pew-sitters?", "Why is the Biblical worldview declining so rapidly in our younger generations?", "What can I do here on earth to enter the fight for truth?" These questions led to this quest to examine discipleship in this hostile, anti-Biblical, anti-Christ, secular-worldview environment. This is why this book exists, and why you and I have spent time with this process. It is my prayer that this book strengthens, emboldens, and equips...in some way... the body of Christ around the world. And like a drop of water in a pond, it is my prayer that God uses it to make ripples for His glory and His Kingdom.

Scripturally-Based Testing

This is not a dissertation, nor is it a traditionally scholarly academic approach to the subject. However, the rest of this section shows the model that I feel the Lord led me to, and how it was tested against Scripture to assure Biblical validity. To avoid accidentally slipping into *Eisegesis* (reading into the texts of Scripture what an interpreter wishes to find or thinks he finds) I worked intentionally to validate the principles gleaned from the interviews were Biblical with a lens of *Exegesis* (reading out of the text, in context, what God and His chosen original authors meant to convey), as well as assuring harmony of the principles to (1) centuries old Biblical teachings and principles (2) trusted advisors who are Biblically grounded, and (3) personal knowledge of Scripture, and (4) much prayer and reflection. *Let's begin!*

In Section 3 there are four main objectives:

1. **Quick review of the Key Principles illustrated in the Interviews**

2. **Showing the process of grouping the *Principles Illustrated* from the interviews into categories**

3. **Testing each category with Scripture, in context, to assure Biblical validity**

4. **Explaining the Disciple-ing Matrix (a model for Biblical Discipleship) that resulted**

KEY PRINICIPLES ILLUSTRATED

Summaries from Interviews

Adam's Key Principles Illustrated

- Loving Others
- Being Christ-Like
- God's Word – Bible Study
- Not Condemning, Forgiving, Encouraging
- Sacrificing for Others, Protecting
- Leading by Example, Shining Our Light
- Confidence, Having Faith in God's promises

Andrew's Key Principles Illustrated

- Coming to faith was a process, beginning with a question by a bold disciple co-worker
- Bold, confident disciple led me
- Responsibility to be the spiritual leader in the home
- Prayer without ceasing
- Kingdom Focus
- Bible Study and Application
- Being *Salt and Light*
- *Chess Board Position* – Prioritization to Share the Gospel
- Seek Opportunities to discuss Faith and Faith-Activities
- Yeast must be Active to spread - engaging others, Spreading the Good News of Jesus

Barb's Key Principles Illustrated

- Kingdom Focus, Christ-Centered
- Follow the Leading of the Holy Spirit
- Trusting God's Leading
- Excellence for the Right Reasons
- Learning to Hear God's voice – Quiet Time with God
- One Life – Not Compartmentalized
- Praying & Speaking into Someone's Life, led by the Spirit

David's Key Principles Illustrated

- Seek the Lord's guidance on what to say
- Using Common Sense as to appropriateness of when to share with people
- Good work ethic = Good witness
- Asking: "Is there anything I can pray for you about?"
- Allowing God to be glorified in your unique circumstances
- Co-worker time – don't waste it!

Devon's Key Principles Illustrated

- Fame and Money did not satisfy the soul's desire…only God
- Being Pure in our *secret life*
- People are watching – be an example
- Three Levels: Be Discipled, Peer Discipling, Disciple others (Paul – Timothy Model)
- God will move you to a *Bigger Tank* so you can grow!

Don and Karol's Key Principles Illustrated

- Discipled through relationships
- Jesus calls people to a personal relationship
- Giving every day to God – asking for His lead
- God will burden our hearts
- Being prepared to pray
- Asking to Pray with Co-workers
- Give God each day
- Caring. Kindness. Love.
- Prayer with focus

Jeff Carson's Key Principles Illustrated

- Gratitude to God for salvation leads to sharing the Gospel
- Mentor encouraged us to study God's Word
- God opens doors
- Disciples are to be *making* disciples
- The more we learn, the more we have to tell others
- We can't save anybody – we can only share the Gospel of Jesus Christ out of Love
- We have to listen to people
- Earn the right to let them see Christ in you
- People watch us as Christian disciples
- God uses ordinary people to do extraordinary things
- Your business *is* your ministry
- The more you learn and do, the more God provides opportunities
- Humbleness is seen

Jim Laidlaw's Key Principles Illustrated

- Not Judging others, meeting them where they are
- Many accept Christ at great risk to themselves
- God's Love in Jesus transforms men's hearts
- Not forcing, Just Being Present
- As business leaders, we have an effect on our team
- We are to *Believe* and *Take Action*
- Urgency - Get with it! – Get on it!
- Get out of your head, and get into your heart

Jim and Anita's Key Principles Illustrated

- Children Seek God
- Growing in faith through the Word and church
- Mentored by a friend
- Encouraged friend to read Gospel – he came to Christ
- Praying for God's guidance
- Baptism was witness for the Lord
- Trusting in the Lord's plan
- Let others see us trusting in Christ
- Asking a question can lead people to seek Jesus Christ
- Conscious effort to talk about the Lord, and live so they see Christ in you.
- Be *real*, become friends with people
- Listen to the Lord's call on your life
- Never stop learning

John Gidman's Key Principles Illustrated

- Relationship with Christ is a *Joy*, not a *Duty*
- Peaceful reconciliation in Christ
- Engage the community creatively for ministry
- Bible reading - the Word is the best teacher
- Surrender to Christ brings Joy

Kyle Condra's Key Illustrations

- Some have never heard the Gospel
- Christians just loved me completely
- Scripturally, relationally, grace-filled, nothing but love
- Honest testimonies are powerful
- Transformational change after encountering Christ
- Bible study - Listening when driving
- Born-Again was so literal – struggled, lost friends
- New Disciples Need a Mentor
- Servant Leadership following Christ
- Different, positive
- Before Christ, After Christ

Scott Beck's Key Illustrations

- *Relationship vs. Religion*
- God calls us to humble ourselves, repent, and *Surrender*
- Starting the day in God's Word, thanksgiving, and Praise
- Engaging children in conversation about God
- Leadership: Servanthood & Stewardship balance
- Providing Optional Educational Opportunities
- Honoring God with our business
- Personally connecting with people
- Biblical Leadership: Humility, Servant Leadership, and Direction

Chapter 26

CATEGORIES

There were 103 *Key Principles Illustrated* identified in the 12 interviews, 14 people. And that was just a few key ones from each interview. As expected in a qualitative interview approach, there was a lot of overlap. By placing similar attributes or principles together, we were able to cluster and identify the following list of *15 Principle Categories*:

15 Principle Categories Identified

1. Loving God, Loving Others
2. Christ is the model
3. Bible Study - the Word
4. Leading by example, Shine the Light
5. Trusting God's promises
6. BOLD Disciple – engaging others with the Gospel
7. Spiritual leader at home
8. Personal Prayer life, Communing with Christ
9. Spirit Led – Give the day to God
10. Kingdom focused, Biblical Worldview
11. Discipling Others, Being Discipled
12. Personal relationship with Christ
13. Christ-Like Leadership, Engaging Culture in Profession
14. Community, Fellowship, Small Groups
15. Missions & Outreach Minded, Reaching the Lost

Category Clusters

On the next eleven pages the Categories are listed with their component *Principles Illustrated* from each of the interviews, showing their parts. While they are individually slightly different principles, you can see their similarities, and hopefully, understand how and why they were grouped together. Following the category clusters, we will examine the Biblical validity for those as attributes for this Disciple-ing discussion:

Loving God, Loving Others (Great Commission)

- Loving Others (because I love God) - Adam
- "Is there anything I can pray for you about?" David H
- Being prepared to pray - Don & Karol
- Asking to Pray with Co-workers - Don & Karol
- Caring. Kindness. Love. - Don & Karol
- We have to listen to people- Jeff C
- Earn the right to share Gospel - Jeff C.
- Be *real*, become friends with people - Jim & Anita
- Peaceful reconciliation in Christ – John G.
- Engage community creatively for ministry – John G.
- Some have never heard the Gospel – Kyle C
- Christians just loved me completely – Kyle C
- Scripturally, relationally, grace-filled, nothing but love – Kyle C
- Personally connecting with people – Scott B
- Not Judging, meeting them where they are –Jim. L

Christ is the Model

- Not Condemning, Forgiving, Encouraging Adam
- Sacrificing for Others, Protecting Adam
- Fame and Money did not satisfy the soul's desire...only God - Devon
- Being Pure in our *secret life* - Devon
- Asking a question can lead people to seek Jesus Christ - Jim & Anita
- Be *real*, become friends with people - Jim & Anita
- Christians just loved me completely – Kyle C
- Scripturally, relationally, grace-filled, nothing but love – Kyle C
- Personally connecting with people – Scott B

Bible Study, Being in the Word

- God's Word – Bible Study - Adam
- Bible Study and Application - Andrew
- Mentor encouraged us to study God's Word- Jeff C
- The more we learn, the more we have to tell others- Jeff
- The more you learn and do, the more God provides opportunities - Jeff C
- Growing in faith through the Word and church - Jim & Anita
- Encouraged friend to read Gospel – he came to Christ - Jim & Anita
- Asking a question can lead people to seek Jesus Christ - Jim & Anita
- Never stop learning - Jim & Anita
- Bible reading - the Word is the best teacher – John G.

- Bible study - Listening when driving – Kyle C
- Starting the day in God's Word, thanksgiving, and Praise – Scott B

Leading by Example – Shine the Light

- Leading by Example, Shining Our Light - Adam
- Good work ethic = Good witness - David H
- Allowing God to be glorified in your unique circumstances - David H
- People are watching – be an example - Devon
- Earn the right to let them see Christ in you- Jeff C
- People watch us as Christian disciples- Jeff C
- Humbleness is seen   - Jeff C
- God's Love in Jesus transforms men's hearts – Jim L
- Baptism was witness for the Lord - Jim & Anita
- Conscious effort to talk about the Lord, and live so they see Christ in you. - Jim & Anita
- Peaceful reconciliation in Christ – John G.
- Scripturally, relationally, grace-filled, nothing but love – Kyle C
- Honest testimonies are powerful – Kyle C
- Transformational change after encountering Christ – Kyle C
- Born-Again was literal, struggled, lost friends – Kyle C
- Engaging children in conversation about God – Scott B
- Honoring God with our business – Scott B

Trusting God's Promises

- Confidence, Having Faith in God's promises – Adam
- Trusting in the Lord's plan - Jim & Anita

- Let others see us trusting in Christ - Jim & Anita
- Listen to the Lord's call on your life - Jim & Anita
- Trusting and believing the Lord's plan – Jim L.

Bold Disciple – Engaging Others with the Gospel

- Coming to faith was a process, beginning with a question by a bold disciple co-worker - Andrew
- Bold, confident disciple led me - Andrew
- Being *Salt and Light* - Andrew
- *Chess Board Position* – Prioritization to Share the Gospel - Andrew
- Seek Opportunities to discuss Faith and Faith-Activities - Andrew
- Yeast must be Active to spread - engaging others, Spreading the Good News of Jesus - Andrew
- Using Common Sense as to appropriateness of when to share with people - David H
- Co-worker time – don't waste it! - David H
- Fame and Money did not satisfy the soul's desire...only God - Devon
- People are watching – be an example - Devon
- Three Levels: Be Discipled, Peer Discipling, Disciple others (Paul – Timothy Model) - Devon
- Gratitude to God for salvation leads to sharing the Gospel- Jeff C
- The more we learn, the more we have to tell others- Jeff C
- We can't save anybody – we can only share the Gospel of Jesus Christ out of Love- Jeff C
- The more you learn and do, the more God provides opportunities - Jeff C

- We are to *Believe* and *Take Action* – Jim L
- Urgency - Get with it! – Get on it! – Jim L
- Encouraged friend to read Gospel – he came to Christ - Jim & Anita
- Let others see us trusting in Christ - Jim & Anita
- Asking a question can lead people to seek Jesus Christ - Jim & Anita
- Conscious effort to talk about the Lord, and live so they see Christ in you. - Jim & Anita
- Be *real*, become friends with people - Jim & Anita
- Engage the community creatively – John G.
- Some have never heard the Gospel – Kyle C
- Christians just loved me completely – Kyle C
- Scripturally, relationally, grace-filled, nothing but love – Kyle C
- Honest testimonies are powerful – Kyle C
- Engaging children in conversation about God – Scott B
- Providing Optional Educational Opportunities – Scott B
- Honoring God with our business – Scott B

Spiritual Leader at Home

- Responsibility to be the spiritual leader in the home - Andrew
- Listen to the Lord's call on your life - Jim & Anita
- Peaceful reconciliation in Christ – John G.
- Some have never heard the Gospel – Kyle C
- Christians just loved me completely – Kyle C
- Scripturally, relationally, grace-filled, nothing but love – Kyle C
- Honest testimonies are powerful – Kyle C

- Transformational change after encountering Christ – Kyle C
- Engaging children in conversation about God – Scott B

Personal Prayer Life, Communing with Christ

- Prayer without ceasing   - Andrew
- Learning to Hear God's voice – Quiet Time with God - Barb
- Praying & Speaking into Someone's Life, led by the Spirit - Barb
- Prayer with focus - Don & Karol
- Praying for God's guidance - Jim & Anita
- Trusting in the Lord's plan - Jim & Anita
- Listen to the Lord's call on your life - Jim & Anita
- Starting the day in God's Word, thanksgiving, and Praise – Scott B

Spirit Led - Give the Day to God

- Follow the Leading of the Holy Spirit – Barb
- Trusting God's Leading - Barb
- Excellence for the Right Reasons - Barb
- One Life – Not Compartmentalized - Barb
- Seek the Lord's guidance on what to say - David H
- God will move you to a *Bigger Tank* so you can grow! - Devon
- Giving every day to God – asking for His lead - Don & Karol
- God will burden our hearts - Don & Karol
- Give God each day - Don & Karol
- God opens doors- Jeff C

- God uses ordinary people to do extraordinary things- Jeff C
- The more you learn and do, the more God provides opportunities - Jeff C
- Praying for God's guidance - Jim & Anita
- Trusting in the Lord's plan - Jim & Anita
- Let others see us trusting in Christ - Jim & Anita
- Conscious effort to talk about the Lord, and live so they see Christ in you. - Jim & Anita
- Be *real*, become friends with people - Jim & Anita
- Listen to the Lord's call on your life - Jim & Anita
- Peaceful reconciliation in Christ – JOHN G.
- Engage the community creatively for ministry – JOHN G.
- Surrender to Christ brings Joy – JOHN G.
- Born-Again was so literal – struggled, lost friends – KYLE C

Kingdom Focused, Biblical Worldview

- Kingdom Focus   - Andrew
- Kingdom Focus, Christ-Centered - Barb
- Being Pure in our *secret life* - Devon
- Let others see us trusting in Christ - Jim & Anita
- Asking a question can lead people to seek Jesus Christ - Jim & Anita
- Conscious effort to talk about the Lord, and live so they see Christ in you. - Jim & Anita
- Listen to the Lord's call on your life - Jim & Anita
- Surrender to Christ brings Joy – John G.
- Before Christ, After Christ – Kyle C
- *Relationship vs. Religion* – Scott B

- God calls us to humble ourselves, repent, and *Surrender* – Scott B
- Honoring God with our business – Scott B

Discipling Others, Being Discipled

- Three Levels: Be Discipled, Peer Discipling, Disciple others (Paul – Timothy Model) - Devon
- Discipled through relationships - Don & Karol
- Mentor encouraged us to study God's Word- Jeff C
- Disciples are to be *making* disciples- Jeff C
- Growing in faith through the Word and church - Jim & Anita
- Mentored by a friend - Jim & Anita
- Asking a question can lead people to seek Jesus Christ - Jim & Anita
- Conscious effort to talk about the Lord, and live so they see Christ in you. - Jim & Anita
- Not Judging others, meeting where they are, Jim L
- Peaceful reconciliation in Christ – John G.
- Engage the community creatively in ministry – John G.
- Some have never heard the Gospel – Kyle C
- Christians just loved me completely – Kyle C
- Scripturally, relationally, grace-filled, nothing but love – Kyle C
- Honest testimonies are powerful – Kyle C
- Transformational change after encountering Christ – Kyle C
- Born-Again was so literal – struggled, lost friends – Kyle C
- New Disciples Need a Mentor – Kyle C
- Before Christ, After Christ – Kyle C
- Engaging children in conversation about God – Scott B

- Providing Optional Educational Opportunities – Scott B
- Personally connecting with people – Scott B
- Honoring God with our business – Scott B

Called to Personal Relationship with Christ Jesus

- Jesus calls people to a personal relationship - Don & Karol
- Children Seek God - Jim & Anita
- Asking a question can lead people to seek Jesus Christ - Jim & Anita
- Relationship with Christ is a *Joy*, not a *Duty* – JOHN G.
- Surrender to Christ brings Joy – John G.
- Transformational change after encountering Christ – Kyle C
- Born-Again was literal, struggled, lost friends – Kyle C
- *Relationship vs. Religion* – Scott B
- God calls us to humble ourselves, repent, and *Surrender* – Scott B

Christ-Like Leadership, Engaging Culture in Profession

- Your business *is* your ministry- Jeff C
- As leaders, we have an effect on our team -Jim L
- Be *real*, become friends with people - Jim & Anita
- Listen to the Lord's call on your life - Jim & Anita
- Some have never heard the Gospel – Kyle C
- New Disciples Need a Mentor – Kyle C
- Servant Leadership following Christ – Kyle C
- Different, positive – Kyle C
- Leadership: Servanthood & Stewardship balance – Scott B

- Providing Optional Educational Opportunities – Scott B
- Honoring God with our business – Scott B
- Personally connecting with people – Scott B
- Biblical Leadership: Humility, Servant Leadership, and Direction – SCOTT B

Community - Fellowship

- All of the individuals interviewed are active in a Church / fellowship
- All of the individuals interviewed are involved in a small group Bible study of some form
- All of the individuals joyfully discuss the blessings, encouragement, support, and growth they experience through their involvement in community

Missions & Outreach Minded, Reaching the Lost

- All of the individuals interviewed expressed an Outreach Mindset – a desire to participate in:
  - Hope given to the hopeless
  - The Good News of the Gospel of Jesus be shared to those who do not know the Lord
  - For the Lost to be Saved by Christ

Chapter 27

Foundation, Method, Expression

Groupings for Scriptural Support & Validation

Now that we have looked at the clusters and have these 15 categories identified, hopefully you will agree that the categories and supporting statements would be in agreement with a Biblical worldview. Thus, the essence of this model needs be in harmony with:

1. **The Biblical worldview is true and vital:**
   a. The Bible is authoritative Word of God
   b. There is only one true and living God, the creator and sustainer of all that is, and Who exists in three persons: the Father, the Son, and the Holy Spirit
   c. Jesus is the Son of God, who is co-eternal with the Father, who was born into this earth by the power of God through a virgin; that he lived a sinless life, was crucified, shed His blood and died a substitutionary death for His people whom He redeemed at the cross; that He was buried and rose from the dead on the third day; that after appearing to His disciples bodily He rose to Heaven where he is the intercessor and advocate for all believers; and that He will bodily return to judge the world and set up His Kingdom.
   d. That every man, woman, and child needs to know the Lord Jesus Christ as Lord, for salvation is by faith alone in Jesus Christ,

and that no one comes to the Father except through Him (John 14:6).

2. That everyone needs the Good News of the Gospel, and that as disciples of Jesus we are called to share the Love of God in Christ to those who are lost.
3. It is important to be a disciple of Jesus.
4. It is important to make disciples of Jesus, whenever and where ever possible.
5. That only God can save people.
6. Our role is to love God and love others, in Christ.

Principle Categories Identified

1. Loving God, Loving Others
2. Christ is the model
3. Bible Study - the Word
4. Leading by example, Shine the Light
5. Trusting God's promises
6. BOLD Disciple – engaging others with the Gospel
7. Spiritual leader at home
8. Personal Prayer life, Communing with Christ
9. Spirit Led – Give the day to God
10. Kingdom focused, Biblical Worldview
11. Discipling Others, Being Discipled
12. Personal relationship with Christ
13. Christ-Like Leadership, Engaging Culture in Profession
14. Community, Fellowship, Small Groups
15. Missions & Outreach Minded, Reaching the Lost

Foundation – Method – Expression

After having written out each of the pages for the 15 categories…. we had a problem…. it was a 50-page chapter! My wife, Tracey, and I both agreed that it needed to be cut into groups. After praying and looking over the categories list, the Lord blessed me with the amazing discovery that resulted in the following table. Thank you, Jesus.

Foundation	Method	Expression
Bible Study - the Word	Christ is the model	Loving God, Loving Others
Trusting God's promises	Spiritual leader at home	Leading by example, Shine the Light
Personal Prayer life, Communing with Christ	Spirit Led – Give the day to God	BOLD Disciple – engaging others with the Gospel
Kingdom focused, Biblical Worldview	Community, Fellowship, Small Groups	Discipling Others, Being Discipled
Personal relationship with Christ	Missions & Outreach Minded, Reaching the Lost	Christ-Like Leadership, Engaging Culture in Profession

Thus, the next three chapters will cover the look at the Scriptural Support & Validation for the **Foundation, Method, and Expression** groupings.

Chapter 28

Foundation Group

Scriptural Support & Validation

Five categories were grouped into Foundations:

- Bible Study – the Word
- Trusting God's Promises
- Personal Prayer Life, Communing with Christ
- Kingdom Focused, Biblical Worldview
- Personal Relationship with Christ

Category: Bible Study – the Word

This category was a compilation of statements in the interview about the importance for any disciple to be well versed in the Scriptures – not because we *have to*...but because it is a joy and a pleasure to soak in God's Word! As Christians we know this. Here are just a few powerful verses to consider when evaluating the importance of this attribute in our lives as Christ-followers, (ESV):

2 Timothy 3:16-17

> **All Scripture is breathed out by God** and profitable for teaching, for reproof, for correction, and for training in righteousness, **that the man of**

God may be competent, equipped for every good work.

Joshua 1:8

This Book of the Law shall not depart from your mouth, but you shall meditate on it day and night, so that you may be careful to do according to all that is written in it. For then you will make your way prosperous, and then you will have good success.

Psalm 119:105

Your **word is a lamp** to my feet and a light to my path.

1 Peter 3:15

But in your hearts honor Christ the Lord as holy, **always being prepared to make a defense** to anyone who asks you for a reason for the hope that is in you; yet do it with gentleness and respect,

Acts 17:11

Now these Jews were more noble than those in Thessalonica; they received the word with all eagerness, **examining the Scriptures daily** to see if these things were so.

Hebrews 4:12

[12] For the **word of God is living and active**, sharper than any two-edged sword, piercing to the division of soul and of spirit, of

joints and of marrow, and discerning the thoughts and intentions of the heart.

Ephesians 6:13-17

[13] Therefore take up the whole armor of God, that you may be able to withstand in the evil day, and having done all, to stand firm. [14] Stand therefore, having fastened on the belt of truth, and having put on the breastplate of righteousness, [15] and, as shoes for your feet, having put on the readiness given by the gospel of peace. [16] In all circumstances take up the shield of faith, with which you can extinguish all the flaming darts of the evil one; [17] and take the helmet of salvation, **and the sword of the Spirit, which is the word of God,**

Proverbs 2:1-5

My son, if you receive my words and treasure up my commandments with you, making your ear attentive to wisdom and inclining your heart to understanding; yes, **if you call out for insight and raise your voice for understanding, if you seek it like silver and search for it as for hidden treasures, then you will understand the fear of the LORD and find the knowledge of God.**

Romans 10:14-17

[14] How then will they call on him in whom they have not believed? And how are they to believe in him of whom they have never heard? And how are they to hear without someone preaching? [15] And how are

they to preach unless they are sent? As it is written, "How beautiful are the feet of those who preach the good news!" **16** But they have not all obeyed the gospel. For Isaiah says, "Lord, who has believed what he has heard from us?" **17 So faith comes from hearing, and hearing through the word of Christ.**

God's Word, the Holy Bible, is our lamp to see, God's teachings to us on how to live, how to love Him and to love our neighbors, and it is the inspired, authoritative Word of God… and it is our sword! Can a soldier go to battle without his sword? Are we spending an appropriate amount of time in God's Word, daily? Are His words constantly on our lips?

Category: Trusting God's Promises

Trusting God's promises is a powerful concept… do we truly *Trust God's Promises*? Completely? That is faith, strong faith. We saw many examples of our disciple friends sharing some very challenging situations…yet, still having faith. One immediate thought is of my dear friend, Jim Laidlaw, who has been diagnosed with stage 4 prostate cancer that has spread to his bones... it has been described as *terminal*. Yet, Jim has faith. He told me "I look forward to being with the Lord!" My brother David is a cancer survivor, and a lifelong sufferer with Cerebral Palsy…but he is trusting in God's promises. We are all moving closer to the day we stand before the Lord… none of us know for certain that we will be here on this planet next Tuesday –

or, even tomorrow. Do you trust the Lord's promises? Let's look at some scripture regarding this topic (ESV):

Romans 8:28

> And **we know** that for those who love God **all things work together for good**, for those who are called according to his purpose.

Psalm 9:10

> And **those who know your name put their trust in you**, for you, O LORD, have not forsaken those who seek you.

Psalm 28:6-8

> Blessed be the LORD!
> For **he has heard the voice of my pleas** for mercy.
> [7] The LORD is my strength and my shield;
> **in him my heart trusts, and I am helped**;
> my heart exults,
> and with my song I give thanks to him.
> [8] The LORD is the strength of his people;
> he is the saving refuge of his anointed.

Joshua 1:9

> [9] Have I not commanded you? Be strong and courageous. **Do not be frightened, and do not be dismayed, for the LORD your God is with you** wherever you go."

Psalm 37 3-6

³ **Trust in the LORD**, and do good;
　　dwell in the land and befriend faithfulness.
⁴ Delight yourself in the LORD,
　　and he will give you the desires of your heart.
⁵ Commit your way to the LORD;
　　trust in him, and he will act.
⁶ He will bring forth your righteousness as the light,
and your justice as the noonday.

Hebrews 11:5-6

⁵ By **faith** Enoch was taken up so that he should not see death, and he was not found, because God had taken him. Now before he was taken, he was commended as having pleased God. ⁶ And **without faith it is impossible to please him**, for whoever would draw near to God must believe that he exists and that he rewards those who seek him.

In this Hebrews 11:5-6 passage we see the word translated as *faith*. The Greek word is: πίστις, which when transliterated is *pistis,* which is a noun – translated into English as *Faith* (and also translated in other places in scripture as *assurance, belief, fidelity).* It's important to

---

Strong's Definition: (from blueletterbible.org)

πιστεύω pisteúō, pist-yoo'-o; from G4102; to have faith (in, upon, or with respect to, a person or thing), i.e. credit; by implication, to entrust (especially one's spiritual well-being to Christ):—believe(-r), commit (to trust), put in trust with.

---

know that the same root word in **verb-form** is πιστεύω, *pisteuo,* which translated is *Believe, to commit to Trust, to trust in !* I dug in there because these two words are vitally important to us in English as Christ-following disciples: In John 3:16, Romans 10:9 and many other "Believe" passages taught by Jesus and His Apostles.

"To Believe in, place our faith and trust upon, to have faith, to TRUST" **- That's what we are called to do as disciples... as "Believers"**

Promises of God that we need to TRUST in:

John 3:16

16 "For God so loved the world, that he gave his only Son, that **whoever believes in him should not perish but have eternal life.** **17** For God did not send his Son into the world to condemn the world, but in order that **the world might be saved through him.** **18** Whoever believes in him is not condemned**, but whoever does not believe is condemned already, because he has not believed in the name of the only Son of God.

Romans 10:9-13

9 because, **if you confess with your mouth that Jesus is Lord and believe in your heart that God raised him from the dead, you will be saved.** **10** For with the heart one believes and is justified, and with the mouth one confesses and is saved. **11** For the Scripture says, **"Everyone who**

believes in him will not be put to shame." **12** For there is no distinction between Jew and Greek; for the same Lord is Lord of all, bestowing his riches on all who call on him. **13 For "everyone who calls on the name of the Lord will be saved."**

John 14:1-7

"Let not your hearts be troubled. **Believe in God; believe also in me. 2 In my Father's house are many rooms. If it were not so, would I have told you that I go to prepare a place for you? 3** And if I go and prepare a place for you, **I will come again and will take you to myself, that where I am you may be also. 4** And you know the way to where I am going." **5** Thomas said to him, "Lord, we do not know where you are going. How can we know the way?" **6** Jesus said to him, **"I am the way, and the truth, and the life. No one comes to the Father except through me. 7** If you had known me, you would have known my Father also. From now on **you do know him** and have seen him."

John 5:21-24

21 For as the Father raises the dead and gives them life, so also the Son gives life to whom he will. **22** For the Father judges no one, but has given all judgment to the Son, **23** that all may honor the Son, just as they honor the Father. Whoever does not honor the Son does not honor the Father who sent him. **24 Truly, truly, I say to you, whoever hears my word and believes him who sent me has**

eternal life. He does not come into judgment, but has passed from death to life.

Thus, **"Trusting God's Promises"** is vital – it is believing and trusting in Jesus Christ, His substitutionary death on the cross on our behalf, that He was buried and rose from the dead bodily on the third day by the power of God, that He defeated death and the grave, that He appeared to many over many days, and ascended to Heaven – and that He is coming back…and that In-Him we pass from death to life, that our sins are washed in His blood, that we have been redeemed, justified, and forgiven… Saved by the Blood of the Lamb of God. Jesus Messiah.

That is what we believe unto salvation. Jesus is whom we trust.

Category: Personal Prayer life, Communing with Christ

As believers and people who are familiar with the Bible, we know that we are instructed and welcomed to spend quality time in prayer with the Lord. It is modeled for us. It is a vital part of the Christ-following journey. Let's look at a few key passages (CSB):

Ephesians 6:16-19

[16] In every situation take up the shield of faith with which you can extinguish all the flaming arrows of

the evil one. [17] Take the helmet of salvation and the sword of the Spirit—which is the word of God. [18] **Pray at all times in the Spirit with every prayer and request, and stay alert with all perseverance and intercession for all the saints.** [19] Pray also for me, that the message may be given to me when I open my mouth to make known with boldness the mystery of the gospel.

Note: Notice how Prayer instruction comes immediately after the "put on the full armor of God" passage for spiritual warfare! Prayer is a mighty weapon for the world of spiritual warfare, and cannot be neglected.

Philippians 4:6-7

[6] Don't worry about anything, but in everything, **through prayer and petition with thanksgiving, present your requests to God.** [7] And the peace of God, which surpasses all understanding, will guard your hearts and minds in Christ Jesus.

Luke 5:16 (Jesus modeled prayer to the Father)

[15] But the news about him spread even more, and large crowds would come together to hear him and to be healed of their sicknesses. [16] **Yet he often withdrew to deserted places and prayed.**

Matthew 6:5-8

[5] "Whenever you pray, you must not be like the hypocrites, because they love to pray standing in the synagogues and on the street corners to be

seen by people. Truly I tell you, they have their reward. **⁶ But when you pray, go into your private room, shut your door, and pray to your Father who is in secret. And your Father who sees in secret will reward you.** ⁷ When you pray, don't babble like the Gentiles, since they imagine they'll be heard for their many words. ⁸ Don't be like them, because **your Father knows the things you need before you ask him.**

James 5:13

¹³ Is anyone among you suffering? **He should pray.** Is anyone cheerful? **He should sing praises.** ¹⁴ Is anyone among you sick? He should call for the elders of the church, **and they are to pray over him,** anointing him with oil in the name of the Lord.

Category: Kingdom Focused, Biblical Worldview

An article by Barna Group titled *Competing Worldviews Influence Today's Christians*, published May 9, 2017, revealed what most of us reading this book already know: that Kingdom-focus and a Biblical worldview is being attacked and eroded by a multitude of factors. At the time of this writing you can find the article at their website, and I would recommend it: **barna.com/research/competing-worldviews-influence-todays-christians/**

The article discusses the infiltration of non-Biblical worldview perspectives into the minds of professing Christians: *New Spirituality, postmodernist views, ideas associated with Marxism, ideas based on secularism.*

After several attempts I could not keep from writing a lengthy chapter or a whole book on this topic! (Maybe that will come later). For the sake of keeping this short and concise – following is a quick summary and three scripture passages for illustration:

We know that in order to be a strong and effective disciple of the Lord Jesus we need:

Biblical Worldview (summary)

- that the Bible is the Authoritative Word of God, and is the source of Truth.
- test all things through Scripture
- that Jesus is the Son of God, the second person of the Trinity – that Jesus is God in the Flesh
- that Jesus is the Way, the Truth, and the Life, and that no one comes to the Father except through Him
- that we are saved by Grace, through faith in the Lord Jesus Christ only
- That Jesus was born of a virgin by the power of God, that He lived a sinless life, that He died a substitutionary death on the cross for those who would believe, that He was buried, and bodily rose from the dead on the third day in defeat of sin and death, that He appeared to many believers, that He ascended to Heaven, that He is living and active, acting as our advocate, and that He will return someday to set up His

Kingdom, will judge all of mankind, ruling for eternity with believers in His presence, and non-believers eternally separated from His presence.

- That disciples here on earth are commanded to trust in Him, receive His love, and to share the gospel of Jesus to our families, communities, and the world in order to bring as many as possible into God's Kingdom.
- See the world through the lens of Scripture

Kingdom Focus

- Understanding that disciples of Jesus are citizens of God's Kingdom
- Desire to follow God's plan for His Kingdom
- Follow God's leading in your life to bear fruit for the Kingdom
- Hunger to see God's Kingdom flourish
- Aligning our life, lifestyle, actions, hobbies, thoughts, and professions to God's Kingdom

John 18:36-37 (CSB)

36 "**My kingdom is not of this world**," said Jesus. "If my kingdom were of this world, my servants would fight, so that I wouldn't be handed over to the Jews. But as it is, my kingdom is not from here." **37** "You are a king then?" Pilate asked. "**You say that I'm a king**," Jesus replied. "**I was born for this, and I have come into the world for this: to testify to the truth. Everyone who is of the truth listens to my voice.**"

Ephesians 2:17-21 (CSB)

> **17** He came and proclaimed the good news of peace to you who were far away and peace to those who were near. **18** For through him we both have access in one Spirit to the Father. **19** So, then, **you are no longer foreigners and strangers, but fellow citizens with the saints, and members of God's household**, **20** built on the foundation of the apostles and prophets, with Christ Jesus himself as the cornerstone.

Luke 4:43 (CSB)

> **43** But he said to them, "It is necessary for me to proclaim the **good news about the kingdom of God** to the other towns also, **because I was sent for this purpose.**

Category: Personal Relationship with Christ Jesus

You have probably heard "Relationship, Not Religion" stated by someone, somewhere. The premise is this: Christianity is NOT about having a *religion*… Christianity is about having a *Relationship* with the one true living God and Savior, Jesus Christ.

I totally agree.

How many people have you known in your life ... and maybe it's you, or has been you in the past... who practice *religion* (they go to a church service or synagogue or a mosque and go through the motions of religious tradition) – but who are empty, hollow regarding their faith and trust in Jesus. They may go to church on occasion to make family members happy (Christmas, Easter), or as a societal-norm to fit into their community, or as a business networking activity – but they don't truly believe in the Bible

> **22 But the fruit of the Spirit is love, joy, peace, patience, kindness, goodness, faithfulness,**
> **23 gentleness, and self-control. The law is not against such things.**
>
> Galatians 5:22-23 CSB

and have a personal relationship of love and trust with Jesus Christ. Do you know someone like that? Is that you? Or a loved one, or friend? Do you see the fruit of the Spirit?

A lack of the fruits of the Spirit showing may be a sign that someone does not have, or is currently distant from, a personal relationship with Jesus. Here are a few Bible verses to consider regarding this topic. (CSB)

Galatians 5:22-23 CSB

> **22** But the fruit of the Spirit is love, joy, peace, patience, kindness, goodness, faithfulness,**23** gentleness, and self-control. The law is not against such things.

1 John 4:16-19

> [16] And we have come to know and to believe the love that God has for us. **God is love, and the one who remains in love remains in God, and God remains in him.** [17] In this, love is made complete with us so that we may have confidence in the day of judgment, because as he is, so also are we in this world. [18] There is no fear in love; instead, perfect love drives out fear, because fear involves punishment. So the one who fears is not complete in love. [19] **We love because he first loved us.**

Even the demons know that Jesus is Lord. But they do not love Him, nor do they have a saving relationship with Him.

James 2:18-19

> [18] But someone will say, "You have faith, and I have works." Show me your faith without works, and I will show you faith by my works. [19] You believe that God is one. Good! Even the demons believe—and they shudder.

Prayer & Relationship

We previously talked about the importance of prayer in a disciple's journey of faith. The question is this: **Can you have a relationship without communication?** Would that work with your spouse, or family, or friends? Not talking or communicating with them is a sign that your relationship is lacking, or non-existent. Thus, a good relationship with the Lord must be grounded in good communication via prayer – as illustrated in the following:

Matthew 6:6 CSB

⁶ But **when you pray, go into your private room, shut your door, and pray to your Father who is in secret.** And your Father who sees in secret will reward you.

Proverbs 8:17 CSB

¹⁷**I love those who love me, and those who search for me find me.**

Jeremiah 29:11-13 CSB

¹¹ For I know the plans I have for you" - this is the LORD's declaration - "plans for your well-being, not for disaster, to give you a future and a hope. ¹² **You will call to me and come and pray to me, and I will listen to you.** ¹³ **You will seek me and find me when you search for me with all your heart.**

Thus, we see the calling to personal relationship with Christ - a crucial component of being His disciple and living the victorious Christian life.

Chapter 29

Method Group

Scriptural Support & Validation

Five categories were grouped into Method:

- Christ is the model
- Spiritual Leader at home
- Spirit Led – Give the day to God
- Community, Fellowship, Small Groups
- Missions & Outreach Minded, Reaching the Lost

Category: Christ is the Model

Like the first category, we as Christians all know this to be true. It's obvious, and we know it is said throughout the Bible. So, let's look at just a few examples, (ESV):

Matthew 16:24-25

> [24] Then Jesus told his disciples, **"If anyone would come after me, let him deny himself and take up his cross and follow me**. [25] For whoever would save his life will lose it, but whoever loses his life for my sake will find it.

John 13:12-17 – Jesus speaking:

¹² When he had washed their feet and put on his outer garments and resumed his place, he said to them, "Do you understand what I have done to you? ¹³ You call me Teacher and Lord, and you are right, for so I am. ¹⁴ If I then, your Lord and Teacher, have washed your feet, you also ought to wash one another's feet. **¹⁵ For I have given you an example, that you also should do just as I have done to you. ¹⁶ Truly, truly, I say to you, a servant is not greater than his master, nor is a messenger greater than the one who sent him.** ¹⁷ If you know these things, blessed are you if you do them.

1 Corinthians 11:1 – Apostle Paul writing:

Be imitators of me, as I am of Christ.

Ephesians 5:1-2 – Apostle Paul writing:

Therefore be imitators of God, as beloved children. ² And walk in love, as Christ loved us and gave himself up for us, a fragrant offering and sacrifice to God.

1 John 2:3-6 – Apostle John writing:

³ And by this we know that we have come to know him, if we keep his commandments. ⁴ Whoever says "I know him" but does not keep his commandments is a liar, and the truth is not in him, ⁵ but whoever keeps his word, in him truly the love of God is perfected. **By this we may know**

that we are in him: ⁶ whoever says he abides in him ought to walk in the same way in which he walked.

1 John 3:15-16 – Apostle John writing:

¹⁵ Everyone who hates his brother is a murderer, and you know that no murderer has eternal life abiding in him. **¹⁶ By this we know love, that he laid down his life for us, and we ought to lay down our lives for the brothers**.

Jesus told us He is the model.
His apostles told us Jesus is the model.

Category: Spiritual Leader in Home

Men and women are equally valuable to God – equally blessed, loved, cherished *imagers* of God – and equally called to share the Gospel of Jesus Christ, to train up and guide our children, and influence our families for Christ. There are some differences in God's plan for the specific *roles* that men and women are called to - the ministry that we are all called to first is in our own home…beginning with us. Being a disciple of Jesus is a very personal thing…an inward thing. We have to have a deep personal relationship with Christ first - *then* we can minister to our family. God's plan in the Bible is not always readily embraced in the modern world and modern human traditions in the western world. Unfortunately, that has caused great problems in our modern society: rampant teen pregnancy, single-parent homes, lack of the God-designed family structure, and all of the problems that come with that – ultimately, societal decay.

If married, God's design is in place with husband, wife, and (possibly) children. Both husband/father and wife/mother are to minister to the family, teach the children, model Christ and Godly values. And, the husband/father is given a very serious responsibility to his wife and family – he is called to be the *spiritual leader* in the home. If not married or single parent homes, then the single mother (and/or father if he is there) has to assume the spiritual leader of the home role. Or, if the father is not a disciple or is not living up to God's expectations for him, then the woman in the home must strengthen and encourage the father to fulfill his duty. And if he is unable or unwilling, then, by default, the wife/mother has to fill that role. Is this view controversial, causing push-back in our modern western culture? Yes. Is it Biblical? Yes, it is – and we will look at scriptural validation shortly.

Please let me reiterate the point for emphasis: men AND women are called to live God-honoring lives, to guide, lead, and teach children in the ways of God, and both are called to serve God as image-bearers of the Lord. In the context of a man's responsibility – he is accountable to God for being the spiritual leader in his home. Far too often the man of the home fails at his role, and his Godly wife must step up and assume leadership. Praise God for faithful women who love the Lord Jesus!

Either way, we must start with our own spiritual condition first - with a solid relationship with Christ - then we can effectively be the Spiritual leader in our family. It is an *inside-to-outside thing* – echoing Jesus' teaching on being *born again* in John chapter three.

If we have a family, then the abundance of Godly love and joy and dedication will spill over into our home and our family. And, even more so when we intentionally pray, are very intentional at spending time in God's Word, teach our families, and ask for God's guidance and blessings.

If there are problems inside us, in our walk with the Lord, then those problems will reduce our effectiveness as ministers of the Gospel to our family and anything else we do. Thus, the *inside-to-outside*. Having struggled with this myself in the past, I can relate and empathize…and also call out and help others to get things right inside first…then God can use you for ministry. Because it does affect our family, and must be dealt with God's way, with His hand of blessing on your family, and other possible ministry efforts.

Let's look at a few verses that support this idea (ESV):

Proverbs 22:6

> **Train up a child in the way he should go**;
> even when he is old he will not depart from it.

Matthew 18:5-6

> [5] **"Whoever receives one such child in my name receives me**, [6] but whoever causes one of these little ones who believe in me to sin, it would be better for him to have a great millstone fastened

around his neck and to be drowned in the depth of the sea.

Regarding men as spiritual leaders in the home. First, it is clear that men and women are equal in God's sight regarding their value and their position as daughters and sons of God in Christ, as we see in Galatians 3:

Galatians 3:28

> [28] There is neither Jew nor Greek, there is neither slave nor free, **there is no male and female, for you are all one in Christ Jesus.**

There are, however, different *roles* seen in God's perfect design, as illustrated and instructed in His Word. Obviously, humans deviate from God's design and create all kinds of problems and variants through human sinfulness and poor choices (sin, lack of faith, lack of obedience to Christ's ways, divorce, marital strife, etc.) Please remember – what we are looking at here… in God's Word… is God's perfect design. (a few examples):

Ephesians 5:22-32

> [22] **Wives, submit to your own husbands, as to the Lord.** [23] **For the husband is the head of the wife even as Christ is the head of the church**, his body, and is himself its Savior. [24] Now as the church submits to Christ, so also wives should submit in everything to their husbands.

> [25] **Husbands, love your wives, as Christ loved the church and gave himself up for her**, [26] that he might sanctify her, having cleansed her by the washing of water with the word, [27] so that he might

present the church to himself in splendor, without spot or wrinkle or any such thing, that she might be holy and without blemish. **²⁸** In the same way **husbands should love their wives as their own bodies.** He who loves his wife loves himself. **²⁹** For no one ever hated his own flesh, but **nourishes and cherishes it, just as Christ does the church, ³⁰** because we are members of his body. **³¹** "Therefore a man shall leave his father and mother and hold fast to his wife, and the two shall become one flesh." **³²** This mystery is profound, and I am saying that it refers to Christ and the church. **³³** However, **let each one of you love his wife as himself, and let the wife see that she respects her husband.**

Colossians 3:18-25

¹⁸ Wives, submit to your husbands, as is fitting in the Lord. ¹⁹ Husbands, love your wives, and do not be harsh with them. ²⁰ Children, obey your parents in everything, for this pleases the Lord. **²¹ Fathers, do not provoke your children, lest they become discouraged. ²²** Bondservants, obey in everything those who are your earthly masters, not by way of eye-service, as people-pleasers, but with sincerity of heart, fearing the Lord. **²³ Whatever you do, work heartily, as for the Lord and not for men, ²⁴ knowing that from the Lord you will receive the inheritance as your reward.** You are serving the Lord Christ. **²⁵** For the wrongdoer will be paid back for the wrong he has done, and there is no partiality.

And, because some might say: "well, that's just Paul's theology…". Here's a similar passage from the Apostle Peter:

1 Peter 3:1-7

Likewise, **wives, be subject to your own husbands, so that even if some do not obey the word, they may be won without a word by the conduct of their wives,** **²** **when they see your respectful and pure conduct.** **³** Do not let your adorning be external—the braiding of hair and the putting on of gold jewelry, or the clothing you wear— **⁴** but let your adorning be the hidden person of the heart with the imperishable beauty of a gentle and quiet spirit, which in God's sight is very precious. **⁵** For this is how the holy women who hoped in God used to adorn themselves, by submitting to their own husbands, **⁶** as Sarah obeyed Abraham, calling him lord. And you are her children, if you do good and do not fear anything that is frightening. **⁷** **Likewise, husbands, live with your wives in an understanding way, showing honor to the woman as the weaker vessel, since they are heirs with you** of the grace of life, so that your prayers may not be hindered.

Obviously, this is a subject that some people struggle to accept. However – please keep these things in mind as you study, pray, and ponder God's Word:

1. It's God's perfect design
2. It's God's perfect Word
3. It calls out men to have greater responsibility and accountability for their spiritual leadership in the home. They are accountable to God to be understanding, obedient, faithful, gentle, loving, Godly husbands and fathers. It is a big calling and responsibility. It is an important ministry!
4. Likewise, women and mothers are called to important ministries unto the Lord, as well! If a mother, then the eternal impact of a mother's love and nurturing and ministry to the children – and to her husband – is profound in its impact in God's plan.

Category: Spirit Led, Give Day to God

Surrendering the day to God is a very difficult thing to do in practicality - moment by moment. So many distractions, so many things to do…busy, busy. However, for those who have learned to live this way – it is fantastically freeing and empowering, increasing effectiveness and the sense of purpose and joy experienced from the Lord throughout the day. I sensed this surrender, especially, when talking with Karol and Barb during the interviews. In reviewing all of the notes multiple times it was very obvious – but ALL of the disciples interviewed talked about "giving it to God", "following the Holy Spirit's lead", "God burdening our hearts to do something", "following God's plan", etc. – Ultimately, giving the day to God and following the Spirit. Let's look at a few verses that illustrate this point (CSB):

John 16:7-14

> **7** Nevertheless, I am telling you the truth. It is for your benefit that I go away, because if I don't go away the **Counselor** will not come to you. If I go, I will send him to you. **8 When he comes, he will convict the world about sin, righteousness, and judgment: 9** About sin, because they do not believe in me; **10** about righteousness, because I am going to the Father and you will no longer see me; **11** and about judgment, because the ruler of this world has been judged. **12** "I still have many things to tell you, but you can't bear them

now. ¹³ **When the Spirit of truth comes, he will guide you into all the truth. For he will not speak on his own, but he will speak whatever he hears. He will also declare to you what is to come.** ¹⁴ **He will glorify me, because he will take from what is mine and declare it to you.**

John 14:15-17, 26

¹⁵ "If you love me, you will keep my commands. ¹⁶ And I will ask the Father, and he will give you another Counselor to be with you forever. ¹⁷ He is the **Spirit of truth. The world is unable to receive him because it doesn't see him** or know him. **But you do know him, because he remains with you and will be in you.**

²⁶ But the **Counselor, the Holy Spirit, whom the Father will send in my name, will teach you all things and remind you of everything** I have told you.

John 15:26

²⁶ "When the **Counselor comes, the one I will send to you from the Father —the Spirit of truth who proceeds from the Father**—he will testify about me. ²⁷ You also will testify, because you have been with me from the beginning.

Romans 8:12-17 (The Holy Spirit's Ministries)

[12] So then, brothers and sisters, we are not obligated to the flesh to live according to the flesh, [13] because if you live according to the flesh, you are going to die. **But if by the Spirit you put to death the deeds of the body, you will live. [14] For all those led by God's Spirit are God's sons.** [15] For you did not receive a spirit of slavery to fall back into fear. Instead, you received the Spirit of adoption, by whom we cry out, *"Abba,* Father!" [16] **The Spirit himself testifies together with our spirit that we are God's children,** [17] and if children, also heirs—heirs of God and coheirs with Christ—if indeed we suffer with him so that we may also be glorified with him.

It is obvious from Scripture that Jesus told us that the Holy Spirit would come (Acts 2 – Pentecost) - and that the Holy Spirit (also referred to as the "Counselor", the "Spirit of Truth", and the "Spirit of Christ") would indwell the believers, instruct the believers, bring conviction of sin, guide the believers, and testify.

Following the lead of the Holy Spirit of God is a vitally important part of the victorious Christian life of a disciple.

Category: Community, Fellowship, Small Groups

One of the classes I teach at church in my role as Connections Director is titled: *CONNECT – Doing Life in Christian Community.* Creative title, right? Well, maybe not...but the title is perfect for the topic at hand!

Can you be a Christ-following disciple alone? For example, you are stuck on a deserted island after a plane crash, all alone with only a volleyball for a friend... and a Bible washes up on shore. Over some months you read through it, believe it, pray to God and accept the free offer of God's grace in Jesus Christ – you trust in Christ – and you are saved, born-again by the Holy Spirit! But you are still alone on the deserted island... can you be a Christ follower, a disciple?

The answer is, of course, yes! But now you have to do the Christian journey alone in the desert, except that you have the Lord with you, the Holy Spirit indwelling you, and you have the scriptures (something many believers around the world and throughout history have *not* had!) The Spirit can minister to you, guide you...and you can spend time in the Word...but you will miss out on the blessings of Christian fellowship, brotherly-sisterly love, having a mentor...

Let's look at some scripture to see the instruction and blessings of being in fellowship and community (NASB):

1 Thessalonians 5:11

[11] Therefore, **encourage one another and build one another up**, just as you also are doing. [12] But we ask you, brothers *and sisters*, to **recognize those who diligently labor among you and are in leadership over you in the Lord, and give you instruction**, [13] and that you regard them very highly in love because of their work. Live in peace with one another.

Hebrews 10:24-25

[24] and let's consider **how to encourage one another in love and good deeds**, [25] **not abandoning our own meeting together, as is the habit of some people, but encouraging** *one another*; and all the more as you see the day drawing near.

Ecclesiastes 4:9-12

[9] **Two are better than one** because they have a good return for their labor; [10] for if either of them falls, **the one will lift up his companion.** But **woe to the one who falls when there is not another** to lift him up! [11] Furthermore, if two lie down together they keep warm, but how can one be warm *alone*? [12] And if one can overpower him who is alone, two can resist him. **A cord of three *strands* is not quickly torn apart.**

Proverbs 27:17

> *As* iron sharpens iron,
> So one person sharpens another.

Matthew 18:20

> [19] "Again I say to you, that if two of you agree on earth about anything that they may ask, it shall be done for them by My Father who is in heaven. [20] **For where two or three have gathered together in My name, I am there in their midst.**"

Acts 2:42-43

> [42] **They were continually devoting themselves to the apostles' teaching and to fellowship**, to the breaking of bread and to prayer. [43] Everyone kept feeling a sense of awe; and many wonders and signs were taking place through the apostles.

As we can see from scripture, meeting together as the body of Christ is strongly encouraged and modeled for us. We could be a disciple on a desert island with a volleyball, but it is much better in fellowship with our brothers and sisters!

Category: Missions & Outreach Minded, Reaching the Lost

My favorite sign over a church exit door:

You Are Now Entering The Mission Field

We were not called to sit around in complacency and form a Christian Country Club. We believers, Christ-following disciples, were commanded by Jesus to **"Go"**:

Matthew 28:18-20 ESV

[18] And Jesus came and said to them, "All authority in heaven and on earth has been given to me. [19] **Go therefore and make disciples of all nations, baptizing them in the name of the Father and of the Son and of the Holy Spirit,** [20] **teaching them to observe all that I have commanded you.** And behold, I am with you always, to the end of the age."

Other passages with this same message are scattered throughout the New Testament:

John 20:21 (ESV)

[19] On the evening of that day, the first day of the week, the doors being locked where the disciples were for fear of the Jews, Jesus came and stood among them and said to them, "Peace be with you." [20] When he had said this, he showed them his hands and his side. Then the disciples were glad when they saw the Lord. [21] Jesus said to them again, **"Peace be with you. As the Father has sent me, even so I am sending you."**

Matthew 9:37-38 (ESV)

[36] When he saw the crowds, he had compassion for them, because they were harassed and helpless, like sheep without a shepherd. [37] **Then he said to his disciples, "The harvest is plentiful, but the laborers are few; [38] therefore pray earnestly to the Lord of the harvest to send out laborers into his harvest."**

Acts 1:8 (ESV)

[8] But you will receive power when the Holy Spirit has come upon you, **and you will be my witnesses in Jerusalem and in all Judea and Samaria, and to the end of the earth."** [9] And when he had said these things, as they were looking on, he was lifted up, and a cloud took him out of their sight.

Luke 24:46-47 (ESV)

44 Then he said to them, "These are my words that I spoke to you while I was still with you, that everything written about me in the Law of Moses and the Prophets and the Psalms must be fulfilled." **45** Then he opened their minds to understand the Scriptures, **46** and said to them, "Thus it is written, that the Christ should suffer and on the third day rise from the dead, **47 and that repentance for the forgiveness of sins should be proclaimed in his name to all nations, beginning from Jerusalem. 48 You are witnesses of these things.**

Romans 10:15 (ESV)

14 How then will they call on him in whom they have not believed? And how are they to believe in him of whom they have never heard? And how are they to hear without someone preaching? **15** And how are they to preach unless they are sent? As it is written, **"How beautiful are the feet of those who preach the good news!"**

Scripture is clear: GO! proclaim the Gospel. GO! Share the Good News. GO! Make disciples.

Being Missions & Outreach Minded is Our Purpose. Reaching the Lost is our Goal

---

DISCIPLE-ing

Chapter 30

Expression Group

Scriptural Support & Validation

Five categories were grouped into Expression:

- Loving God, Loving Others
- Leading by Example, Shine the Light
- BOLD Disciple – engaging others with the Gospel
- Discipling Others, Being Discipled
- Christ-Like Leadership, Engaging Culture in Profession

Category: Loving God, Loving Others

Anyone who grew up around church or is familiar with the Bible will know this principle exists - It is found throughout the New Testament teachings. As well, Jesus was quoting from Old Testament scriptures when he answered the question in Matthew 22:34-40 (ESV) in what we know as *The Great Commandment*, Jesus answering:

> [34] But when the Pharisees heard that he had silenced the Sadducees, they gathered together. [35] And one of them, a lawyer, asked him a question to test him. [36] "Teacher, which is the great

commandment in the Law?" **³⁷** And he said to him, **"You shall love the Lord your God with all your heart and with all your soul and with all your mind.** **³⁸** **This is the great and first commandment.** **³⁹** **And a second is like it: You shall love your neighbor as yourself.** **⁴⁰** On these two commandments depend all the Law and the Prophets." (Matthew 22:34-40 ESV)

This same teaching is recorded in Mark 12:28–34 as:

²⁸ And one of the scribes came up and heard them disputing with one another, and seeing that he answered them well, asked him, "Which commandment is the most important of all?" **²⁹** **Jesus answered, "The most important is, 'Hear, O Israel: The Lord our God, the Lord is one.** **³⁰** **And you shall love the Lord your God with all your heart and with all your soul and with all your mind and with all your strength.'** **³¹** **The second is this: 'You shall love your neighbor as yourself.' There is no other commandment greater than these."** **³²** And the scribe said to him, "You are right, Teacher. You have truly said that he is one, and there is no other besides him. **³³** And to love him with all the heart and with all the understanding and with all the strength, and to love one's neighbor as oneself, is much more than all whole burnt offerings and sacrifices." **³⁴** And when Jesus saw that he answered wisely, he said to him, "You are not far from the kingdom of God." And after that no one dared to ask him any more questions. (Mark 12:28–34 ESV)

And the teaching is also recorded in Luke 10:2-28 (ESV), which is either a separate event – or, with a slightly different perspective – focusing more on the <u>response of the lawyer in verse 27</u>, who was testing Jesus:

> **25** And behold, a lawyer stood up to put him to the test, saying, "Teacher, what shall I do to inherit eternal life?" **26 He said to him, "What is written in the Law? How do you read it?" 27 And he answered, "You shall love the Lord your God with all your heart and with all your soul and with all your strength and with all your mind, and your neighbor as yourself." 28 And he said to him, "You have answered correctly; do this, and you will live."**

> **29** But he, desiring to justify himself, said to Jesus, "And who is my neighbor?"   (after which Jesus tells him and the crowd the *Parable of the Good Samaritan*)

Jesus was answering their questions quoting from the Old Testament Hebrew scriptures, (the Torah / Tanakh) in two parts:

Part 1: "The most important" from the Mark 12 passage:

> **29 Jesus answered, "The most important is, 'Hear, O Israel: The Lord our God, the Lord is one. 30 And you shall love the Lord your God with all your heart and with all your soul and with all your mind and with all your strength.'**

Jesus quoted from the Shema confession that the Jews all knew well, from Deuteronomy 6:4-5 (ESV)

⁴ "Hear, O Israel: The LORD our God, the LORD is one. ⁵ You shall love the LORD your God with all your heart and with all your soul and with all your might.

Part 2: Second part from the Mark 12 passage:

³¹ The second is this: 'You shall love your neighbor as yourself.' There is no other commandment greater than these."

Jesus quoted from Leviticus 19:18 (ESV)

¹⁸ You shall not take vengeance or bear a grudge against the sons of your own people, **but you shall love your neighbor as yourself**: I am the LORD.

Thus, we have easy scriptural validation for this category: *Love God, Love Others*

...from Jesus' own words

Category: **Lead by Example, Shine the Light**

The interviews illustrated Christ-followers who led in their families, their churches, their communities, their jobs, businesses, and careers. They talked about "shining a light into dark places" and "having an impact on their co-workers". Let's look at scriptures that point to these attributes of a disciple of the Lord (ESV)

Matthew 5:14-16

> [14] "You are the light of the world. A city set on a hill cannot be hidden. [15] Nor do people light a lamp and put it under a basket, but on a stand, and it gives light to all in the house. [16] In the same way, **let your light shine before others, so that they may see your good works and give glory to your Father who is in heaven.**

1 Peter 2:9

> [9] But you are a chosen race, **a royal priesthood**, a holy nation, a people for his own possession, that you may proclaim the excellencies of him who **called you out of darkness into his marvelous light**.

1 Peter 5:1-3

> So I exhort the elders among you, as a fellow elder and a witness of the sufferings of Christ, as well as a partaker in the glory that is going to be revealed: [2] **shepherd the flock of God that is among you, exercising oversight, not under compulsion, but willingly, as God would have**

you; not for shameful gain, but eagerly; [3] not domineering over those in your charge, but being examples to the flock.

Hebrews 13:7

Remember your leaders, those who spoke to you the word of God. **Consider the outcome of their way of life, and imitate their faith.**

Titus 2:1-8

But as for you, **teach what accords with sound doctrine.** [2] Older men are to be **sober-minded, dignified, self-controlled, sound in faith, in love, and in steadfastness.** [3] Older women likewise are to **be reverent in behavior, not slanderers or slaves to much wine.** They are to teach what is good, [4] and so train the young women to love their husbands and children, [5] to be self-controlled, pure, working at home, kind, and submissive to their own husbands, that the word of God may not be reviled. [6] Likewise, urge the younger men to be self-controlled. [7] **Show yourself in all respects to be a model of good works, and in your teaching show integrity, dignity,** [8] **and sound speech that cannot be condemned, so that an opponent may be put to shame, having nothing evil to say about us.**

Lead by example and Shining our light are clearly scriptural concepts.

Category: BOLD Disciple, Engaging Others with the Gospel

If you are a disciple of Jesus Christ, you are called to shine your light and share the Good News of the Gospel. If we have friends and family who do not know the Lord, who have not humbled themselves, repented of their sin and turned to God, placing their faith and trust in the atoning work of Jesus Christ on the cross... they are lost. If they die, they will spend eternity separated from God (and us).

I am not saying this lightly, or dismissively.... I have friends who do not know the Lord Jesus. I have family members who do not know the Lord Jesus. I have neighbors and co-workers who do not know the Lord. They have turned away from or resist the one-true God, from the one-true Gospel, from the one-true Savior... they reject the Gospel. And it breaks my heart...and I'm sure it breaks yours as well. THAT is why we must be BOLD! That is why we must do everything we can to engage others with the Gospel – out of love, with patience, with gentleness. But BOLDLY!

In the interviews, there were many different *styles* of evangelism outreach expressed:

- The soft, gentle, warmth of friendship, love, and caring style
- The inviting others to a dinner party, concert, church event, Bible study, etc. style
- The intellectual style
- The passionate "can I tell you my story of how God saved me?" approach

- The "serve others in desperate need, show them the love of Christ through action" style
- The "how can I pray for you?" conversational style
- The BOLD, Direct "do you know the Lord Jesus Christ as your personal Savior?" style

The word "BOLD" as defined by *dictionary.com* as:

bold

Adjective

1. Not hesitating or fearful in the face of actual or possible danger or rebuff; courageous and daring: *a bold hero*
2. Not hesitating to break the rules of propriety; forward; impudent: *He apologized for being so bold as to speak to the emperor.*
3. Necessitating courage and daring; challenging: *a bold adventure*
4. Beyond the usual limits of conventional thought or action; imaginative: *Einstein was a bold mathematician.*
5. Striking or conspicuous to the eye; flashy; showy: *a bold pattern*
6. Steep; abrupt: *A bold promontory*

Being *Bold* could be jumping up and down, screaming… though, that probably is not the correct approach in most situations. Or like the incredibly BOLD sermon by the disciple Stephen to Sanhedrin in Acts chapter 7 that infuriated the leaders to the point of having him stoned to death! That was BOLD! But, being a *Bold* disciple could be just overcoming your fear of rejection and a fear of damaging a relationship - by praying for courage and guidance, stepping out of your comfort zone and asking a friend "You seem troubled...can I pray for you?" And, if possible, praying over your friend out-loud, hand on their shoulder - that takes boldness! Getting out of your own way, and allowing the Holy Spirit to move through you into someone else's life. That's bold.

Let's look at a few key verses, (ESV):

Matthew 28:18-20 - known as *The Great Commission*

> **18** And Jesus came and said to them, "All authority in heaven and on earth has been given to me. **19 Go therefore and make disciples of all nations, baptizing them in the name of the Father and of the Son and of the Holy Spirit, 20 teaching them to observe all that I have commanded you.** And behold, I am with you always, to the end of the age."

Note: This does *not* say: "**to all those with the gift of evangelism, go therefore and make disciples...**" This command was given to all of the disciples when Jesus ascended. And I would also tell you that it is applicable to ALL disciples of Jesus Christ – regardless of your spiritual gifts. We can ALL use our own style, with our own personality and behavioral temperament, within our own circle of family, friends, and co-workers to witness in a way that is *bold* for us...just a little out of our comfort zone. Asking to pray for them… inviting them… being a friend, being present, caring, nurturing, telling them you will pray for them, giving them a Gospel of John booklet, writing them a Christ-honoring Christmas card, etc.

Acts 14:1-7 Paul and Barnabas at Iconium

¹Now at Iconium they entered together into the Jewish synagogue and **spoke in such a way that a great number of both Jews and Greeks believed.** ² But the unbelieving Jews stirred up the Gentiles and poisoned their minds against the brothers. ³ **So they remained for a long time, speaking boldly for the Lord, who bore witness to the word of his grace**, granting signs and wonders to be done by their hands. ⁴ But the people of the city were divided; some sided with the Jews and some with the apostles. ⁵ When an attempt was made by both Gentiles and Jews, with their rulers, to mistreat them and to stone them, ⁶ they learned of it and fled to Lystra and Derbe, cities of Lycaonia, and to the surrounding country, ⁷ **and there they continued to preach the gospel.**

1 Peter 3:15

¹⁵ but in your hearts regard Christ the Lord as holy, **ready at any time to give a defense to anyone who asks you for a reason for the hope that is in you**.

Psalm 96:3

Declare his glory among the nations, his marvelous works among all the peoples!

Mark 16:15

¹⁵ And he said to them, "Go into all the world and proclaim the gospel to the whole creation.

Romans 10:14-17

¹⁴ How then will they call on him in whom they have not believed? And how are they to believe in him of whom they have never heard? And how are they to hear without someone preaching? ¹⁵And how are they to preach unless they are sent? As it is written, **"How beautiful are the feet of those who preach the good news!"** ¹⁶ But they have not all obeyed the gospel. For Isaiah says, "Lord, who has believed what he has heard from us?" **¹⁷ So faith comes from hearing, and hearing through the word of Christ.**

The Lord has blessed me with the great joy and opportunity to be a bi-vocational Minister of the Gospel as the *Connections Director* at my church (and working towards ordination as a Pastor). I also am a professional Business Sales & Leadership Coach, and busines speaker. As a coach, one of the main hurdles my clients struggle with is fear. Yes, FEAR. And poor mental toughness, or self-talk…and confidence problems. These are successful business people across the country. Many are *very* successful, but they still struggle with confidence, self-talk,

and fear. Helping them get out of their comfort zones....
"getting comfortable being uncomfortable" - that is how
people grow. Growth happens OUTSIDE of your comfort
zone.

Understanding your identity in Christ is very important to increasing your boldness as a disciple in sharing the gospel, in offering to pray...to inviting someone to a Bible study.

If you are *in Christ Jesus*... then you are Saved, Sanctified, Justified, Forgiven, and Free from condemnation! You are a child of God, you are loved! No one can snatch you from your Father's hand. Your name is written in the Lamb's book of life. You are free. You are saved!

> "being a *Bold* disciple could be just overcoming your fear of rejection and a fear of damaging a relationship by praying for courage and guidance, stepping out of your comfort zone and asking a friend "You seem troubled...can I pray for you?"

Do you want that for your friends? Your family? Is getting a little uncomfortable worth being used by God to gently, lovingly share the love of God to them? Maybe they will accept the free gift of Jesus... maybe they will reject it... but you tried.

That is what being BOLD is about.

Doing what you can do...and praying that God do the rest.

Category: Personal Prayer life, Communing with Christ

As believers and people who are familiar with the Bible, we know that we are instructed and welcomed to spend quality time in prayer with the Lord. It is modeled for us. It is a vital part of the Christ-following journey. It's how we grow in and maintain relationship with the Lord. Let's look at a few key passages (CSB):

Ephesians 6:16-19

> **16** In every situation take up the shield of faith with which you can extinguish all the flaming arrows of the evil one. **17** Take the helmet of salvation and the sword of the Spirit—which is the word of God. **18 Pray at all times in the Spirit with every prayer and request, and stay alert with all perseverance and intercession for all the saints.** **19** Pray also for me, that the message may be given to me when I open my mouth to make known with boldness the mystery of the gospel.

Note: Notice how prayer instruction comes immediately after the "put on the full armor of God" passage for spiritual warfare! Prayer is the mighty weapon for the world of spiritual warfare, and cannot be neglected!

Philippians 4:6-7

> **6** Don't worry about anything, but in everything, **through prayer and petition with thanksgiving, present your requests to God.** **7** And the peace of

God, which surpasses all understanding, will guard your hearts and minds in Christ Jesus.

Luke 5:16 (Jesus modeled prayer to the Father)

> [15] But the news about him spread even more, and large crowds would come together to hear him and to be healed of their sicknesses. [16] **Yet he often withdrew to deserted places and prayed.**

Matthew 6:5-8

> [5] "Whenever you pray, you must not be like the hypocrites, because they love to pray standing in the synagogues and on the street corners to be seen by people. Truly I tell you, they have their reward. [6] **But when you pray, go into your private room, shut your door, and pray to your Father who is in secret. And your Father who sees in secret will reward you.** [7] When you pray, don't babble like the Gentiles, since they imagine they'll be heard for their many words. [8] Don't be like them, because **your Father knows the things you need before you ask him.**

James 5:13

> [13] Is anyone among you suffering? **He should pray.** Is anyone cheerful? **He should sing praises.** [14] Is anyone among you sick? He should call for the elders of the church, **and they are to pray over him,** anointing him with oil in the name of the Lord.

Category: Discipling Others, Being Discipled

This book is about Being a Disciple and Making Disciples. This category has a *nuance* – the importance of *Being Discipled by others* – having a mentor. We saw many of the interviews discuss the importance of have a mentor in your Christian walk…to help you navigate the journey, and hopefully avoid pitfalls. Kyle, Jeff, and Devon were very passionate in talking about the importance of being mentored, being discipled their journey by other Christ-followers who were solid in the Word and in their faith. Obviously, we see that model very prevalent in the work place. Senior leading Junior, helping them grow.

Devon and Jeff both talked about the *Paul-Timothy-Barnabas* model where everyone needs to (1) have a mentor; (2) have a peer-mentor; (3) be mentoring someone else. There is no question that this model of discipleship works – both in our Christian journey, and also in our professional career journeys. Let's look here at a few scripture passages (CSB):

John 14:25-26

> **25** "I have spoken these things to you while I remain with you. **26 But the Counselor, the Holy Spirit, whom the Father will send in my name, will teach you all things and remind you of everything I have told you.**

It is important to remember that our #1 Mentor is:
The Holy Spirit

Proverbs 27:17 (ESV)

Iron sharpens iron, and one man sharpens another

Titus 2:1 -3-5 (CSB)

But you are to proclaim things consistent with sound teaching. **² Older men are to be self-controlled, worthy of respect, sensible, and sound in faith, love, and endurance.** ³ In the same way, **older women** are to be reverent in behavior, not slanderers, not slaves to excessive drinking. **They are to teach what is good, ⁴ so that they may encourage the young women to love their husbands and to love their children,** ⁵ to be self-controlled, pure, workers at home, kind, and in submission to their husbands, so that God's word will not be slandered.

Proverbs 22:6 (CSB)

Start a youth out on his way;
even when he grows old he will not depart from it.

2 timothy 2:2 (CSB)

You, therefore, my son, be strong in the grace that is in Christ Jesus. **² What you have heard from me in the presence of many witnesses, commit to faithful men who will be able to teach others also**.

Category: Christ-like Leadership, Engaging the Culture in Your Profession

The Apostle Paul worked making tents with Aquila and Priscilla *because he was of the same trade*, and he did the ministry work he was called to do by the Lord on the weekends – Acts 18 ESV: (underline emphasis added)

> **18** After this Paul left Athens and went to Corinth. **²** And he found a Jew named Aquila, a native of Pontus, recently come from Italy with his wife Priscilla, because Claudius had commanded all the Jews to leave Rome. And he went to see them, **³** and because he was of the same trade he stayed with them and worked, for they were tentmakers by trade. **⁴** And he reasoned in the synagogue every Sabbath, and tried to persuade Jews and Greeks.

And in 2 Thessalonians 3 we see Paul warning against idleness, and encouraging people to work hard for their provisions (and not sit around waiting for Jesus to come back): 2 Thessalonians 3:7-8 ESV:

> **⁷** For you yourselves know how you ought to imitate us, because we were not idle when we were with you, **⁸** nor did we eat anyone's bread without paying for it, but with toil and labor we worked night and day, that we might not be a burden to any of you.

We know from the New Testament writings that Paul was a diligent worker. And throughout we see strong leadership attributes, persistence, work ethic, and passion to serve the Lord. And he had a deep understanding of his mission – the apostle to the Gentiles, to bring the people back to God - despite the danger, despite the risks. He lived outside his comfort zone! He was completely on a mission to fulfill his calling by God – no matter the costs, no matter the peril. Led by a personal encounter with Jesus Christ and empowered by the Holy Spirit, the Apostle Paul had full-blown, all-in Biblical Worldview and Kingdom focus!

Questions for us to ponder

When Paul was making tents or other activity... do you think his passion and enthusiasm for the Lord Jesus overflowed into his conversations with people?

Do you think they came to know that he was a disciple of Jesus?

Do you think he shared the Gospel with them?

Do you think he prayed for the Lord to guide him into conversations with people?

Do you think he was ever out of his comfort zone?

Do you think he was ever told he was wrong?

Christian Leadership in Business

There are many examples of Christ-honoring businesses in the marketplace. Some are very high profile that we hear about, usually from anti-God, anti-Christ organizations complaining about their faith-centric approach to doing business (i.e. *Chik-fil-A, Hobby Lobby*). Their businesses were founded on and run according to Christian principles, and they unashamedly professed Biblical Worldview and faith in Jesus Christ – and were greatly blessed.

There are many other businesses scattered around the world that are not as well-known publicly, but whom are wonderful businesses run by Christian disciples, honoring God with their business and their lives. And God blesses that. My friend and past college roommate and fraternity brother, Scott Beck and his family are a perfect example of that. Knowing Scott and his father for 35 years now, and living in close proximity to their business I can tell you… they walk the talk. That is their reputation… and they live up to that standard. Like all people, they are not perfect either…but there is a sincerity and depth of character and faith that is pervasive in that organization, and God has blessed their business over the generations.

The interview with Scott Beck was very helpful, and I especially liked Scott's response regarding Biblical Leadership:

Question: what are the main Biblical leadership principles that God's Word has presented to you?

That breaks down into three main categories: *Humility, Servant Leadership*, and *Direction.*

Humility – God is opposed to the proud, but gives grace to the humble. Hebrews says: "Let us come boldly to the throne of grace that we may obtain mercy and find grace to help in the time of need."

Servant Leadership – Leaders don't lord over their people. They work along with them and support them with the tools, training, and encouragement to do their work.

Direction – Clarity of communication. "Without vision, the people perish" (Proverbs 29:18). People need direction and purpose and to know that their work is meaningful and that their values align with mine.

Proverbs 16:3 ESV

> Commit your work to the LORD,
> and your plans will be established

Colossians 3:23-24 ESV

> [23] Whatever you do, work heartily, as for the Lord and not for men, [24] knowing that from the Lord you will receive the inheritance as your reward. You are serving the Lord Christ.

Chapter 31

The DISCIPLE-ing Matrix

There are many words that could be used to express the shape that came from this study: *model, flow-chart, table, array, grid, source*...but the one that stuck was *Matrix*. In mathematics, it usually has a rectangular arrangement of rows and columns. In the biological sciences it implies that in which other things are imbedded into. A general definition designates it as: *something within or from which something else originates, develops, or takes form* (source: Merriam-Webster.com).

This seemed to be the best choice: *DISCIPLE-ing Matrix*

It is a visual correlation of the interconnectedness of

God – the Father, the Son, the Holy Spirit

Belief and Trust in the LORD

Relationship with the LORD

The Fruits of the Spirit

Being a disciple of the LORD, Jesus Christ

Making disciples of the LORD, Jesus Christ

The 15 Categories Identified in the Interviews

Author's Conclusions

Twenty years ago, I became a disciple of Jesus Christ - beginning November 19, 2000. Jesus has completely transformed me – how I think, react, love, give, say, what I do, and what is important in my life. I praise Him for that, and give Him all the glory and honor and praise!

Working on this book project over the last two years has been a great joy, with incredible discussions with amazing people – disciples of the Lord Jesus, and much learning, Bible study, research, and hundreds of hours of writing.

Over the last twenty years of growing as a disciple I have read the Bible many, many times. I spent three years earning a *Master of Ministry in Pastoral Ministry* degree, reading what seemed like hundreds of books, and writing thousands of papers (an exaggeration, but that's what I felt like). My bookshelves are filled with books on evangelism, theology, apologetics, discipleship, and church growth. Yet, I wanted to better understand the Biblical model of being a disciple of Jesus and bringing others to Christ, making disciples. Thus, this quest... the interviews...this book. After nearly two years of study, evaluation, prayer, and writing - my conclusions and observations follow:

Conclusion #1:

BEING a disciple **and** *MAKING disciples* are *distinctly separate yet totally inseparable actions* by a follower of Jesus Christ. They are interwoven in their essence and expression - you cannot do one without the other. They are functions of each other. Like *being alive and breathing* at the same time. Or, your *heart beating and blood pumping* through your arteries and veins at the same time. You can't make disciples without being a disciple; and, you can't truly be a disciple without discipling others through your example and witness, because that's what disciples *do*...or at least, that's what they *are supposed to do*. A better way to state it might be this:

Conclusion #1

We cannot properly fulfill our God-given *purpose* as a disciple if we are not actively engaged in the process of making disciples.

It may seem like common sense... or a simple truth. Or, you might disagree with the statement. Thus, let's look deeper:

Ephesians 2:8-10 (ESV) (bold emphasis added)

> [8] For by grace you have been saved through faith. And this is not your own doing; it is the gift of God, [9] not a result of works, so that no one may boast. [10] For we are his workmanship, **created in Christ Jesus for good works, which God prepared beforehand, that we should walk in them.**

This passage is most likely very familiar to those reading this book. In breaking it down deeper, we can see the component parts as:

1. We were created in Christ Jesus for good works

2. Those good works were *prepared beforehand* by God for us to *walk in them* (to do them)
3. Thus, we have that as a *purpose* as disciples

So, what IS our God-given purpose(s)?

Conclusion #2

We Have *Purpose* as Disciples:

- **Trust in Jesus as Lord** (Jn 3:16-18)
- **Glorify God with our lives** (Mt 5:16)
- **Love God, Love Others** (Mt 22:35-40)
- **Make disciples, baptize, teach**
  (Mt 28:19-20)
- **Seek to fulfill the good works that God has prepared** (Eph 2:8-10)
- **Abide/Remain in Jesus** (Jn 8:31-82)

In thinking through the various interviews, Bible verses that have been discussed, and through much prayer and study and reflection during this time, I surmised that list of items that would make up the **Purpose** that all disciples are called to live out. There are probably additional ones that are not mentioned, but this seems to comprise a good description of what we are instructed and encouraged to do. **Think about this list...read the verses. How does it speak to you? In the next short chapter, you will be** asked to identify an *Action Plan* for you to pray about and implement in your journey of DISCIPLE-ing.

The third conclusion came about immediately after a prayer where I called out to the Lord: *"Oh, Lord...15 categories, 50 pages... please help me break this down!"* Literally, within five minutes this happened:

Foundation	Method	Expression
Bible Study - the Word of God	Christ is the model	Loving God, Loving Others
Trusting God's promises	Spiritual leader at home	Leading by example, Shine the Light
Personal Prayer life, Communing with Christ	Spirit Led – Give the day to God	BOLD Disciple – engaging others with the Gospel
Kingdom focused, Biblical Worldview	Community, Fellowship, Small Groups	Discipling Others, Being Discipled
Personal relationship with Christ	Missions & Outreach Minded, Reaching the Lost	Christ-Like Leadership, Engaging Culture in Profession

After praying I started looking for any pattern... and there it was. It literally jumped off the page at me. Here's what it means:

Foundation: These categories related to *foundational* beliefs or practices of a disciple that make for a strong foundation of their Christian life and journey.

1. Bible Study – the Word of God
2. Trusting God's promises
3. Personal Prayer life, Communing with Christ
4. Kingdom focused, Biblical Worldview
5. Personal relationship with Christ

Method: These categories related to the *method* with which we approach life, interaction in the world, and live out our daily lives as a disciple. (personal & professional)

1. Christ is the model
2. Spiritual leader at home
3. Spirit Led – Give the day to God
4. Community, Fellowship, Small Groups
5. Missions & Outreach Minded, Reaching the Lost

Expression: These categories related to the expression of how we lived out God's purpose in our lives, and how we shine the light of Jesus to the world in our lives (personal & professional)

1. Loving God, Loving Others
2. Leading by example, Shine the Light
3. BOLD Disciple – engaging others with the Gospel
4. Discipling Others, Being Discipled
5. Christ-Like Leadership, Engaging Culture in our Professions

Conclusion #3

Foundation

Bible Study – the Word of God
Trusting God's promises
Personal Prayer life, Communing with Christ
Kingdom focused, Biblical Worldview
Personal relationship with Christ

Method

Christ is the model
Spiritual leader at home
Spirit Led – Give the day to God
Community, Fellowship, Small Groups
Missions & Outreach Minded, Reaching the Lost

Expression

Loving God, Loving Others
Leading by example, Shine the Light
BOLD Disciple – engaging others with the Gospel
Discipling Others, Being Discipled
Christ-Like Leadership, Engaging Culture in our
Professions

Built on the Love of God in Christ and His substitutionary sacrifice on our behalf, with the Fruits of the Spirit, and the categories identified in this study, following is the visual depiction of the results - the *Disciple-ing Matrix:*

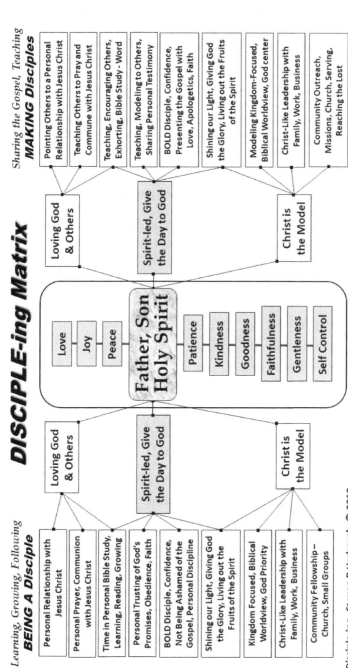

Disciple-ing, Steven R Harbaugh © 2019

Chapter 32

TAKING ACTION
Foundation – Method – Expression

In the previous Chapter we looked at the three conclusions:

Conclusion #1 - We can't properly fulfill our God-given *purpose* as a disciple if we are not activity engaged in the process of making disciples.

Conclusion #2 - We Have *Purpose* as Disciples:

- Trust in Jesus as Lord (Jn 3:16-18)
- Glorify God with our lives (Mt 5:16)
- Love God, Love Others (Mt 22:35-40)
- Make disciples, baptize, teach (Mt 28:19-20)
- Seek to fulfill the good works that God has prepared (Eph 2:8-10)
- Abide/Remain in Jesus (Jn 8:31-82)

Conclusion #3 – Disciples are called to 15 categories in **Foundation, Method, Expression**.

Question – So now what? What are you going to do now? *If you're a disciple*, let's look at how you can continue to grow in your journey as a disciple. *If you are not a believer in Jesus yet* – thank you for reading this book! Please don't stop. *The last chapter was written for you!*

Please prayerfully use the following ACTION PLAN to plot out strategies and steps to grow in your discipleship.

DISCIPLE-*ing* ACTION PLAN

Area to Grow	What You Will Do
Bible Study	
Trusting God	
Personal Prayer	
Kingdom Focused Biblical Worldview	
Jesus Relationship	
Christ is the Model	
Spiritual Leader	
Give the day to God	
Community, Small Group	
Missions, Outreach, Reaching the Lost	
Loving God, Loving Others	
Lead by Example, Shine the Light	
BOLD Engage others with Gospel	
Discipling Others, Being Discipled	
Christ-Like Leadership, Engaging Culture in our Professions	

Chapter 33

Spirit vs. Flesh – Choices & Consequences, and the Good News of Jesus Christ

God loves you!... and He desires a personal relationship with you – and that is a beautiful thing. He even provided, through his chosen men as writing-vessels and prophets, a message to you. God's Word, the Holy Bible, contains unmeasurable wisdom, instruction, and guidance for those who seek relationship with Him and to understand reality from a biblical and Godly perspective.

Bad News, and Good News

As well, the Holy Bible speaks of the actions and thoughts of those who do *not* wish to follow God – who reject God and His message, His ways. One of the most profound passages, in my opinion, is in Paul's letter to the church at Galatia – Galatians 5:16-26 ESV

> *16 But I say, walk by the Spirit, and you will not gratify the desires of the flesh. 17 For the desires of the flesh are against the Spirit, and the desires of the Spirit are against the flesh, for these are opposed to each other, to keep you from doing the things you want to do. 18 But if you are led by the Spirit, you are not under the law. 19 Now the works of the flesh are evident: sexual immorality,*

impurity, sensuality, [20] idolatry, sorcery, enmity, strife, jealousy, fits of anger, rivalries, dissensions, divisions, [21] envy, drunkenness, orgies, and things like these. I warn you, as I warned you before, that those who do such things will not inherit the kingdom of God. [22] But the fruit of the Spirit is love, joy, peace, patience, kindness, goodness, faithfulness, [23] gentleness, self-control; against such things there is no law. [24] And those who belong to Christ Jesus have crucified the flesh with its passions and desires. [25] If we live by the Spirit, let us also keep in step with the Spirit. [26] Let us not become conceited, provoking one another, envying one another.*

In pondering these verses, it is apparent that Paul (and the Holy Spirit of God who inspired him) gives dire warnings for a life characterized by living in *the works of the flesh.* I am definitely not advocating the belief structure that Christians are *sinless* - we are not - there are many verses that speak of this (1 John 1:7-9 et al). However, a life characterized by blatant, on-going, unrepentant sin is a sign-post of serious problems and a distance from the Spirit of God. It is a red-flag to the spiritual condition.

Choices matter. Choices affect our relationship with the Lord, with our loved ones, our families, friends, neighbors, and anyone we have contact with…but especially those closest to us. The choice to follow sinful desires of the flesh, *temptations*, is nothing new to mankind –

succumbing to sin temptations goes back to the Garden of Eden in Genesis 3 and chases us daily, believers and unbelievers alike. As the apostle Paul wrote in Romans 7:14-25: (NASB, italics and underline emphasis added)

[14] For we know that the Law is spiritual, but I am of flesh, sold into bondage to sin. [15] For what I am doing, I do not understand; for I am not practicing what I would like to do, but I am doing the very thing I hate. [16] But if I do the very thing I do not want to do, I agree with the Law, confessing that the Law is good. [17] So now, no longer am I the one doing it, but sin which dwells in me. [18] For I know that nothing good dwells in me, that is, in my flesh; for the willing is present in me, but the doing of the good is not. [19] <u>For the good that I want, I do not do, but I practice the very evil that I do not want.</u> [20] <u>But if I am doing the very thing I do not want, I am no longer the one doing it, but sin which dwells in me.</u>

[21] I find then the principle that evil is present in me, the one who wants to do good. [22] For I joyfully concur with the law of God in the inner man, [23] but I see a different law in the members of my body, waging war against the law of my mind and making me a prisoner of the law of sin which is in my members. [24] <u>Wretched man that I am! Who will set</u>

me free from the body of this death? [25] *Thanks be to God through Jesus Christ our Lord! So then, on the one hand I myself with my mind am serving the law of God, but on the other, with my flesh the law of sin.*

It is a WAR! A war between walking in the Spirit of God and walking in the flesh. A war between doing things God's way, and doing things our way. A war between good and evil. A war of choice. For sure, it is difficult – even Paul struggled to the point of exasperation evident in this passage. And it is, likewise, difficult for us. Daily. And there will be, inevitably, times when we trip and fall into sin.

How does this manifest in our lives? How does this manifest in our families? Or in our communities? It is the war of making good choices. It is the war of trusting in God's guidance, and fleeing from temptations in the areas of '...*sexual immorality, impurity, sensuality, idolatry, sorcery, enmity, strife, jealousy, fits of anger, rivalries, dissensions, divisions, envy, drunkenness, orgies, and things like these...*' *(Gal 5:19-21)* Think pornography, adultery, placing inordinate value on things other than God, hatred towards others, jealousy towards others, anger, dissensions and divisions between people, drug and alcohol abuse, sexual sin... as well as dishonesty, thievery, murder/hatred/abortion, etc. etc. It is rampant in our world. It is a tsunami of anti-God, anti-Bible, anti-morality, anti-righteousness sin against the Holy and Perfect God of the Bible. This war is real – and it destroys families, marriages, relationships, and lives. If you don't see this war happening all around you, it is because you have closed your eyes to it and are making the choice to follow the ways of the world and the world system. Satan and his minions are leading this war against the Holy God... and they have successfully sought to destroy so many billions of people throughout the years. It is heart-breaking.

THE GOOD NEWS!

Jesus said:

"These things I have spoken to you, that in Me you may have peace. In the world you will have tribulation; but be of good cheer, I have overcome the world."
John 16:33 NKJV

Though the battles rage on, Jesus has overcome the world. The war has, ultimately, been won... yet, there are choices that need to be made by us. As human beings on this planet in this space-time continuum, and even as believers – followers of Jesus Christ – there are choices to be made: to follow God's way, or to follow the ways of the world... the ways of Satan... the ways of the flesh.

Mankind's sin has separated us from God. And the great problem is that a perfectly Holy, pure, righteous, and just God cannot have anything sinful and impure in His presence. Thus, the separation. Our sinfulness is infinitely opposed to God's perfect being, and nothing we do, no acts of our own can purify us of our imperfection and sinfulness. It is a great dilemma! Sin and its filthy lawlessness and transgression against God's ways must be dealt with by Justice. So, the great problem question is: *How can a Holy, perfect, pure, righteous, and just God be true to His Holy nature, but allow sin against Him to go unpunished - and still be considered just?* If a human judge allowed a murderous thief who killed your family to walk free without punishment, you would scream "unjust!!!" You would come unwound with a deep sense of moral outrage and injustice, and would declare that: "the judge is corrupt! Paid off by bribes! This isn't right!" Your human sensibilities could not comprehend how such a travesty of justice could happen! And we are only humans... yet, we can recognize this outrage. That's a problem. How much more is that problem existent when the Judge is the Holy, perfect, pure, all-knowing, and just Creator of the Universe? Justice must occur for lying, stealing, murder, slander, idolatry, hatred, sexual sin, and the myriad of sins against God. Justice must happen, otherwise God is not just – or, to phrase it differently... *unjust.* And that cannot be. In order for God to be true to His perfect nature, justice must be dealt. Do you see the direness of the situation? A just God cannot just ignore sin...or just passively *forgive* sin. Justice must happen.

There is the *Good News*...the "Gospel". And that is that the one, true God of the Bible is a loving Creator and Father – and He provided a Way. God, Himself, the Creator, would step into space and time, into His creation, and become one of us...*God with us*...He would become man. The Creator would become a child, foretold in the Hebrew scriptures, would live a perfect sinless life, and would take on the punishment for our sin - because we could not save ourselves! No earthly sacrifice could pay the price of the justice that was demanded to redeem us from that sin. Jesus, the Son of God – God become flesh, came to save us. God loves you so much that He provided the way: on the cross of Christ, Jesus took on the sin of all mankind, of all time, and bore the punishment for that sin unto His death. He was crucified for you... He died for you. His love was poured out for you on that cross. As His blood poured out, so did his Grace, Mercy, and Love.

As recorded by the eyewitness John and author of the Gospel of John, Jesus in his last moments before death on the cross said, "It is finished" (John 19:30). Justice was paid - the punishment for sin was complete. After the Roman executioners verified Jesus' death by a spear thrust into his chest, His dead body was removed from the cross and laid in a tomb. The Son of God, the Creator of the Universe who had become mankind had just died for you. On the third day, He rose from the dead - victorious over sin, and victorious over death. He appeared, bodily, to hundreds of witnesses after His resurrection. He ascended to Heaven where He is our advocate, and He will return to the earth as King of kings and will judge the living and the dead.

And, most miraculously, He gives you and I the free gift of salvation from your sin against God. Not because you and I deserve it...not because you and I earned it...but because He loves us. And all He asks in return is that we love Him back. To love Him, to accept His gift of grace and mercy, and to believe in and place our faith and trust in Him and His atoning sacrifice on our behalf. As Jesus tells us in John 3:16-18

¹⁶ "For God so loved the world, that he gave his only Son, that whoever believes in him should not perish but have eternal life. ¹⁷ For God did not send his Son into the world to condemn the world, but in order that the world might be saved through him. ¹⁸ Whoever believes in him is not condemned, but whoever does not believe is condemned already, because he has not believed in the name of the only Son of God.

We have many choices in life. Our choices impact our families, our children, our loved ones – some for good, some for bad. Some for evil, but some for God. There is no greater choice that you and I and our families and friends will ever make than how we respond to the Good News of God, the Gospel of Jesus Christ. Our choice has eternal implications for us and our loved ones. The Creator of the universe, God incarnate, the Son of God, Jesus Christ, came to save you from your sin and from the consequences of your sin. To take care of the Justice required, in love. What is your response to that free gift?

What is your choice?
How do you respond to the love of God in Jesus Christ?

Most of you who have read through this book are likely believers... and for that I praise God! It is my hope and prayer that this book has moved you, strengthened your faith, sharpened your focus...Iron sharpens iron, so one man sharpens another!

For those of you who have read this who do *not* believe... who have *not* placed your faith and trust in *Yeshua*

Hamashiach, Jesus Messiah. Thank you for joining on this journey. It is my sincerest prayer and hope that you recognize our state, that we are sinners in need of the Savior…that you would humble yourself, repent, and call upon His name and place your faith and trust in Jesus Christ and the sacrifice that He made for you. Love Him back, trust in Him, and you will be redeemed.

May God bless you in your relationship with Him,
Steve Harbaugh   email: DISCIPLEing2819@gmail.com

And He shall be called

Wonderful Counselor, Mighty God, Everlasting Father, Prince of Peace, Son of God, Son of Man, Son of David, Lamb of God, Christ, Messiah, *Yeshua Hamashiach*, Lord of Lords, King of kings, The Resurrection and the Life, Name above all names, The Word, Man of Sorrows, Head of the Church, Master, Teacher, Faithful & True Witness, The Rock, The Door, The Branch, The Good Shepherd, The Alpha & Omega, The True Vine, The Light of the World, The Lion of the Tribe of Judah, The Only Begotten Son, Redeemer, Savior, I Am, Bridegroom, Image of the Invisible God, LORD, The Word Become Flesh, The Amen, The King of the Jews, Bread of Life, High Priest, Chief Cornerstone, Living Water, The Holy One of Israel...

JESUS

Made in the USA
Monee, IL
21 June 2021

71599741R00223